THE FALL OF
BERLIN

THE FALL OF BERLIN

THE FINAL DAYS OF HITLER'S EVIL REGIME

ANTHONY TUCKER-JONES

Picture credits

All photographs courtesy of Alamy Stock Photo.
All maps by David Woodroffe.

This edition published in 2024 by Arcturus Publishing Limited
26/27 Bickels Yard, 151–153 Bermondsey Street,
London SE1 3HA

AD008026UK

Printed in the UK

Contents

Introduction

Capital of the World

Although he ruled over and died in Germany, Adolf Hitler was not German. He was born in Austria in 1889, not far from the German border, which made Vienna his native capital city, not Berlin. Indeed, he lived in Vienna as a young man, and it was there that his virulent anti-Semitism and extreme nationalism first developed. Then, shortly before the start of the First World War, he moved to Munich in Germany. During that conflict, he served in a Bavarian infantry regiment on the Western Front, where he survived being wounded and gassed. Afterwards, he returned to Munich and embarked on a political career that culminated in him becoming leader of the National Socialist German Workers' Party (Nationalsozialistische Deutsche Arbeiterpartei) in 1921 and then German Chancellor 12 years later. From that point on, Berlin was his seat of power.

The city after the First World War was the scene of constant political and social upheaval. Berlin and Munich in 1919 endured poorly co-ordinated communist uprisings that were crushed by ex-soldiers of the Free Corps. The following year, a leftist-led general strike in Berlin thwarted an attempted coup by the Free Corps. The weak German government sought to prop up the shattered economy by frantically printing money. In the face of ensuing rampant inflation, many Germans became poverty-stricken, but from the chaos emerged a new generation of entrepreneurs. They became immensely wealthy by building business empires based on credit.

Berlin during the 1920s, like many other European capitals, was a centre for hedonistic pleasures. For a time, it was a place where anything went. At night, bohemians, tourists and the wealthy thronged the streets seeking entertainment. Prostitution proliferated and nudity was commonplace in the city's clubs, on theatre stages and on the flickering screens of cinemas. Homosexuals, lesbians and transvestites were openly tolerated. One visitor described the neon lights on Friedrichstrasse as 'the pornographic shop-window of Germany's shame.'[1] Such venues as the Adlon Hotel, Eldorado nightclub, Monokel bar, Scala Theatre and the Technical ballroom all became places to be seen. In the latter, also known as the Residenz-Casino, each table had a telephone to encourage flirting. Berliners embraced American-style dance bands and jazz music with great enthusiasm. Socialites flaunted their beauty and wealth with gay abandon. All this behaviour was soon to change.

Berlin's decadence ended abruptly when Hitler came to power in 1933. Instead, the city was plunged into a puritanical nightmare. Berliners were overawed by the sight of the massed ranks of Hitler's thuggish Brownshirts holding a triumphant torchlit parade through the iconic Brandenburg Gate. 'Berlin, of course, is a city vibrating with energy; it has all the faults of youth,' said Hitler, 'but it will learn.'[2] What he wanted was 'not a city of feasting and carousing, but a city beauteous and gracious to live in.'[3] This inevitably came at a price. Prostitutes were forced into state-sanctioned brothels frequented by senior Nazis, jazz was banned and homosexuals were jailed or shot. Lesbians were consigned to state maternity homes or brothels. At the infamous Berlin Salon Kitty, the prostitutes were forced to spy on their clients. The burning of books deemed undesirable by the Nazis in front of Berlin University that year further illustrated the nature of the regime that had come to power. Hitler wanted nothing that in his view would sap national strength.

Leading German intellectuals were rapidly driven from Berlin. Novelist Lion Feuchtwanger had his home seized and was forced into exile in France after he publicly criticized Hitler's book *Mein Kampf*. Famous Jewish mathematician Albert Einstein was forced to step down from his directorship at Berlin's Kaiser Wilhelm Institute and move to America. The Berlin State Opera lost Jewish conductor Otto Klemperer, whose property was confiscated, and he also went to America. As did caricaturist George Grosz, who was driven from his Berlin studio after he lampooned the Nazis once too often. Hitler cared little about the impact this brain drain had on the city.

Despite Hitler's authoritarian regime, German national pride swelled when Berlin hosted the Summer Olympic Games in 1936. Hitler used the Games as an opportunity to showcase how modern and progressive the city was after just three years of Nazi rule. In this he was successful, with few people appreciating that the German capital and the rest of the country had fallen into the hands of extreme racists. Hitler ordered Joseph Goebbels, his propaganda minister, to play down the Nazis' rabid anti-Semitism to avoid displeasing the International Olympic Committee. Goebbels dutifully launched a glossy public relations campaign designed to beguile the world. Any dissenting voices were quickly silenced.

Nazi preparations for the Games included an enormous purpose-built sports complex complete with Olympic stadium and village. The stadium could accommodate a crowd of up to 100,000 spectators. Hitler hoped his athletes would demonstrate the racial superiority of Aryan Germany. Black American athlete Jesse Owens proved him wrong. Nonetheless, to Hitler's delight, German athletes won by far the most medals. After the Games, the Olympic village was repurposed for military use. All the facilities were to become the scene of bitter fighting in 1945.

Hitler soon set about remodelling Berlin. On 30 January 1937, the fourth anniversary of his appointment as chancellor, he signed the 'Decree for a General Building Inspector for the Imperial Capital'.[4] Albert Speer, Nazi minister and architect, was placed in charge of the city's grandiose urban renewal and glorification. No expense was to be spared. Hitler and Speer agreed on two grand throughfares: the East–West and North–South Axis. At the heart of these was to be built a Great Hall of the People with a capacity of 180,000. Neither Hitler nor Speer ever envisaged that these new roads could potentially provide penetration points into the city for an invader.

Austria's Anschluss ('connection' or 'joining') with Germany in 1938 meant that the country became part of the German Reich. 'I will not tolerate any rivalry between Vienna and Berlin,' Hitler warned. 'Berlin is the capital of the Reich and will remain the capital of the Reich.'[5] Furthermore, he said, 'I shall see to it that Berlin acquires all the characteristics of a great capital.'[6] He planned for it to be the centre of a Greater German Reich and to that end it was to be renamed Germania. Hitler ordered Speer to construct a new chancellery in the

Vossstrasse to reflect the grandeur of his expanding empire. 'Whoever enters the Imperial Chancellery,' boasted Hitler, 'must have the sense of approaching the lord of the world.'[7] When the ridgepole for the New Chancellery was erected, he ordered, 'Berlin must change its face in order to adapt to its great new mission.'[8]

That same year, many Berliners were dismayed and disgusted by the events that took place on Kristallnacht on 9/10 November 1938. Hitler, after a Polish Jew had shot a member of the German embassy staff in Paris, unleashed his Nazi thugs upon Jewish businesses, homes and synagogues. These were smashed, ransacked and in some cases burnt down. Some Berliners took the opportunity to loot their neighbours' wrecked shops. This orgy of violence spread throughout Germany. Everywhere, the streets were left strewn with shattered glass – hence Kristallnacht or 'Crystal Night'. The pogrom did not bode well for the future of Berlin or Germany's Jews. Almost overnight, Jewish Berliners were eliminated from the city's economic, political and social life. All this was done in the name of Hitler's goal of achieving Aryan purity.

'Look at Paris, the most beautiful city in the world. Or even Vienna,' Hitler had told Speer. 'Those are cities with grand style. Berlin is nothing but an unregulated accumulation of buildings. We must surpass Paris and Vienna.'[9] He sent architects to Paris to seek inspiration and looked to Budapest, which he thought was also one of the most beautiful cities in the world. Work started in Berlin in the late 1930s and Speer completed the East–West Axis highway in time for Hitler's 50th birthday in 1939. German troops marked his birthday by holding a midnight ceremonial torchlit parade amid Nazi regalia outside the Old Chancellery building. All of this was part of the Nazis' highly seductive rituals.

The following year, Speer finished the New Chancellery. Hitler, fearful of possible future riots, ordered that the doors should be made of thick steel and the windows fitted with bulletproof steel shutters. He wanted a barracks for his guard regiment to be close by. 'It must be possible to defend the centre of the Reich like a fortress,'[10] Hitler instructed Speer. He also envisaged using tanks on the widened streets. Referring to the army, he observed, 'If they come rolling up here in their armoured vehicles … nobody will be able to put up any resistance.'[11] Although he was referring to civil unrest in these prophetic comments, he almost seemed to foresee the coming of the Red Army in April 1945.

Over the next few years, Hitler's plans of expansion saw the Third Reich getting bigger and bigger. 'The name Germania for the capital of the Reich in its new representative form would be very appropriate,' said Hitler in the summer of 1942, 'for it would give every member of the German community, however far away from the capital he may be, a feeling of unity and closer membership.'[12] His delusions did not stop there as he claimed, 'Berlin will one day be the capital of the world.'[13] Clearly, he was intoxicated by his surge of conquests, blind to the possibility that one day the tide might turn. 'Berlin, as a world capital, can make one think only of ancient Egypt, it can be compared only to Babylon or Rome.'[14] Hitler wanted to make Berlin the centre of the universe, with all the civic gaudiness of imperial Rome.

'The Reich must get a worthy capital,' insisted Hitler. 'I know we shall make a magnificent city of it.'[15] The East–West Axis and the New Chancellery were just the start of Hitler's vision for Germania. There were to be new cinemas, government buildings, an opera house, plazas, shops and theatres as well as an indoor swimming baths to rival those of ancient Rome. 'As early as 1939 many old buildings in the vicinity of the Reichstag were razed to make room for our Great Hall,' recalled Speer, 'and the other buildings that were to surround the future Adolf Hitler Platz.'[16] Speer sought to knock down the fire-damaged Reichstag, but

Hitler refused, wanting to retain it for social events. 'Hitler liked the structure,'[17] he noted with some disappointment.

Although Speer commissioned many grand-looking models of Germania, the Second World War ensured that the redevelopment of Berlin soon came to a halt. On the night of 25 August 1940, the Royal Air Force bombed the city in retaliation for an accidental raid on London. This was the first time that bombs had ever fallen on Berlin. However, little damage was done and there were minimal casualties. The Royal Air Force returned on 28 August, this time in greater strength, and killed Germans on the streets of the Reich's capital.[18] These were to prove to be the opening salvoes of many attacks to come. Stalin's Red Air Force the following August launched a series of raids on Berlin and the Royal Air Force began to escalate its assault.

These raids proved highly embarrassing to Reichsmarschall Hermann Göring, commander of the Luftwaffe, who had vowed no enemy aircraft would ever reach Berlin. He was first shamed on 1 October 1939 when British bombers conducted a test run to the city. 'Do you think that Germany would give in if Berlin were in ruins?' Göring had asked Luftwaffe General Hans Jeschonnek in the summer of 1940. 'Of course not,' responded Jeschonnek. 'That is where you are wrong,'[19] replied Göring knowingly. Thanks to the growing intensity of the Allied bomber campaign, construction of Germania was scrapped in early 1943. After the war, Speer's interrogators asked him if he regretted not being able to fulfil his grandiose plans. 'God, no; they were awful!'[20] he exclaimed in response. Despite the Luftwaffe's best efforts, British and American bombers made certain that central Berlin was a wasteland by the time the Red Army arrived.

The reality of Hitler's war really came home to Berliners in late November 1943 when Allied bombers killed almost 3,800 people, made 500,000 homeless and destroyed over 68,000 buildings. Air Marshal Sir Arthur Harris' RAF Bomber Command by March 1944 had destroyed 21.6 sq km (5,340 acres) in night-time attacks on the city while the Americans destroyed another 4 sq km (1,000 acres) during daylight raids. However, it was impossible to flatten all 72.5 sq km (28 sq miles) of Berlin. 'Judged by the standards of our attacks on Hamburg,' conceded Harris reluctantly, 'the [aerial] Battle of Berlin did not appear to be an overwhelming success.'[21] What it did do, though, was distract the Luftwaffe from the Eastern and Western Fronts. Defence of the Reich's skies became a priority.

Hitler always believed he would win the Second World War and made no preparations for the protection of Berlin other than enhancing its air defences. Crucially, little thought was given to creating new defences on the Rhine or the Oder rivers until it was too late. In 1944, the Red Army delivered a decisive blow to the German armed forces, putting it on the road to the Vistula and Oder rivers, the Seelow Heights and, ultimately, Berlin.[22] Once the Soviets were over both rivers in 1945, the Third Reich's days were numbered. The defences on the Oder were so weak that Berlin's home guard, known as the Volkssturm, were sent out from the city to help reinforce them. Tearful schoolboys of the Hitler Youth found themselves crouching in foxholes facing Soviet tanks.

Once the Soviets had established their Küstrin bridgehead and the rumble of guns could be heard in Berlin, fear of defeat began to permeate the city. Although some Berliners had fled the bombing and were staying with relatives elsewhere, Berlin was still packed with thousands of trapped civilians. Hitler's last-minute, frantic efforts to get his tattered armies to rescue Berlin from encirclement ended miserably. To the south of the city, few German troops escaped an area called the

Halbe pocket. Those caught in the surrounding forests were massacred in an orgy of violence.

Soviet leader Joseph Stalin was determined to make Berlin his prize and his alone. He wanted to occupy the city not only to punish Germany for the despoliation of the Soviet Union, but also to ensure it could never threaten his country again. To that end, Stalin did not want the assistance of Britain and America in capturing Berlin. As far as he was concerned, the Red Army should take all the glory for storming the shattered Nazi lair. Stalin was pleased that neither British Prime Minister Winston Churchill nor American President Franklin Roosevelt made a separate peace deal with Germany despite secret talks being held in Switzerland. Likewise, he was pleased that the Allies were distracted on the flanks, leaving the Red Army to conduct the battle on its own. To urge it on to final victory, Stalin deliberately encouraged competition between Marshals Georgy Zhukov and Ivan Konev to see who would be first into the city.

Instead of making Berlin one of the greatest cities that ever was, Hitler's lust for conquest ensured it became a ruin and the scene of one of the bloodiest battles in history. His refusal to surrender, even when staring defeat in the face, meant that the Red Army had to fight its way inch by inch into the city to capture the Reichstag and Reich Chancellery. This consigned both sides to terrible bloodletting, with the long-suffering Berliners caught in the crossfire. Zhukov and Konev's men simply bludgeoned their way in using brute force. After the unspeakable horrors inflicted on the Soviet Union's cities, the Red Army demanded its pound of flesh in retribution. Hitler, with his remaining troops scattered, decided it was best to take his own life among the rubble of his capital on 30 April 1945. By that point, Nazi rule extended to just a few city blocks, making continued resistance futile.

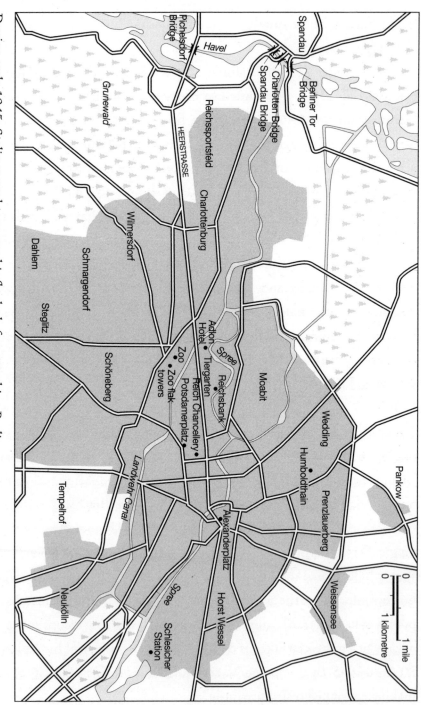

During early 1945, Stalin moved to secure his flanks before attacking Berlin.

Prologue

Last Flight from Berlin

The pilot tightly gripped the stick of his Focke-Wulf (Fw) 190 trainer aircraft as he rose from the airfield at Rechlin–Lärz on 26 April 1945. Looking out the cockpit canopy, he noted the circling escort of Fw 190 fighters. They were there not to guard him, but rather his VIP passengers: Luftwaffe General Ritter von Greim and his mistress test pilot, Hanna Reitsch. The aircraft was only a two-seater so Reitsch had crawled into the confined space in the rear of the fuselage. General von Greim had been summoned to Berlin on urgent business by Adolf Hitler. The pair had flown from Neubiberg near Munich on 24 April but were then stranded at Rechlin for a day. Their immediate destination was Gatow in southwest Berlin, which was the capital's only remaining airfield still in German hands. The air around and over Berlin was swarming with

Russian fighters,' recalled Hitler's personal pilot, Hans Baur. 'Many Luftwaffe pilots were refusing to fly into Berlin from Rechlin.'[1]

General von Greim was not the first to make this perilous journey. Albert Speer, the Nazi munitions minister, had departed Berlin on 20 April, but returned five days later using the same route. He had flown from Rechlin to Gatow in the trainer aircraft escorted by a squadron of fighter bombers who were off to attack the Red Army south of Potsdam. From the air, Speer noted it did not look as if much was happening apart from the odd flash of artillery. 'But on the eastern boundary of Berlin,' he observed, 'far off in the mist, larger billows of smoke could be discerned.'[2] At Gatow, he and his entourage had climbed aboard two Fieseler Fi 156 Storch light reconnaissance planes, which landed before the Brandenburg Gate. Hitler's staff wanted him to fly to Berchtesgaden, but Speer advised the Führer to stay in Berlin. Shortly after, Speer flew out of Berlin alone.

General von Greim and Hanna Reitsch's pilot on reaching Gatow spotted enemy fighters and plunged their aeroplane into a steep dive. 'I was certain that our aircraft had been hit,' recalled a frightened Reitsch, 'and now I waited for us to impact the ground or explode.'[3] Instead, their pilot pulled out of the dive and landed safely at Gatow. The pair then clambered into a waiting Storch. Von Greim took the controls with Reitsch crouched behind him. The plan had been to fly into central Berlin using a *Hubschrauber*, a German helicopter, that could land in the gardens of the Reich Chancellery or the nearby streets but it had been destroyed on the runway.

Flying low over Berlin, von Greim could see plumes of smoke rising from Germany's devastated capital. He was in command of the Luftwaffe's 6th Air Fleet defending the Eastern Front so was not responsible for fending off the Allies' strategic bomber campaign that had wrought so much damage. He was not entirely happy at the thought of landing on an improvised airstrip in Berlin's Tiergarten near the Brandenburg Gate, especially as the Red Army had overrun much of the city.

Reitsch reassured him that the Storch, known as a go-anywhere aircraft thanks to its short take-off and landing capabilities, would get them there. They were entering a Dante-esque inferno. For miles and miles, entire city blocks were scorched and blasted. Roofs, floors and windows had vanished, reducing buildings to miserable shells. Many of the walls that remained looked as if they would topple into the streets at the slightest breeze. Terrified Berliners cowered in their basements and cellars awaiting the terrible whims of their vengeful conquerors.

The plane passed over the Havel river and the Grunewald forest, skimming the treetops. Just south of the Olympic Stadium, it was violently buffeted by Soviet anti-aircraft fire and von Greim was hit by shrapnel in his right foot. Bleeding profusely, he kept passing out and Reitsch, reaching over his shoulders, grabbed the controls. Glancing to the side, she could see that fuel was flowing freely from the punctured wing tanks. Nonetheless, she expertly brought the stricken plane down on a shell-pitted road not far from the Brandenburg Gate. There was no reception party and they had to wait with artillery shells landing all around them until a truck arrived. They were driven down Unter den Linden and along Wilhelmstrasse and delivered to the Reich Chancellery air raid shelter. There, Dr Ludwig Stumpfegger treated von Greim's wound.

Afterwards, von Greim was carried deep into the Führerbunker to be confronted by Hitler. 'He was very stooped, both his arms trembled,' observed Reitsch, 'and he had a glazed, distant look in his eyes. He greeted us in an almost flat voice.'[4] Hitler, turning to Reitsch, exclaimed,

'You brave woman! There is still loyalty and courage in the world.'[5] When Hitler asked von Greim if he knew why he had been summoned to Berlin, he replied he did not. 'Because Hermann Göring has betrayed both me and his Fatherland,' said Hitler bitterly. 'Behind my back he has established connections with the enemy.'[6] To make matters worse, Göring had declared himself Hitler's successor and that if he did not hear from Hitler by 2200 hours he would assume control of Nazi Germany. 'An ultimatum! A crass ultimatum!' continued Hitler. 'It is the end…'[7]

In response, the usurper Göring had been sacked as the commander-in-chief of the Luftwaffe and von Greim was to replace him. Furthermore, von Greim was to be promoted to field marshal. 'Commander-in-Chief of a Luftwaffe which no longer existed!'[8] noted Reitsch. Major Bernd Freytag von Loringhoven, who was in the Führerbunker, was aghast at the danger von Greim had put himself in. 'I found it absolutely crazy for the new head of the Air Force to run such a risk,' he remarked, 'simply for the pleasure of receiving the halo of loyalty from Hitler.'[9] Hitler could have radioed his orders; instead, von Greim had been obliged to risk his life, been wounded and would be trapped in the Führerbunker for three days. Despite the enormity of the situation, von Greim bizarrely claimed that seeing Hitler was like being exposed to the 'fountain of youth.'[10]

Later, Reitsch met with Hitler. 'His head sagged, his face was deathly pallid,'[11] she recalled. 'The army of General Wenck is moving up from the south,' he reassured her. 'He must and will drive the Russians back long enough to save our people.'[12] Elements of General Wenck's 12th Army to the southwest of Berlin were indeed fighting their way east, not to relieve the capital, but to rescue General Busse's 9th Army, which was facing annihilation.

The Luftwaffe tried in vain to resupply Berlin's beleaguered garrison. Junkers Ju 52 transport aircraft flying from Gatow resorted to landing on sections of the city's 48 km (30 mile)-long East–West axis. This was achieved by removing the streetlamps, but only limited numbers of anti-tank rounds were flown in. The Luftwaffe also hoped to fly in reinforcements but the East–West Axis was blocked when a Ju 52 crashed into a house. By the end of 27 April, the defenders in the central areas had been squeezed into a pocket some 16 km (10 miles) wide and 5.6 km (3.5 miles) across.

The Luftwaffe's famous tank-busting Stuka pilot, Lieutenant Colonel Hans-Ulrich Rudel, answering Hitler's call, tried to land on the East–West Axis early on 28 April. He was flying in a Heinkel He 111 bomber and as it approached the city his aircraft came under fire. 'It was very difficult to recognize the features of the capital,' said Rudel, 'because of enormous clouds of smoke and a thin layer of mist.'[13] He also found the fires dazzling, which further obscured visibility. 'We then received a message saying that landing was impossible as the East–West Axis was under heavy artillery fire and the Russians had already taken Potsdamer Platz.'[14]

Göring was not the only one to betray Hitler. Joseph Goebbels' Propaganda Ministry on 28 April picked up a Reuters report announcing that Reichsführer Heinrich Himmler, Hitler's right-hand man, had offered to surrender the German armies on the Western Front. Hitler took the news extremely badly. 'He raged like a madman,' said Reitsch. 'His colour rose to heated red and his face was virtually unrecognisable...'[15] At least Göring had informed Hitler of his intentions, whereas Hitler felt that Himmler had stabbed him in the back. 'Men and women alike screamed with rage, fear and desperation,' added Reitsch, 'all mixed into one emotional spasm.'[16] Furthermore, the Red Army steadily overwhelming Berlin's garrison had reached the Potsdamer Platz just a block away from the Chancellery. It was anticipated that their final assault would begin in 30 hours. Reitsch recalled Hitler pacing like a caged tiger, 'waving a road map that was fast disintegrating from the sweat of his hands and planning Wenck's campaign with anyone who happened to be listening.'[17]

Hitler in the early hours of 29 April married his mistress, Eva Braun. 'Poor, poor Adolf,' she said to Reitsch, 'deserted by everyone, betrayed by all. Better that ten thousand others die than he be lost to Germany.'[18] Both von Greim and Reitsch wanted to stay in Berlin with the Führer, but Hitler had other plans. After undergoing surgery on his shattered foot, von Greim was to join Admiral Dönitz, whom Hitler had appointed as his official successor. Dönitz was trying to establish a new Nazi government at Plön. Before they parted, Hitler presented them each with cyanide capsules. He also insisted that Himmler be arrested and instructed von Greim, 'A traitor must never succeed me as Führer, you must go out to ensure that he does not.'[19] Hitler's parting words to them were, 'God protect you.'[20] His staff were dismayed. 'I was totally downcast,' recalled SS-Senior Squad Leader Rochus Misch, the Führer's bodyguard. 'I had been hoping secretly that Hitler would fly out with Greim. Now the last hope floated – or better put, flew away.'[21]

Reitsch and von Greim were flown out of Berlin just after midnight on 29 April in an Arado Ar 96 advanced trainer aircraft by the same pilot who had delivered them to Gatow. Taking off from the Tiergarten, they again came under Soviet fire until they were able to dart above the cloud. The men of the Soviet 3rd Shock Army who were in the Tiergarten watched in dismay, fearing that Hitler had just slipped their grasp. 'Soon we spotted bright streamers, the Havel and its chain of silvery lakes, through black breaks in the clouds,'[22] observed Reitsch. This was to be the very last flight out of Berlin. At Rechlin, von Greim gave orders for the Luftwaffe to use every available aircraft to attack the Soviet tanks on the Potsdamer Platz in a futile effort to save the defenders of the Chancellery. The pair then reached Dönitz's headquarters in Schleswig-Holstein and after a few days flew to Klagenfurt in Austria. Having been arrested by American troops, the last head of the Luftwaffe took his own life in Salzburg prison on 24 May 1945, possibly using the cyanide Hitler had given him.[23] General von Greim had done the world a favour by not rescuing the man responsible for the deaths of millions of people on the last flight from Berlin.

Part 1

The Gathering Storm

Chapter 1

Delay at Küstrin

By the end of 1944, Nazi Germany had suffered a series of catastrophic defeats. The Western Allies had landed in Normandy and reached the German city of Aachen. On the Eastern Front, the Red Army had stormed its way to Warsaw and the Vistula. During the winter, Hitler launched his surprise offensive into the Ardennes on the Western Front in the hope of taking Antwerp. He reasoned this would force the Americans and British to pause, whereupon he could turn east with his rejuvenated armies and deliver a similar blow to the Red Army. However, his assault through the Ardennes ground to a halt in a matter of weeks thanks to American tenacity, a lack of fuel, and Allied air power. By the New Year it was obvious that Stalin was preparing an enormous offensive – one that would inevitably take his troops to the gates of Berlin.

The Red Army launched an offensive from its Baranov bridgehead in Poland on the western bank of the Vistula on 12 January 1945 with the aim of getting to the Oder. This was the last great natural barrier on the Eastern Front protecting Berlin. Küstrin, nestled between the Oder and Warta rivers east of the capital, lay on the most direct route. North of Baranov the Red Army also struck from its bridgeheads at Pulavy and Magnuszev. To the north of Warsaw, it drove to the northwest with the aim of reaching Elbing and the Baltic coast. German intelligence assessed that the Soviets had an enormous 15:1 superiority on the ground and 20:1 in the air. Common sense dictated that nothing could withstand such a steamroller of firepower. However, by this stage, Hitler's grasp on the reality of his situation was sketchy at best.

Stalin, once the Red Army had crossed the Vistula, felt it imperative to first crush the German Baltic balcony in East Prussia and Pomerania, which stretched from Stettin on the Oder in the west to Königsberg in the east. Between these two points lay the ports of Kolberg, Gdynia, Danzig and Pillau. Stalin reasoned that the strong German forces in this region posed a serious threat to the Red Army's right flank as it drove on the Nazi capital. By 14 January it was evident that Stalin also intended to overrun the industrial area of Upper Silesia in Poland as the Red Army had again swung in a northwesterly direction. The loss of this region would be crippling to Hitler's war effort. As far as Stalin was concerned, nothing was to be left to chance when it came to capturing Berlin.

On the Soviet far right, General Ivan Chernyakhovsky's 3rd Belorussian Front tore into East Prussia with the aim of crushing German forces in the Königsberg area. To his south, Marshal Konstantin Rokossovsky's 2nd Belorussian Front in northern Poland headed for Danzig. Marshal Georgi Zhukov's 1st Belorussian Front in central

Poland thrust towards the heart of Germany, while Marshal Ivan Konev's 1st Ukrainian Front spread out in southern Poland, pushing on Silesia. South of him, four other Soviet fronts were slowly pushing the Germans out of the Balkans and eastern Europe. On the Western Front, Hitler's Ardennes and Alsace offensives had completely run out of steam, wasting Germany's dwindling resources, which would have been much better employed defending the Rhine and the Oder.

In a desperate attempt to stop the Soviets' Vistula–Oder offensive, Hitler created Army Group Vistula, which initially consisted of the 2nd and 9th Armies and the weak 11th SS Panzer Army. The 2nd Army would end up trapped in Danzig. Reichsführer Heinrich Himmler was placed in command of this new army group, a job for which he was woefully underqualified. However, ever since the attempt on Hitler's life on 20 July 1944 he had increasingly relied on the SS as he no longer trusted the regular armed forces.

Hitler hoped that if the Soviet breakout from Baranov reached the Oder the Red Army could be held at Breslau and Oppeln. At the end of the month, the Soviets crossed the Oder near Lüben and created a bridgehead. On the German left flank, Army Group Courland on the Baltic coast, with 22 divisions and over 630 panzers, was trapped in the Courland peninsula, while Army Group North, with 24 divisions, was squeezed into the Samland Peninsula and Königsberg. A terrified German prisoner told his captors, 'There is not much enthusiasm amongst the troops who have been ordered to defend Königsberg to the last.' When he was pressed for more information on the condition of the garrison he said, 'All the schools, theatres and railway stations are packed with wounded.'[1] In mid-January, Hitler begrudgingly gave General Heinz Guderian, the army's chief-of-staff, permission to withdraw seven divisions from Courland by sea, but no more. Among them was the 11th SS Panzergrenadier Division Nordland under SS-Brigadier Joachim Ziegler.

The Red Army reached the Oder near Küstrin on 1 February 1945, though the town still remained in German hands. It became the responsibility of SS-Major General Heinz Reinefarth and was defended by four battalions of SS troops. The garrison also had a limited quantity of artillery and flak guns. Reinefarth was a decidedly unsavoury character who had helped brutally crush the Warsaw Uprising the previous summer. Guderian noted, 'he was a good policeman, but no general.'[2] As far as Hitler was concerned, he was just the man for the job. Küstrin was an ancient Prussian stronghold with part of the Old Town located on a narrow headland between the Oder and the Warta, which made it an ideal defensive position. In contrast, the area on the eastern bank of the Warta was much more exposed.

Shortly after arriving at Küstrin, the Red Army established bridgeheads over the Oder to the north and south of the town, in the Kienitz and Reitwein Spur areas, which were held by units of the 5th Shock Army and 8th Guards Army respectively. The Germans were caught by surprise at the speed of the Soviets crossing. 'At the moment the detachment burst into the town of Kienitz,' reported Zhukov, 'German soldiers were blissfully walking the streets, and officers were sitting at a restaurant.'[3] Even the Berlin trains were running normally, until the station master was informed that all services were to be terminated until the end of the war. To the south of Küstrin, the Soviet 44th Guards Tank Brigade got over the river. When word reached the capital that Soviet armour had crossed, panic spread quickly. Joseph Goebbels, the Nazi propaganda minister, would have rather kept this news hushed up, but it was not long before all the German towns and cities along the

Oder knew what had happened. To the south, the Germans maintained a small bridgehead on the eastern bank at Frankfurt-on-the-Oder.

Remarkably, Stalin did not move on Berlin for another two and a half months because of the perceived need to secure his flanks. General Vasily Chuikov, commander of the 8th Guards Army, considered this was a grave error. 'I think that it would have been more correct to throw five Armies from the 1st Byelorussian Front against Berlin,' he reasoned, 'instead of sending them north.'[4] He felt that Zhukov should also have been reinforced by three or four armies from the 1st Ukrainian Front. This could have sealed Berlin's fate in early February. Instead, Zhukov was forced by Stalin to consolidate his position.

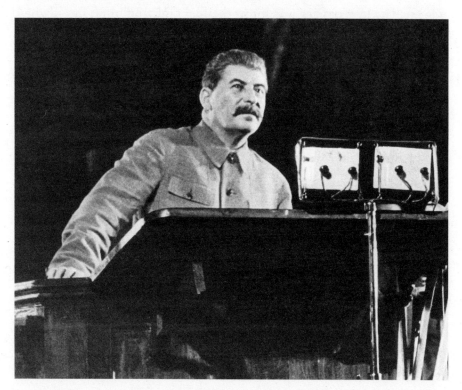

During early 1945, Stalin moved to secure his flanks before attacking Berlin.

Recovering from the shock, the Germans reacted violently against the bridgehead at Kienitz, which was defended by elements of the Soviet 266th Rifle Division supported by tanks. On the morning of 2 February, it was heavily shelled and mortared. Then the Luftwaffe swarmed into the skies. 'The hurricane of fire raged for about an hour,' recalled Zhukov. 'Then enemy troops, supported by armour, attacked our advanced detachment from three directions.'[5] The panzers rolled through the Soviets' gun positions and almost reached the river. An anti-tank battery under the command of Captain Kravtsov with a single gun remaining only had 13 rounds to fend off eight panzers. The gunners had concealed their weapon in a barn and caught the enemy tanks side on. The first panzer was hit in the fuel tank and burst into flames. The second was immobilized when a track was knocked off. After five panzers had been destroyed, the survivors withdrew.

Following this German attack, the Soviet 26th Guards Rifle Corps moved to expand the Kienitz bridgehead, sending over the 94th Guards Division, which included the 199th Guards Artillery Regiment and the 301st Rifle Division. They were met by repeated German counterattacks and the Luftwaffe, which was operating from all-weather concrete runways in the Berlin area. 'On February 2 and 3, the Luftwaffe continually bombed the combat formations of Berzarin's 5th Shock Army at its bridgehead on the Oder,' noted Zhukov. 'During those two days, the German aircraft flew over 5,000 combat missions, inflicting heavy losses on the 5th Army.'[6] In contrast, the Red Air Force was unable to take off from its forward airfields because the ground was thawing. Zhukov's orders to Berzarin were 'to dig in deep' and 'to organize massive anti-aircraft fire.'[7]

The Germans likewise struggled to contain Chuikov's southern bridgehead that soon extended into the Reitwein Spur. Weak battle groups were put together that included members of the 6th Fortress Regiment from Frankfurt, Hitler Youth and units of the civilian Volkssturm home guard. Walter Beier, who was on leave from deployment in East Prussia, found himself put in charge of a detachment on the grounds that he was a combat veteran. Beier watched in horror as 350 Hitler Youth were mown down by accurate Soviet fire. Some of the Volkssturm, fearful for the fate of their families, fought tenaciously. 'Among the Fritzes that we took prisoner,' recalled one Soviet officer, 'was a fifty-nine-year-old German, and he didn't have a tooth in his head, but this bastard was fighting like some kind of brainless automaton.'[8] All counterattacks by these forces on 2 February were easily beaten off, so the Germans contented themselves with mortaring Soviet positions. On 4 February, a single tank battalion from the newly formed Kurmark Panzergrenadier Division launched a counterattack despite warnings about the thawing ground. This operation failed when the tanks kept slipping back down the southern slopes of the Reitwein Spur.

That day, Chuikov was attending a meeting with Zhukov when Stalin telephoned wanting to know what was going on. 'We are planning the operation against Berlin,'[9] said Zhukov. There was a pause on the line. 'You are wasting your time,' said Stalin. 'After first consolidating on the Oder, you must turn as many forces as possible to the north.' An unwelcome 97 km (60 mile) gap had opened up between Zhukov and Rokossovsky that was only thinly defended. Furthermore, there were problems getting ammunition and fuel forwards from the Vistula. Zhukov ultimately agreed with Stalin and felt that Chuikov took a much too simplistic and ill-informed view of the situation. 'We understood,' recalled a bitterly disappointed Chuikov, 'that the offensive against Berlin was being postponed for an indefinite period.'[10]

Stalin took Elbing and 9,000 prisoners on 10 February, though some of the garrison managed to reach Danzig before the coastal road was severed. Three days later, Hitler lost control of Budapest. By mid-month, Breslau was completely surrounded. German forces in Hungary, in the meantime, were under heavy attack in the Lake Balaton area. Hitler intended to counterattack there using the 6th Panzer Army that had been withdrawn from the Ardennes. General Guderian reasoned with Hitler that it would be much better to attack the Soviet spearhead between Küstrin and Frankfurt. This, Guderian hoped, would help protect Berlin and buy time to permit armistice negotiations with the Americans and British. To facilitate such a counteroffensive, Guderian wanted all the divisions in the Balkans, Italy, Norway and Courland withdrawn to Germany. 'I can see no other way left to us of accumulating reserves,' he told Hitler, 'and without reserves we cannot hope to defend the capital.'[11] In response, Hitler flew into a rage at such defeatism and flatly refused.

Hitler's dictum was that no ground was ever to be willingly given up, regardless of the strategic cost. Thanks to this stance, although he could muster some 260 divisions, only 75 were available to face Stalin's thrust directed at Silesia and Berlin. About 30 were cut off in the Baltic states and another 28 were fighting to hold on to the remains of German-occupied Hungary. There were 76 divisions on the Western Front and 24 in Italy facing the Allies. There were 17 in Scandinavia on pointless occupation duties and 10 in Yugoslavia trying to contain the advancing partisans and Red Army.

Hitler turned to Heinrich Himmler's tough Waffen-SS to save Küstrin. In mid-February, Himmler was meant to oversee a counteroffensive, launched from Stargard using the 11th SS Panzer Army, with the aim of relieving first Arnswalde and then Küstrin. SS-

General Felix Steiner, commander of the 3rd SS Panzer Corps, was ordered to take charge of what was largely a paper army. Although a successful corps commander, he was promoted well above his abilities, just as SS-General Sepp Dietrich had been when Hitler put him in charge of the 6th Panzer Army in the Ardennes.

Guderian, fully aware of Himmler's shortcomings as a military leader, managed to get his deputy, General Walther Wenck, appointed to the Reichsführer's headquarters to oversee the operation. Wenck declined to have lunch with Himmler on the grounds it was a waste of time and instead made his way to the front to assess the situation. An affronted Himmler, suffering from a heavy cold, chose that very moment to go on sick leave to the SS hospital at Hohenlychen, north of Berlin. From his bed, where he was tended to by his favourite doctors, he issued what he thought was a stirring Order of the Day. 'Forward through the mud! Forward through the snow!' Himmler urged. 'Forward by day! Forward by night! Forward for the liberation of German soil!'[12] In the event, this was his sole contribution to trying to protect Berlin. Wenck and Steiner's attack involved elements of six very understrength SS divisions, of which four were armoured with fewer than 300 panzers and tank destroyers. Four weak army divisions were also committed and a division was on its way from Norway but didn't arrive in time.

Despite the almost complete lack of artillery support and air cover, some of the assault force successfully reached Arnswalde. Just two days into the attack, after Wenck broke his shoulder in a car crash on the evening of 17 February, the assault quickly ground to a halt in the face of stiff Soviet opposition. Two days later, Arnswalde was lost. Steiner had been an army commander for just a matter of days, though to be fair to him, his command never really amounted to such. He immediately lost one of his better units when the 4th SS Police Panzergrenadier

Division was sent to try and save Danzig. Hitler became fixated with Steiner's supposed abilities just as he had with Dietrich. However, the operation was not an entire waste of time as it helped convince Stalin that he must first clear East Prussia and Pomerania. Furthermore, the city of Poznan, defended by 60,000 German troops, held out in the rear of Chuikov's 8th Guards Army until 23 February. This meant Stalin postponed his assault on Berlin for six weeks, which gave the defenders valuable time to prepare their defences.

Behind the scenes, increasingly desperate measures were suggested to try to protect Berlin. Brigadier Reinhard Gehlen, who was in charge of Eastern Front intelligence, proposed to Guderian on 3 March setting fire to 644 sq km (400 sq miles) of pine forest. He thought the area between Görlitz and Guben was ideal. 'To achieve our objective of annihilating the enemy's equipment and personnel,' he wrote, 'the fires must be started in such a way that the enemy has no chance of escape.'[13] Gehlen's staff calculated that 360 sorties by the Luftwaffe dropping incendiaries would do the trick. Guderian was not receptive to the idea and did not respond. Gehlen then pointed out to the Luftwaffe that only four railway bridges across the Vistula were intact. If these were cut, it would hamper the Red Army's operations on the Neisse and Oder rivers. When General Karl Koller, the Luftwaffe's chief-of-staff, put this to the Hitler he was not receptive. He preferred the idea of an attack on western Soviet electricity supplies. Gehlen then tried the SS to see if their commandos could take out the bridges. He was advised an operation against a single bridge was under consideration, but nothing happened.

On 4 March, the Red Army reached the Baltic between Kolberg and Köslin, cutting off the German forces in the Baltic balcony. Five days afterwards, southwest of Kolberg, it reached the Oder either side of Stettin. This posed a threat to the vital synthetic oil plant at nearby Pölitz. The Soviets then commenced their attack on Küstrin on 10 March and pushed towards the Warta. They encountered determined resistance around the railway station and the road bridge that led to the area between the two rivers. Artillery was used to relentlessly pound the town's old forts. By 12 March, on the southern reaches of the Oder there was heavy fighting at Breslau. The Soviets also reached Oppeln in Upper Silesia. The latter, as well as the cities of Stettin, Kolberg, Danzig and Königsberg, continued to defiantly hold out.

Guderian's headquarters at Zossen, to the southeast of Berlin, was bombed on 15 March and General Hans Krebs, his second in command, was wounded. His previous deputy, General Wenck, was still out of action. Guderian, determined to be rid of the ineffectual Himmler, on 20 March managed to get General Gotthard Heinrici, who was commanding the 1st Panzer Army in the Carpathians, appointed to take charge of Army Group Vistula. In the meantime, the Western Front continued to crumble. 'I received the news that British troops had crossed the Rhine…' wrote Nazi Armaments Minister Albert Speer. 'Germany was being overrun.'[14] Speer was grappling with Hitler's ridiculous decree that all of Germany's industries and infrastructure must be destroyed to deny them to the advancing enemy. Speer quite rightly was worrying about the impact of this on a post-war Germany.

Chapter 2

Busse is Not to Blame

Hitler, in response to the growing threat at Küstrin, ordered five divisions from General Theodor Busse's 9th Army to attack northwards from the Frankfurt bridgehead on the east bank of the Oder to relieve the town. He hoped that after the destruction of the enemy-held bridgeheads on the west bank near Küstrin he could then strike into the rear of Zhukov's 1st Belorussian Front. In theory, this was a sound plan; in practice, it was impossible. Guderian was against this enterprise as Busse had insufficient troops but was as usual overruled by Hitler. 'I felt that such an attack was pointless,' explained Guderian, 'and proposed that our first step must be the elimination of the Russian bridgehead near Küstrin and the re-establishment of direct contact with the besieged garrison.'[1] Instead, a frustrated Guderian had to carry out the Führer's wishes.

When General Heinrici, the new commander of Army Group Vistula, learnt of the plan while visiting Zossen, he was aghast. At Frankfurt, there was only a single bridge that would be vulnerable during the German build-up and the bridgehead on the eastern bank was simply not big enough to hold five divisions. Furthermore, Soviet artillery on the nearby heights would be able to accurately shell the massing attack force. Intelligence on the strength of Soviet forces in the area indicated that the operation would never get to Küstrin. Looking at the map, Heinrici told Guderian, 'It's quite impossible.' Guderian shrugged; Hitler had made his mind up. 'Our troops will be pinned with their backs to the Oder,' warned Heinrici. 'It will be a disaster.'[2] Guderian was about to head off to Berlin to brief Hitler and suggested he go with him. 'If I'm supposed to launch this insane attack the day after tomorrow,' grumbled Heinrici, 'I'd better get to my headquarters as soon as possible.'[3]

Preparations for this operation made the situation worse. The 25th Panzergrenadier Division was pulled out of the corridor leading to Küstrin and replaced by elements of the 20th Panzer Division. The idea was that the 25th Panzergrenadier, which was one of Busse's better formations, take part in the offensive. This was not saying much as this division had been destroyed the previous summer during the collapse of Army Group Centre and subsequently re-formed. The 20th Panzer Division had been badly mauled at the same time. However, before this redeployment could be completed, Berzarin's 5th Shock Army and Chuikov's 8th Guards Army attacked on 22 March and completely cut Küstrin off. This left part of 20th Panzer and the SS garrison trapped. The situation showed that Guderian had been right in his assessment of German priorities.

Sure enough, attempts to fight through to Küstrin from Frankfurt failed. Busse launched two attacks on 23 March and both were stopped.

When Heinrici reported this, Guderian replied, 'There must be another attack.'[4] In response, Heinrici suggested that the panzers in Küstrin be allowed to break out. Guderian insisted, 'The attack must be mounted.'[5] Three days later, Guderian noted, 'Our attempt to re-establish contact with the defenders of Küstrin failed.'[6] Some of Busse's panzers catching the 8th Guards by surprise did get to the town on 27 March but were quickly deluged in Soviet shells. 'The attack,' said Heinrici, 'is a massacre. The Ninth Army has suffered incredible losses for absolutely nothing.'[7]

SS-Major General Reinefarth was ordered to defend Küstrin to the last man, but instead he chose to withdraw while the fleeting opportunity to escape remained. Hitler reacted to this by ordering his arrest. Three days later, the last of Küstrin's old forts were captured. Despite Reinefarth's actions, the Red Army took about 3,000 prisoners and killed a similar number. Reinefarth was sentenced to death and knew that his only salvation lay in surrendering to the British or the Americans. At the head of his men, he headed westwards. Stalin now had one long bridgehead on the western banks of the Oder threatening Berlin rather than two.

Hitler held Busse responsible and once more Guderian found himself embroiled in a heated row. As far as Hitler was concerned, the operation failed due to an inadequate artillery bombardment. 'I pointed out to him that Busse had had no more ammunition to hand,' recalled Guderian, 'and therefore was not in a position to fire more shells than he had in fact done.'[8] Hitler turned on Guderian, claiming it was his fault, but Guderian stated that all the ammunition he had was issued to Busse. Hitler then blamed the troops despite the fact they had suffered appalling casualties.

Guderian returned to Zossen and wrote a critical report on why he thought Hitler's plan would not work. On 28 March, he and Busse were summoned to the Führerbunker. Hitler proceeded to berate Busse, which greatly angered Guderian. 'Explanations! Excuses! That's all you give me!' yelled Hitler. 'Well! Then you tell me who let us down at Küstrin – the troops or Busse?'[9] 'I explained to you yesterday thoroughly,' said Guderian, 'both verbally and in writing – that General Busse is not to blame for the failure of the Küstrin attack.'[10] He then asked Hitler to desist from criticizing Busse.

Furthermore, Guderian wanted the 200,000 German troops needlessly trapped in the Courland pocket hundreds of miles behind enemy lines evacuated by sea. They had remained there because Admiral Karl Dönitz, with over a hundred new U-boats under construction, wanted access to the Gulf of Danzig for training. The reality that the war at sea was now a strategic irrelevance seemed to have passed Hitler and Dönitz by. There were another 400,000 men kicking their heels in Norway supposedly guarding iron-ore supplies and supporting the redundant U-boat campaign.

This defiance was too much for Hitler. His response was to sack Guderian on medical grounds and replace him with General Krebs. Looking intently at Guderian, he said, 'General, for the sake of your health you must take six weeks of convalescence immediately.'[11] When Heinrici phoned Zossen to say that 8,000 men had been lost trying to get to Küstrin he found himself talking to Krebs. Dismayed, Heinrici turned to his staff and said, 'It's not like Guderian. He didn't even say goodbye.'[12] For Guderian, the war was over. He was the last of the senior generals prepared to stand up to the Führer and from now on Hitler was completely surrounded by yes-men. Key among these was Field Marshal Wilhelm Keitel, who was known as 'nodding Keitel' and was accused of having 'the brains of a cinema usher.'[13] It did not help that he held the top job as head of the armed forces.

This was illustrated just two days later when General Heinrici met Hitler for the very first time. He requested that two of his divisions holding Frankfurt-on-the-Oder be redeployed for operations elsewhere. Hitler instantly flew into a rage. Captain Gerhard Boldt, who was present, witnessed Heinrici's stupefied expression. 'Thunderstruck, he looked questioningly from one bystander to another,' recalled Boldt. 'But none of the military, chosen as they were by Hitler and constantly in his presence, were prepared to take Heinrici's part.'[14]

In the meantime, Zhukov arrived in Moscow on 29 March to discuss the Red Army's coming assault on Berlin. When he met with Stalin the Soviet leader said in one of the understatements of all time, 'I think it's going to be quite a fight...'[15] Shortly after, Konev joined them and all three agreed that Küstrin was the key to the city. 'It was decided to launch the main attack from the Küstrin bridgehead with four infantry and two tank armies,'[16] said Zhukov. This was to commence on 16 April. At the same time, Konev would attack in order to keep Hitler's Army Group Centre away from Berlin, thereby protecting Zhukov's left flank. However, Konev was also told that in the event of Zhukov's 1st Belorussian Front being stalled on the eastern approaches of Berlin, his 1st Ukrainian Front should be poised to assault the city from the south.

Zhukov was unhappy that Marshal Rokossovsky's 2nd Belorussian Front to the north would be unable to join the general offensive until 20 April. It meant he would have to initially advance with an unsecured right flank. This could potentially leave him exposed to counterattack by the 3rd Panzer Army. He felt it would have been much better to wait until all three Fronts were ready, but Stalin would not countenance any further delay. 'It was decided to commit the tank armies to the battle after the Seelow Heights were captured,'[17] noted Zhukov after a series of planning exercises. The big question was how long the Germans could hold out on the heights.

Stalin could not wait because he was convinced the Allies were going to attempt to take Berlin before him. During the meeting with Konev and Zhukov, the Red Army's chief of operations General S.M. Shtemenko read out an intelligence warning. Konev recalled that it stated, 'The chief grouping was being formed under the command of Field Marshal Montgomery. The direction of the main strike was planned north of the Ruhr along the shortest route separating the main British forces and Berlin.'[18] The report ended by stating that the Allies firmly believed they could get there first. Stalin told his generals, 'I

To assault Berlin, Zhukov first had to clear Küstrin and the Seelow Heights.

think Roosevelt won't violate the Yalta accords, but as to Churchill, he wouldn't flinch at anything.'[19]

Stalin stared intently at Konev and Zhukov for a few moments. 'Well, then, who is going to take Berlin,' he asked them, 'we or the Allies?' It was Konev who responded with conviction, 'It is we who will be taking Berlin and we shall take it before the Allies.'[20] If there was a race then the Red Army was going to win it. Furthermore, Stalin deliberately moved the demarcation line between Konev and Zhukov further north to encourage them to openly compete for the ultimate prize. Shtemenko claimed that Stalin later admitted this when he said, 'Whoever reaches Berlin first – let him take it.'[21] Küstrin, though, would give Zhukov a head start. 'Events developed in such a way,' observed Shtemenko, 'that both [their] Army Groups took Berlin.'[22]

By this point, Gdynia, Danzig, Kolberg and Oppeln had all been captured by the Red Army. Only battered Breslau and Königsberg remained defiant, though the latter was finally forced to surrender on 9 April. Hitler sentenced the Königsberg garrison commander to death *in absentia*. Vienna was overwhelmed four days later and Hitler was incensed that SS-General Sepp Dietrich and his men did not choose to die in the rubble of the Austrian capital. He felt this was the final betrayal by Himmler's SS.

In the meantime, Armaments Minister Albert Speer vainly tried to save the Berlin Philharmonic Orchestra from being conscripted into the Volkssturm. The orchestra came under Joseph Goebbels' Propaganda Ministry and as it was good for morale, the musicians had been exempted from military service. Now that the Red Army was approaching, the orchestra's manager, Dr Gerhart von Westermann, sought Speer's help to prevent its members being mobilized for the defence of Berlin. Speer discovered that the propaganda minster was not at all sympathetic about the fate of the musicians. 'My initiative and my money made it what it has become…,' snapped Goebbels over the telephone. 'Those who come after have no right to it. It can go under along with us.'[23]

In response, Speer sent his liaison officer, Lieutenant Colonel Manfred von Poser, to destroy the musicians' call-up papers. Then, in further defiance of Goebbels, he planned to secretly evacuate all of the 105-strong orchestra. He informed Westermann that the signal for the orchestra to flee would be them finishing with Wagner's 'The Twilight of the Gods' – 'Die Götterdämmerung'. The music was hardly uplifting but for Speer it was suitably symbolic of the disaster engulfing the Third Reich. He felt it was 'a rather pathetic and also melancholy gesture pointing to the end of the Reich.'[24]

On the night of 12 April, the Berlin Philharmonic conducted their last performance in the Beethoven Hall. At the end, the mood of the audience was even further dampened when they were passed cyanide capsules by the Hitler Youth as they filed out of the building. No one noticed that under their overcoats the musicians were not wearing their normal tuxedos nor playing their best instruments. These had already been sent west into the path of the advancing Americans. In the event though, the orchestra was so fearful of retribution against their families that it voted to stay. Only a single violinist, Gerhard Taschner, and his family took Speer up on his offer to escape. 'That was the last music I would hear for a long time to come,'[25] lamented Speer. Many of the musicians, still in their overcoats, dutifully reported to the Volkssturm. Their conscription was a death sentence.

Chapter 3

Firestorm on the Seelow

Clearly, one of Stalin's greatest concerns was that the Allies would beat him into Berlin. After all the bloodletting endured by the Red Army on the Eastern Front, he did not want the Allies taking the glory. Furthermore, a large Allied military presence in the city would complicate his plans. At the Tehran conference held in 1943 there was consensus that a defeated Germany be divided to stop it waging war again in central Europe. It was then agreed at the Yalta conference in February 1945 that Germany and Berlin be divided into four occupied zones under the control of America, Britain, France and the Soviet Union. Berlin posed a serious problem in that it was to be in the heart of the Soviet-occupied zone. Stalin did not want the Allies carving out a large land corridor to the city as this could compromise his domination of eastern Germany. If he could restrict access into Berlin, it would leave the Allies' enclaves permanently reliant on the good will of the Soviet Union. To accomplish this, he needed the Red Army to get into Berlin first.

The Allies' rapid gains on the Western Front were fuelling Stalin's anxieties. In late March, they had stormed over the Rhine and the Americans swiftly trapped Field Marshal Walter Model's Army Group B in the Ruhr. General William Simpson's US 9th Army then reached the Elbe near Magdeburg on 11 April. The following day, his advance units crossed the river and were about 80 km (50 miles) from the Nazi capital. Although the Americans were within the approved future Soviet occupation zone, crucially no military stop line had been agreed upon. General Simpson wanted to thrust the tough 'Hell on Wheels' US 2nd Armored Division and the 'Thunderbolt' 83rd Infantry Division over the river and up the road to Berlin overnight. 'My mistake was in not doing this more promptly,' said Simpson, 'immediately after we got across the Elbe.'[1]

The Germans responded to the American crossing by holding Magdeburg and blowing up the bridge at Schönebeck, southeast of the city. Attempts by American engineers to build a pontoon bridge over the Elbe were thwarted by intense German shell fire. The Germans then gathered three ad hoc divisions, which forced Simpson to abandon his two weak bridgeheads. The spearhead of the 2nd Armored, unable to get its tanks over the river, came under counterattack from the hastily assembled Scharnhorst Division supported by panzers and self-propelled guns. Lacking armour and air support, the battered infantry of 2nd Armored withdrew back over the river. For its continued defiance,

Magdeburg was bombed and shelled on 17 April before the Americans stormed in. The following day, the garrison blew up the last remaining bridge and then surrendered.[2] In the meantime, Hitler created the new German 12th Army under General Wenck to defend the Elbe.

'At the time we could probably have pushed on to Berlin,' explained General Omar Bradley, commander of the US 12th Army Group, 'had we been willing to take the casualties Berlin would have cost us.'[3] He estimated that the Western Allies would lose about 100,000 men cutting their way from the Elbe to Berlin.

'A pretty stiff price to pay for a prestige objective,' Bradley told General Dwight Eisenhower, the Allied supreme commander, 'especially when we've got to fall back and let the other fellow take over.'[4] Simpson, though, felt that the Allies had lost a golden opportunity, 'I really believe that the 9th Army could have captured Berlin with little loss well before the Russians reached the city.'[5] Instead, the Red Army was about to take it.

Key to the defence of Berlin were the Seelow Heights on the western bank of the river Oder. 'This natural defence line dominated over the surrounding terrain,' noted Marshal Zhukov, 'had steep slopes and was a serious obstacle on the way to Berlin in all respects.'[6] Nazi propaganda dubbed them 'Berlin's Castle'.[7] The Seelow Heights sat astride the Reichsstrasse I that ran westwards to the capital through the towns of Seelow, Diedersdorf and Müncheberg. This was the most direct route of attack for Zhukov's 1st Belorussian Front. The horseshoe-shaped heights ranged from 30.5–61 m (100–200 ft) in height and overlooked the Oder Bruch valley. From them, German guns could shell the valley as well as the Red Army's Oder bridges and bridgeheads. 'It stood like a wall before our troops,' adds Zhukov, 'blocking the plateau where the battle at the nearest approaches to Berlin was to take place.'[8]

General Heinrici, commanding Army Group Vistula, appreciated that Zhukov would want to take the Seelow Heights as quickly as possible. He also knew that Zhukov would deluge his forward positions with a huge artillery bombardment. Heinrici, expecting trouble, on the night of 15 April ordered most of his forces back to their second line of defence. Much to Heinrici's annoyance, some of his generals did not like the idea of retreating. However, Heinrici wanted to preserve as much of his combat power as possible to face Zhukov's onslaught so was happy for the Red Army to waste ammunition on abandoned positions.

Hitler had proclaimed in his very last order of the day, 'In these hours, the whole German people looks to you, my fighters in the East, and hopes that, thanks to your resolution and fanaticism ... the Bolshevik assault will be choked in a bath of blood.'[9] Heinrici, though, was simply playing for time – as his Army Group was so weak, he was unable to conduct any large-scale counterattacks. Furthermore, his artillery only had enough ammunition for two and a half days. In the north, General Hasso von Manteuffel's 3rd Panzer Army was preoccupied countering the threat posed by Marshal Rokossovsky's 2nd Belorussian Front. This left only General Busse's 9th Army facing Zhukov and Konev. To bolster Busse, Heinrici redeployed von Manteuffel's panzer divisions.

Looking further afield around Berlin, if Zhukov also hooked north to cross the river Havel, which was likely, then this would place Oranienburg in danger. A hook south over the Spree would put Zossen in the firing line. Further south, once over the Neisse river, Konev's 1st Ukrainian Front would have to cross the Spree, which would put Spremberg, Cottbus, Baruth and Zossen in their line of advance to the German capital. Privately, Konev wanted to beat Zhukov into Berlin and hoped that Zhukov would be held up on the Seelow Heights.

Konev wanted the glory of reaching Berlin first.

Zhukov already had bridgeheads over the Oder at Kienitz and Küstrin that could act as springboards for his offensive against Berlin. By late March, he had expanded his bridgeheads so that they were 16 km (10 miles) deep and 48 km (30 miles) wide. From there, General Chuikov's 8th Guards Army could launch its attack on the Seelow Heights. Captain Sergei Golbov, a war correspondent with the Red Army, was with the build-up on the eastern bank of the Oder to the north of Küstrin. He surveyed the masses of tanks, troops, boats and pontoons in awe. 'Everywhere the bank of the river was jammed with men and equipment,' Golbov noted, 'and yet there was complete silence.'[10]

Zhukov and Chuikov set up their command post in a bunker on the Reitwein Spur overlooking the Küstrin bridgehead ready for their assault. This commenced at 0400 hours on 16 April 1945 when over 20,000 Soviet guns and rocket launchers opened fire. Soviet engineer Petr Sebelev saw that 'the sky was as bright as day from horizon to horzion.'[11] Zhukov watched through his binoculars as the land before him erupted into volcanic destruction. The sound of the guns and the resulting explosions was deafening and the ground shook for miles as shockwaves expanded to smash anything in their path. The intention was that this massive barrage would pound the German defences into oblivion. 'It seemed as if there were not a single living creature left on the enemy side,' remarked Zhukov.[12] However, many veterans of the Eastern Front knew better.

After 30 minutes, the Red Army ceased its shelling and in the air thousands of aircraft belonging to the Red Air Force began to make attacks. The Red Army then switched on 140 searchlights with the aim of dazzling the Germans and lighting the way. Colonel-General Mikhail Katukov, commander of the 1st Guards Tank Army poised

Soviet guns shelling the Seelow Heights.

to exploit Chuikov's breakthrough, exclaimed, 'Where the hell did we get all the searchlights?'[13] War correspondent Lieutenant Colonel Pavel Troyanoski recalled that the scene was like 'a thousand suns joined together.'[14] Unfortunately, the attackers themselves were soon blinded by the light reflecting off the great clouds of dust and smoke thrown up by the bombardment.

Facing the full force of Zhukov's assault was General Helmuth Weidling's 56th Panzer Corps. This consisted of the 20th Panzergrenadier Division and the 9th Parachute Division, with the ad hoc Müncheberg Panzer Division in reserve. None of these units was anywhere near up to strength. To Weidling's right was the 11th SS Panzer Corps with three divisions, though none of them was armoured. Its reserve was the ad hoc Kurmark Panzergrenadier Division. The latter had only come into existence at Cottbus in January and was never at full strength. It had gone into combat piecemeal for the very first time at Küstrin the following month. On Weidling's left was the 101st Corps with three infantry divisions supported by the 25th Panzergrenadier Division.

The 9th Parachute Division, which had been formed in February 1945, only received the last of its units eight days before Zhukov struck. Even then, two of its more experienced battalions were flown to Breslau to help with the city's defence. Most of the men were former Luftwaffe ground personnel, not jump-qualified paratroopers, who did not want to fight as infantry. General Heinrici had little faith in them. 'The 9th Parachute Division worries me,' he had told Hitler before battle commenced. 'Its commanders and non-commissioned officers are nearly all former administration officers both untrained and unaccustomed to lead fighting units.'[15]

The division was still in the process of regrouping when Soviet shells began to rain down on its positions on the Seelow Heights. Gerd Wagner, serving with the 27th Parachute Regiment, was blown into a crater and knocked unconscious. When he woke up, he discovered he was wounded and that 'all my ten comrades were dead.'[16] Dusting himself off, he managed to reach his regiment's second defence line. In response to the bombardment, Colonel Menke, Wagner's regimental commander, withdrew his headquarters from Schloss Gusow to a bunker hidden in some trees behind the village. However, Captain Finkler was left behind to liaise with their forward positions.

Zhukov launched six armies north of Küstrin into his offensive across the Oder Bruch and towards the Alte Oder. To the south, three armies struck across the Reitwein Spur towards Dolgelin and Seelow. 'Today no one is thinking about death,' said Petr Sebelev, 'but everyone is only thinking about how quickly they can roll into Berlin.'[17] Chuikov's men were able to push forwards from the western bank, but such was their frenzy for revenge, those on the eastern bank did not wait for the pontoon bridges to be assembled. Instead, some paddled across in assault boats while others simply leapt into the water using logs and empty petrol cans to keep them afloat. Captain Golbov watched 'a huge army of ants, floating across the water on leaves and twigs.'[18] Zhukov's great Oder crossing has since been described as 'a shambles.'[19]

Zhukov's assault on the Seelow Heights, 16–19 April 1945.

Forward artillery spotter Lieutenant Vasily Filimonenko and his five-man signals team crossed on a homemade raft constructed from fence posts and doors. They were about to capsize when some engineers in a boat came to their rescue. As they headed for the far bank, they watched in horror as German shells landed in the midst of some sappers trying to assemble a pontoon bridge. Filimonenko and his men, one of whom was wounded, were trapped in the water for 30 minutes before they came ashore. Fortunately, their radio was unharmed and they began to spot German muzzle flashes for their own batteries.

War correspondent Vassili Subbotin, serving with the 150th Rifle Division, part of the 79th Rifle Corps, 3rd Shock Army, recalled that their area of the river was flooded. He waited for two hours to use a swaying pontoon bridge. 'Then we crossed the Oder in our vehicle,' said Subbotin, 'the pontoon sinking into the water.'[20] Once safely over, he noted with some surprise, 'The ground was churned up, but no barbed wire, none of the concrete defensive walls that we had been told about, and no anti-tank ditches.'[21] The first German dead he saw were not in their trenches but lying in the open.

At 0655 hours, Konev's 1st Ukrainian Front launched its attack across the Neisse, which was spearheaded by five armies, with the 3rd and 4th Guards Tank Armies poised to exploit the breakthrough. Konev's attack added a sense of greater urgency as it was known that the Western Allies were now within 64 km (40 miles) of Berlin. This fuelled a growing concern within the Soviet High Command that Hitler might attempt to separately surrender Berlin to the Americans and the British. Konev had no bridgeheads over the Neisse, which meant he had to gain ground quickly if he was to beat Zhukov and the Western Allies to the German capital.

Konev's riflemen, under the cover of a smokescreen and artillery fire, crossed the river to create small bridgeheads from which the engineers could operate. Within 15 minutes of the first troops reaching the far bank, anti-tank guns were ferried over to be followed by tanks. The guns were instructed to fire at point-blank range at any approaching panzers. Within 50 minutes, the first pontoon bridges were completed and over the next four hours, sturdier bridges were also constructed that were capable of taking either 30-ton or 60-ton loads. It was soon apparent that the 4th Panzer Army, which formed part of Field Marshal Ferdinand Schörner's Army Group Centre, would not be able to stop Konev.

In the meantime, Zhukov had been lulled into a false sense of security. 'The enemy did not make a single shot during the 30-minute powerful artillery barrage,' he later wrote. 'This showed that the enemy was completely suppressed and the defence system disrupted.'[22] He was therefore furious with Chuikov when he was informed that the 8th Guards Army had stalled in the face of German artillery fire from the Seelow Heights. 'The further we got, the tougher the resistance became,'[23] observed Lieutenant Filimonenko.

The Soviet searchlights, instead of hampering the Germans had simply served to illuminate the advancing Red Army. German gunners also targeted the lights, killing many of their female crews. 'I shall never forgive Zhukov for that folly,' said Major Yury Ryakhovsky angrily. 'Everyone warned him what would happen, and begged him not to use the lights.'[24] That day, the 88th Guards Rifle Division, under Major General Pankov, successfully pierced a forward German trench network, forcing the defenders to withdraw. This unit belonged to the 28th Guards Rifle Corps, which formed part of Chuikov's 8th Guards Army. Soviet riflemen outflanked the Germans, forcing the survivors to

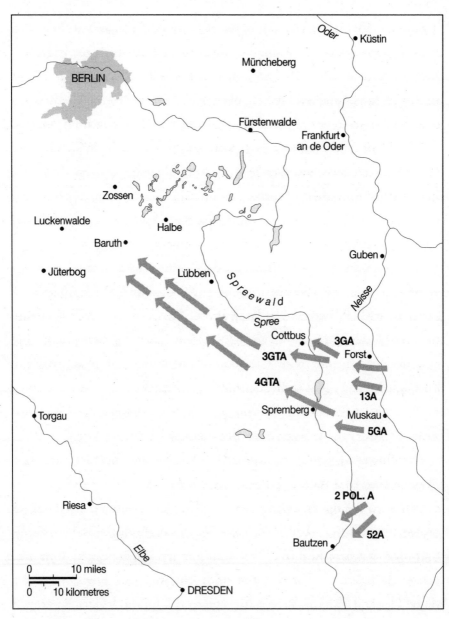

Konev's assault on the Neisse river, 16–20 April 1945.

retreat to a nearby village, which the Soviets took after bitter hand-to-hand fighting. Soviet armour supporting the infantry struggled to clear the marshy ground of the Oder Bruch and came under fire. Zhukov's solution was to order the Red Air Force to target German gun positions, while Soviet artillery continued to shell the heights.

The weather probably saved Armaments Minister Albert Speer's life on 16 April when he decided to indulge in war tourism. Early in the morning, he and Lieutenant Colonel Manfred von Poser, his liaison officer to the General Staff, travelled to the heights overlooking the Oderbruch near Wriezen to watch the historic opening of the Red Army's assault on Berlin. Dense fog on the Alte Oder meant that they could not see anything. 'A few hours later,' recalled a frustrated Speer, 'a forester brought us word that all the troops were retreating and that the Russians would soon be here. So we retreated also.'[25] They headed northwest to Schorfheide and Speer made it to General Heinrici's headquarters at Dammsmühl without mishap.

Way to the south, Konev crossed the Spree and reached Cottbus ready to hook north. It was not long before he was 34 km (21 miles) from Lübben, the town designated the boundary between the 1st Ukrainian and 1st Belorussian Fronts.

When he spoke to Stalin, he was given permission to push on Zossen, the headquarters of the German General Staff, less than 32 km (20 miles) south of Berlin.

Chapter 4

Get Moving

Zhukov had realized by 1300 hours that his battle plan was not having the desired effect. 'After a discussion with the army commanders, late on April 16,' he recalled, 'we decided to reinforce the thrust of the field armies with a powerful strike by all our planes and tank armies.'[1] He ordered Katukov's 1st Guards Tank Army and General Bogdanov's 2nd Guards Tank Army into the attack to force the issue. Katukov, who was in Zhukov's command post, stood blinking. His tanks were supposed to exploit Chuikov's breakthrough, not create it. When Zhukov saw him hesitate he yelled, 'Well! Get moving!'[2]

Katukov knew exactly what to expect as he had gone forwards to consult with Chuikov before the attack commenced. On the way, he found all the roads blocked by the 8th Guards Army. 'Taking those damned heights on the move is just about impossible,' explained an exasperated Chuikov when the pair met. 'Just see what the Germans have constructed.'[3] Katukov remembered, 'Chuikov rolled out on the table several large aerial photographs of the Seelow Heights, on which one could clearly see the dense net of rifle, communication and anti-tank trenches.'[4] The photos also showed deep east–west gullies and the steep slopes. Katukov warned that his tanks could do nothing until the infantry reached the crest. 'I was not enchanted with the idea of setting our vehicles against the still unsuppressed nests of fire,' grumbled Katukov, 'although I saw that the marshal could not decide otherwise under the circumstances.'[5]

Zhukov called Stalin at 1500 hours to inform him of the change of plan. 'So, you've underestimated the enemy … And I was thinking that you were already on the approaches to Berlin,' said Stalin reproachfully, 'yet you're still on the Seelow Heights.'[6] He had now decided to play his commanders off against each other. 'The enemy defence on Konev's Front has proved to be weak,' Stalin told Zhukov pointedly. 'He has easily crossed the Neisse and is advancing hardly meeting any resistance.'[7] This had the desired effect as Zhukov was more determined than ever to get to Berlin first. He gave an undertaking to break through by the end of the day. Stalin, however, did not change his orders to Konev.

The challenge facing Zhukov's men was getting up the steep slopes of the Seelow Heights that formed the second belt of the German defence. These presented a problem not only for Soviet tanks but also the infantry. The heights, as Chuikov and Katukov knew, were covered in bunkers, trenches and foxholes, protected by anti-tank ditches that in places were almost 3 m (9.8 ft) deep and 3.5 m (11.5 ft) wide. These positions overlooked the river valley below and were protected by sweeping crossfire from German artillery, flak guns and machine guns. The approach roads were mined and blocked with felled trees and metal hedgehogs. All the buildings overlooking the roads had been turned into fortified strongpoints concealing more anti-tank guns and machine guns.

This meant that the attackers would be subjected to a deadly deluge of fire as they struggled to reach the base of the heights in full view of the German gunners. The problem the defenders faced was that without constant Luftwaffe cover and counter battery fire they would be vulnerable to air attack and artillery bombardment. Most of the trees on the summit were by now shattered stumps. Soviet photographs of prefabricated concrete German pillboxes showed them to be horribly exposed. This indicated they had been positioned in a hurry or that the Germans were very confident they could withstand direct hits.

In Berlin, there was an air of unreality. As people trudged the ruined streets trying to find something with which to feed their families, they could hear the distant rumble of the guns. Many preferred not to believe what was happening. Surely the Führer would save the city in its hour of need? However, those who understood military matters appreciated that the Luftwaffe had failed to protect the city from devastation. It seemed unlikely to the more cynically minded that the army would fare any better on the Seelow Heights.

The German defenders on the Seelow Heights hung on with remarkable tenacity, knocking out 150 Soviet tanks and shooting down 132 aircraft. Despite this success, though, they could not hold out for much longer, as their casualties mounted and their ammunition rapidly dwindled without much hope of resupply. The 9th Parachute Division's 3rd Battalion, 26th Parachute Regiment and 2nd Battalion, 27th Parachute Regiment were swiftly destroyed while trying to hold their positions. To make matters worse, in the opening hours of the attack, the Red Army broke through the defences of Major General Heinrich Voigtsberger's 309th Infantry Division, which formed part of the 101st Corps. This posed a threat to Weidling's left flank. Then, later in the day on his right flank, the Red Army pierced the positions of Colonel Scheunemann's 303rd Infantry Division, commanded by 11th SS Panzer Corps.

General Busse despaired of Hitler's orders that insisted on no retreat, no surrender. Anyone caught not doing so was to be shot on the spot. Busse knew that it was only a matter of time before the Red Army broke through the Seelow Heights. His headquarters was inundated with requests for ammunition, fuel and reinforcements. As far as Busse was concerned, his job was to hold long enough for the Americans to arrive in Berlin. When he discussed this hope with Heinrici, the latter had said he doubted that the Americans would cross the Elbe.

Towards the end of the day, the Soviet 23rd Guards Rifle Division forming part of the 12th Guards Rifle Corps with Kutznetsov's 3rd Shock Army broke through. The division then approached a heavily defended railway embankment. It was decided that the 63rd Guards Regiment would storm it at night following a brief artillery bombardment. When the 1st Company's commander was killed, female Senior Sergeant Kravets took over. For her actions in taking the enemy position, she was awarded the title of Hero of the Soviet Union.

Katukov appreciated that although Chuikov's forces had secured the enemy positions in no man's land, their failure to penetrate the second line of defence meant that Zhukov's assault was in danger of collapsing. He ordered Major General Yushchuk's 11th Tank Corps to deploy on his right wing, Colonel Babadshanian's 11th Guards Tank Corps in the middle and Major General Drygemov's 8th Guards Mechanized Corps on the left. However, because of the terrain and the size of the bridgehead it was impossible for Katukov to commit all his forces at the same time.

That evening, Zhukov spoke with Stalin again. He tried to reassure the Soviet leader that the Seelow defences would be pierced by the end of 17 April. Stalin had grown angrier about the delay and announced that he was going to order Konev and Rokossovsky's armies to drive on Berlin. While this strategically made sense as it would trap the German armies arrayed around the city, it could also be seen as a snub to Zhukov's leadership. 'Konev's tank armies have every possibility to advance rapidly, and they should be directed to Berlin,' agreed Zhukov, 'but Rokossovsky won't be able to start the offensive before 23 April, because he will be delayed in forcing the Oder.'[8] Stalin did not like Zhukov's tone and hung up.

Just before midnight on 16 April, the Soviets gained a lodgement in the town of Seelow when they captured three houses in the northern suburbs. The fighting continued all night with German gunners continuing to take a terrible toll on their attackers. 'In the early hours on April 17 units of my corps,' reported General Weidling, 'suffering heavy losses, were forced to retreat to the heights east of Seelow.'[9] Despite Zhukov's exhortation to get forward, Katukov was soon informed that his lead tank brigade was making no progress. Katukov decided the only thing he could do was go forwards and see what the hold-up was.

From his command post, Katukov had watched as Babadshanian's tanks struggled round the shell holes and ditches. When they could not get up the steep slopes of the Seelow Heights, they had to trundle along the narrow gullies under heavy fire. Once Babadshanian had achieved a breach, Katukov ordered Drygemov to exploit it. He also committed Yushchuk's 64th Guards Tank Brigade to the breach. Babadshanian's forces, though, were met by counterattacks on the front and his left wing and the 64th Guards Tank Brigade had to be used to repel them.

In the meantime, Yushchuk's 11th Tank Corps circled round Seelow and cut the Reichsstrasse I, while south of Seelow, Soviet tanks rolled into Dolgelin and Friedersdorf at midday. When Chuikov reached Seelow, due to the ferocity of the resistance, he estimated it would take another day to break through to Berlin. That night, the Seelow Heights were taken. 'The enemy threw all that he could into the battle,' records Zhukov, 'but by sunset on April 17 and the morning of April 18, we nevertheless succeeded in shattering the defensive forces on the Seelow Heights and began to move forward.'[10] Katukov noted 'our tank troops advanced at the most only 4 kilometres per day on the 17th and 18th April.'[11]

By now, General Busse's men were at breaking point. His left flank was giving way in the face of Katukov's tanks, while his right flank was facing encirclement by Konev. Once Katukov was clear of the Seelow Heights he could begin his charge towards Berlin. General Weidling's 56th Panzer Corps had held for 48 hours, but when reinforcements in the shape of two panzergrenadier divisions failed to arrive in time it was unable to counterattack. When SS-Major General Jürgen Ziegler, commander of the 11th SS Panzergrenadier Division Nordland, arrived at Weidling's headquarters at Müncheberg he apologized for the absence of his troops. They had run out of fuel. The 18th Panzergrenadier Division should have arrived on 17 April but was a day late. Instead of taking part in a counterattack, it joined the German retreat.

To add to Busse's woes, the 9th Parachute Division, which had been mauled on the Seelow Heights, failed to hold their secondary defences. As Katukov's tanks cleared the heights, the paratroopers broke and ran. Their commander, General Bruno Bräuer, tried to stop them but it did no good. Weidling's senior artillery officer, Colonel Hans-Oscar Wöhlermann, who happened to be on the scene, drew his pistol but the paratroopers took no heed of him either. He noted that Bräuer was 'completely shattered by the flight of his men.'[12] Bräuer, who was a veteran of the invasion of Crete in 1941, suffered a nervous breakdown and had to be replaced. Although he survived the war, he was subsequently shot for war crimes.

The commander of the 27th Parachute Regiment, Colonel Menke, did not escape the chaos as he was killed when Soviet tanks rolled through his regiment's positions close to his headquarters. At Schloss Gusow, Captain Finkler gathered ten men and led a futile counterattack. Most of them were killed almost immediately. Bräuer's unfortunate division scattered in all directions. The 25th Parachute Regiment under Lieutenant Colonel Harry Herrmann fled into northern Berlin, while the 26th Parachute Regiment was driven to the northeast. Other units from the division withdrew into the southern suburbs. Herrmann would end up in command of the remains of the division and was given responsibility for Berlin Defence Sectors G and H in the north. The destruction of the 9th Parachute Division came as no surprise to General Heinrici. 'Experience has taught me that untrained units – especially those led by green officers,' he noted, 'are often so terribly shocked by their first exposure to artillery bombardment that they are not much good for anything thereafter.'[13]

By early on 18 April, the Red Army had broken through at Dieders-dorf to the west of Seelow and were on the road to Müncheberg. This meant that Weidling would have to abandon his headquarters. To the northwest of Müncheberg, the Soviet 5th Shock Army was approaching Strausberg, forcing the 11th SS Nordland Division back. 'As Babadshanian reported, there was some hard fighting at Müncheberg, halfway between Seelow and Berlin,' wrote Katukov. 'The SS people fought despairingly, the town changing hands three times.'[14] At the airfield near Müncheberg, a Soviet reconnaissance unit captured

38 intact planes. The Luftwaffe had simply run out of fuel and pilots. The Soviets kept pressing the 56th Panzer Corps flanks, repeatedly encircling it, while in the air, Soviet ground attack aircraft continued to press home their air strikes. Lieutenant Colonel Theodor von Dufving, Weidling's chief-of-staff, was forced to take cover from Soviet air strikes some 30 times in the space of four hours. Each time, he cursed the Luftwaffe for its absence.

As if all this were not bad enough, Hitler received devastating news from the Western Front on 18 April. He was informed that Army Group B, numbering some 325,000 troops, caught in the Ruhr pocket had surrendered. Three days later, its commander, Field Marshal Model, who had escaped, shot himself. This loss of such manpower was comparable to the German defeats at Stalingrad, Tunis and Falaise. Army Group B, which had fought so doggedly in Normandy and the Ardennes, ceased to exist, along with 21 divisions. German fortunes in Italy were also flagging after the Allies launched a decisive breakthrough of the Gothic Line.

Italian leader, Benito Mussolini, Hitler's one-time ally and now his puppet, on 18 April sent a congratulatory message in anticipation of the Führer's birthday. In his reply, Hitler tried to put a brave face on things. 'In the spirit of dogged contempt for death,' he said, 'the German nation and all those who are similarly minded will halt this attack.'[15] Hitler's claim in light of what was happening to the east of the capital was pure fantasy.

On 19 April, Weidling authorized his men to retreat to the outer perimeter of the Berlin defence area. 'They had suffered tremendous losses…,' he said in justifying his decision, 'they were worn down and exhausted, and were no longer able to resist the tremendous thrust of the superior Russian forces.'[16] Taking the Seelow Heights cost Zhukov over 30,000 dead; the Germans lost 12,000.

To the north, the 101st Corps tried to hold Bernau in the face of the advancing Soviet 47th Army. On the morning of 20 April, the Soviet 125th Rifle Corps launched its attack and swiftly overwhelmed the dispirited defenders. Just to the south of the town, the Soviet 1st Mechanized Corps reached Elisenau. Busse was led to believe that the Red Army was now 40 km (25 miles) from the capital and closing. His biggest concern was that Konev would cut him off to the south, so it was imperative that he retreat. General von Manteuffel was expecting his 3rd Panzer Army to be attacked on 20 April and when it was, he also intended to conduct a fighting withdrawal. The same day, the 79th Rifle Corps, belonging to the 3rd Shock Army, and the 30th Guards Gun Brigade from the 47th Army began to shell Berlin.

On 21 April, elements of the 3rd Shock, 2nd Guards Tank, 5th Shock and 47th Armies finally fought their way into Berlin's suburbs. Stalin remained worried that the Americans might beat him to the ultimate prize. However, that very day, General Eisenhower, the Allied supreme commander, advised him that he was halting his armies on the rivers Elbe and the Mulde, its southern tributary. This gave Stalin exactly the free hand he wanted to take Berlin unhindered.

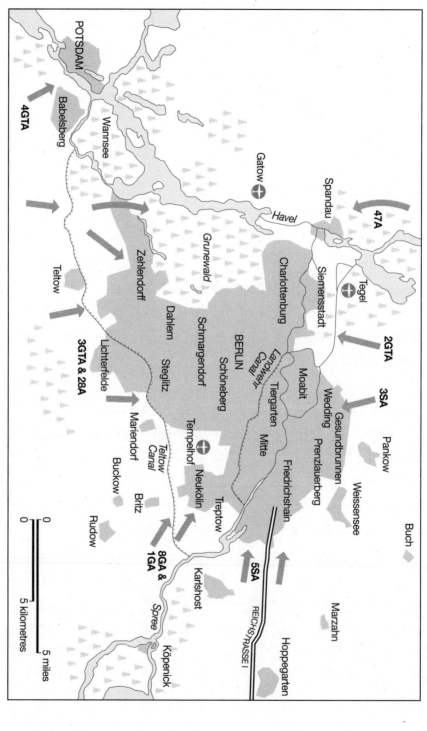

Assault on Berlin, 20 April 1945.

Chapter 5

The Poison Chalice

In early March 1945, when Major General Helmuth Reymann had been appointed the commandant of Berlin, he was handed a poison chalice. Reymann was a former divisional commander with no corps-level experience. Upon arriving from the shattered remains of Dresden he discovered that few defensive preparations had been made, nor was there an evacuation plan for the civilian population. The chain of command was a complete muddle with all the different elements of the armed forces answering to competing masters. His predecessor, Bruno Ritter von Hauenschild, had succumbed to illness, probably brought on by stress. His loss was a blow as he was a veteran panzer commander, so at least would have had a better idea of how to stop Soviet tanks on the streets.

Trying to defend all 515 sq km (200 sq miles) that the city of Berlin covered was an impossible task. It was assessed that about 200,000 troops would be needed, but they were all on the Oder, leaving just a 60,000-strong garrison comprised largely of the elderly Volkssturm home guard and Hitler Youth. To Reymann's horror, he discovered that a third of his men were unarmed and the rest were equipped with old, captured weapons that required a whole range of different types of ammunition.

Zhukov's intelligence erroneously estimated that the Germans had a million men along the Oder plus a 200,000-strong garrison being formed in Berlin. Soviet intelligence also claimed that the city had 200 battalions of Volkssturm trained for street fighting and 600 anti-aircraft guns deployed for ground fighting. In reality, Reymann only had 40 Volkssturm battalions and half of them had yet to be mustered. He also had to hand six miscellaneous army battalions, which included the Grossdeutschland Guard Regiment and an SS police battalion. There were various air defence units and supporting auxiliaries in the city, but they reported to the Luftwaffe's chain of command.

Berlin's police, numbering some 12,000, could fight, but their main task was keeping some semblance of law and order. If they were subsumed into the Waffen-SS or the Volkssturm then inevitably hungry Berliners would take advantage and loot the marshalling yards and warehouses for food. Dresden in February 1945 had been stripped of its police to create the 35th SS Police Division, which was deployed on the Neisse. Berlin also had manpower serving with 1,400 fire brigades commanded by Major General Walter Golbach. Once the fighting for the city commenced, those firemen not obliged to serve with the Volkssturm were withdrawn west to prevent their equipment falling into Soviet hands. The police were controlled by the SS and the Fire

Department; Hitler Youth and Volkssturm answered to the Nazi Party. This meant that Reymann had to work with Berlin's gauleiter Joseph Goebbels, who as well as being the Nazi propaganda minister was also the grand-sounding commissioner of Reich defence.

Hitler was determined to hold Berlin and sacked anyone who disagreed

Reymann and Colonel Hans Refior, his chief-of-staff, knew that they were completely and utterly reliant on Army Group Vistula to help them in their task. When General Heinrici replaced Himmler as commander of Army Group Vistula, he was told that he was not only responsible for the defence of the Oder but also Berlin. Heinrici refused this dual role on the grounds that he did not have the resources to do both jobs and that his primary concern was the Oder. It fell to Lieutenant General Eberhard Kinzel, Heinrici's chief-of-staff, to deliver the bad news to Refior. He explained that neither the army High Command nor the armed forces High Command would accept responsibility for Berlin. Each argued it was the other's job. Kinzel was firmly of the view that the mess was all the fault of Hitler and his inner circle for failing to face up to reality. 'As far as I am concerned,' he said angrily, 'those madmen in Berlin can fry'.[1] Refior was left dumbfounded. He now knew that Berlin would remain 'a rejected orphan'.[2] As for Kinzel, he was sacked and replaced by a Hitler appointee, Major General Thilo von Trotha. Heinrici understandably felt that he was there to spy on him. 'I know this von Trotha,' he remarked acidly. 'Maybe he's intelligent, but he embellishes the facts; he has a kind of flashy optimism'.[3]

When Reymann approached Goebbels about evacuation plans, he was instantly rebuffed. 'My dear General,' said Goebbels, 'when and if an evacuation becomes necessary I will be the one to make the decision'.[4] When Reymann pointed out that there were still around 110,000 children in Berlin under the age of ten, Goebbels claimed livestock would be brought into the city to provide milk. After leaving the meeting, Reymann turned to Refior and said, 'God help the Berliners'.[5] Goebbels, like so many other senior Nazis, naively hoped that the Red Army would be held on the Oder and that Reymann was worrying needlessly.

Such views were egged on by the likes of General Busse, who simply said what the politicians wanted to hear. On 12 April, Goebbels met with Busse, who told him he was playing for time and 'holding out until the British kick us in the ass'.[6] News that US President Franklin Roosevelt had just died also offered hope that America might lose heart in the war. Goebbels was, according to his secretary, in a state of 'ecstasy' when he phoned Hitler to tell him.[7] He also called Busse to say, 'The Czarina is dead.'[8]

Neither Reymann nor von Hauenschild had been the first choice for the role of commandant. Major General Max Pemsel, who had served as the chief-of-staff of the 7th Army in France, had also received the call. He was one of the first senior officers to raise the alarm over the D-Day landings and to appreciate their true significance. His reward for being involved in the German defeat in Normandy was to be posted to Finland to command the 6th Mountain Division. This had withdrawn into Norway when the Germans were forced to evacuate. To his surprise, on 2 April, Pemsel was instructed to fly to Berlin, but thanks to atrocious weather it took him ten days to get there. Driving through the city, he saw that the defensive preparations were 'utterly futile, ridiculous!'[9] When he arrived at armed forces headquarters, he found he was in trouble. 'You know, Pemsel,' said General Jodl, 'you were supposed to be appointed commander of Berlin, but you've arrived too late.'[10] Instead, he was now told to report to the Italian front. Pemsel was grateful for this change of heart and later remarked, 'I thanked God for allowing this bitter chalice to pass from me.'[11]

Preparing city defences felt like nugatory work to many Berliners. The plan was to mobilize 100,000 civilians to dig anti-tank ditches, gun positions and trenches. In the event, only some 30,000 actually turned up for work. Again, Soviet intelligence was faulty as Zhukov claimed, 'More than 400,000 people toiled on the defences of Berlin.'[12] West of the Oder and the Seelow Heights there was no convenient natural north–south barrier to anchor a further defensive line on except for great swathes of dense forest. The only other major north–south barrier was the river Havel, which bordered the city to the west. Cutting Berlin in half and running east–west was the river Spree, which met the Havel at Spandau. The southern part of the city was also divided by the Teltow Canal that joined the Spree and the Havel.

Berlin was organized into eight defence sectors, classified A to H, with each under the command of a colonel. The extent of their defensive measures was in practice one of personal discretion. The innermost government district was known as the Citadel, which was the responsibility of the SS. It was clear that Reymann did not have the resources to hold the forward defence line behind the Seelow or the outer defence ring on the city boundary. At best, these would be able to offer token resistance if the army gave ground. All Reymann could do was concentrate on trying to fortify the inner defence ring based on the S-Bahn railway and the Citadel. This meant barricading the streets and setting up strongpoints in buildings and their cellars on the key road junctions. A use was found for the city's burned-out trams – they were filled with cobbles and rocks to create imposing roadblocks. Zhukov

Berliners barricaded the streets with anything they could find.

knew all about these preparations. 'Berlin's defence,' he wrote, 'prepared in advance with its sectors, districts and sections, was countered by a detailed plan of the offensive.'[13]

In some places, the remains of Berlin's once grand buildings were dynamited to deny them to the Red Army. The massive Karstadt department store on Hermannplatz suffered this fate. Once a symbol of Berlin's modernity and opulence, it was now locked up to keep looters out. Guarded by the Volkssturm, the bomb-damaged building was being used for storage by the SS and as an observation post. However, the authorities decided that its imposing twin 61 m (200 ft)-high towers could provide the enemy with a vantage point, so ordered their destruction. An SS demolition team moved in and completed what the Royal Air Force had started. The blast was such that there were civilian fatalities when the building spilled a sea of rubble out into the street. The ruins would become one of the last strongholds of the French fascist Charlemagne 33rd SS Division.

Reymann's task was made even more impossible when Hitler ordered him to destroy Berlin's 950 bridges. Such an act would inevitably cut off the garrison in isolated pockets. It would also stop any units from Army Group Vistula withdrawing through the city. Reymann met with Heinrici and Albert Speer on 15 April – the day before Zhukov commenced his assault on Seelow. Both Heinrici and Speer were steadfastly against destroying the bridges, but Reymann would not be dissuaded from following orders. He knew only too well what happened to those who did not obey the Führer's dictates. In response, Heinrici said he would issue orders that bridges were to only be blown up if it became militarily necessary. Heinrici reiterated that Reymann could not count on Army Group Vistula for support. If he was pushed back, said Heinrici, he would bypass the capital. 'These instructions will assure that no bridges will be destroyed in Berlin,' explained Heinrici. 'For there will not be any battle for Berlin.'[14]

Reymann's forces were considerably weakened when he was forced to provide reinforcements for Busse's 9th Army once Zhukov's assault commenced across the Oder. Initially, it was proposed that he should send Busse four battalions, but Goebbels argued this was insufficient and instead Reymann was obliged to send everyone. Goebbels confirmed this order on 18 April: 'all forces available, including Volksturm, have been requested by the 9th Army to hold second-line positions.'[15] The city had already given up about 120 heavy anti-aircraft batteries for the defence of the Oder. Reymann could only watch as the ten best-equipped Volkssturm battalions and the Grossdeutschland Guard Regiment deployed east. There were no military vehicles to move them so buses and taxis had to be used instead. In a fury, Reymann said, 'Tell Goebbels that it is no longer possible to defend the Reich capital.'[16] Zhukov, after taking the Seelow Heights, was aware of this development. 'Then the Germans moved up from Berlin substantial forces,' he noted, 'including anti-aircraft artillery, which slowed the offensive to some extent.'[17]

Heinrici on 20 April was once again informed that he was not only responsible for Army Group Vistula but also Berlin. One of the first things he did was to call Reymann and instruct him not to destroy any bridges that were intact. In the event, 84 were blown up. Heinrici also asked for the last of the Volkssturm to be sent to him. When Reymann pointed out that this would leave Berlin utterly defenceless, Heinrici responded, 'I'm trying to make sure that fighting takes place outside the city, and not in it.'[18] Such sentiments were wishful thinking.

The following day, Reymann, who never got on well with Goebbels, found himself sacked. 'I am being replaced,'[19] Reymann told Heinrici over the telephone. Heinrici could only roll his eyes at Hitler's ever-

Volkssturm deploying to defend Berlin.

revolving door. Reymann was packed off to take charge of the German forces in Potsdam, which at least offered the prospect of surviving the war. Initially, General Wilhelm Burgdorf, Hitler's chief adjutant, recommended the Berlin post be assigned to a lieutenant colonel who was a decorated combat veteran from the Grossdeutschland Division. However, he was in hospital after being wounded.

Instead, a completely unknown and unqualified Nazi Party official was given the job as Berlin commandant. Colonel Ernst Kaether found himself being immediately promoted to major general. His previous role had been chief-of-staff for Nazi representatives within the armed forces. Kaether's only combat experience was as a regimental commander. Instead of immediately assessing his resources, he reportedly spent all his time boasting to his friends. 'Several hours were sufficient to evaluate the capacities of this man to fulfil his arduous mission,' noted Major Bernd Freytag von Loringhoven, 'and to cancel his appointment.'[20] That night, Kaether went the same way as Reymann and Hitler decided to assume command himself.

General Weidling, in the chaos of the withdrawal of 56th Panzer Corps from the Seelow Heights, lost all communication with Berlin. Hitler, on the assumption that he had deserted, sentenced him to death. When Weidling turned up at the Führerbunker on 23 April to protest his innocence Hitler promptly appointed him Berlin commandant. A dumbfounded Weidling, bumping into Krebs in the corridor, let his feelings be known. 'It would have been better if you had ordered me shot,' he said gloomily, 'then this cup would have passed from me.'[21] As he headed off to assume his new post he muttered, 'I'd rather be shot than have this honour.'[22]

By this stage, Soviet intelligence was assessing that Berlin had been reinforced by 80,000 regular troops retreating from the forward defences, as well as 32,000 police. This the Soviets estimated had pushed the strength of the garrison to over 300,000. Such numbers seem highly fanciful. It is anyone's guess where the Soviets thought the additional police had come from unless they were counting the tatty remnants of the 4th SS and 35th SS Police Divisions.[23] Furthermore, there remained no coherent chain of command in Berlin, making it impossible to co-ordinate all the disparate units. The battle for the Nazi capital would degenerate into a series of very bitter struggles for the various city districts. 'Defence Zone Headquarters is under heavy fire,' Weidling wrote in his diary. 'The account for the sins of past years has arrived.'[24]

Part 2

Beyond Help

Chapter 6

Boys on a Bridge

In the dying days of the Third Reich, Hitler deluded himself that his once all-conquering armies were coming to the rescue of Berlin. If help came from the west, he reasoned that it was vital to keep open the bridges over the Havel running north to south at Berliner Tor, Charlotten, Spandau and Pichelsdorf. All four were adjacent to the district of Spandau on the western bank of the river. The first three were not ideal because of the proximity of the river Spree running east. Therefore, the Pichelsdorf or Frey bridge, which formed the junction of Heerstrasse and the East–West Axis, offered the most direct route into the city centre. Although Hitler would not countenance such a move, holding the bridges also offered an escape route out of the capital. To the south, holding on to Wannsee Island in the Havel kept communications open with Potsdam.

Spandau was under threat from Lieutenant General Perkhorovich's 47th Army circling in from the northwest. The bridge's first line of defence just to the north was the ancient Spandau Citadel, which was located on an island in the Havel. This formidable brick edifice built in the late 1500s was protected by four bastions and would be difficult to storm. The only way in was over the brick bridge across the moat, which was blocked by a knocked-out Tiger tank. The garrison, commanded by Colonel Edgar Koch and Lieutenant Colonel Gerhard Jung, were confident they would withstand both assault across the moat and heavy bombardment. It was estimated that they could hold out for at least a week. Looking south, their guns could easily dominate the first three bridges. The garrison were not inactive, as tank hunter teams issued forth to attack the 2nd Guards Tank Army on the approaches from Siemensstadt district to the east.

Hitler did not have the troops to defend the approaches to the bridges, so this task was assigned to the Hitler Youth and Volkssturm. The so-called Hitler Youth Regiment or Division, which numbered about 3,000[1] to 5,000[2] teenagers, were trained at the Reich Sports Field stadium just to the northeast of Pichelsdorf. 'You see very young boys, baby faces peeping out beneath oversized steel helmets,' observed one Berliner. 'They're fifteen years old at the most, standing there looking so skinny and small in their billowing uniform tunics.'[3] A number of early sources claim that only about 1,000[4] Hitler Youth took part in the defence of Berlin, but in light of their widespread deployment this is much too conservative. This figure may only refer to those in the city centre. Their principal weapon was the hand-operated *Panzerfaust* anti-tank weapon. Fifteen-year-old boys such as Willy Feldheim, Klaus Küster and Lothar Loewe were handed what the Soviets called '*Faustpatronen*'[5] (anti-tank weapons) and given scant instruction on how to use them.

A battalion of boys aged from 12 to 15 was sent to defend Pichelsdorf and others were deployed to Charlotten. They were ordered to dig in either side of the Heerstrasse in front of the bridges. There, they were to lie either in pairs or on their own at irregular intervals, ready to fight off Soviet tanks. They were a pitiful sight. Dorothea von Schwanenflügel came across some of them and questioned one of the boys. 'Tears were running down his face, and he was obviously very frightened of everyone,' she observed. 'He ... told me that he had been ordered to lie in wait here, and when a Soviet tank approached he was to run under it and explode the grenade.'[6] The boy also confessed that he did not really know how to fire the *Panzerfaust*. 'In fact,' concluded von Schwanenflügel, 'this frail child didn't even look capable of carrying such a grenade.'[7] Hitler Youth units were also instructed to defend Zehlendorf to the east of Wannsee and Schöneberg south of the Landwehr Canal.

Artur Axmann, the head of the Hitler Youth, tried to inspire them by saying, 'There is only victory or defeat.'[8] The boys then watched as he drove off in his staff car. Axmann personally preferred the safety of the Führerbunker. They were left under the command of regional leader Dr Schlünder. Marshal Konev noted, 'These last defenders of the Third Reich, including some very young boys, regarded themselves as the final hope for a miracle that would take place at the very last moment against all odds...'[9] Thus the defence of western Berlin rested in the hands of little more than schoolchildren.

Axmann also moved to help with the defence of eastern Berlin. General Weidling was dismayed by Axmann's arrival at his headquarters in Waldsieversdorf, northwest of Müncheberg, late on 18 April. Axmann announced that his Hitler Youth were deploying on the roads behind the 56th Panzer Corps. Weidling was flabbergasted. What use were teenage boys on bicycles carrying *Panzerfausts* against the well-equipped Red Army? 'You cannot sacrifice these children,'[10] he angrily told Axmann. The latter was taken aback as he had assumed the general would be pleased. 'I will not use them,' added Weidling, 'and I demand that the order sending these children into battle is rescinded.'[11] The spineless Axmann promised to issue the order and disappeared. The hapless Hitler Youth, though, were not pulled out of the line. Willy Feldheim and 130 other boys were deployed in the Klosterdorf area east of Berlin. In the face of continued terrifying Soviet attacks, they fell back. Exhausted, some of them fell asleep in a bunker and when they awoke, they found the war had passed them by, though the ground was strewn with their dead.

Two days later, on Hitler's birthday, Axmann presented some of his boy soldiers from a 'Tank Destruction Unit'[12] to the Führer in the grounds of the Reich Chancellery. He proudly told Hitler that they had 'recently distinguished themselves at the front.'[13] Hitler, looking visibly unwell, managed to muster a weak smile and gently tugged at one of the lad's ears. 'All you could hear,' noted Axmann, 'was the distant rumbling from the front, now scarcely nineteen miles away.'[14] Although Axmann regularly briefed Hitler in the Führerbunker, until 26 April his command post was located at 86 Kaiserdamm and then for the next four days it was in a cellar under the Chancellery at 64 Wilhelmstrasse.

SS-Brigadier Gustav Krukenberg, leading a battalion into Berlin from his 33rd SS Division Charlemagne, reached Pichelsdorf on 24 April. Approaching from Gatow, he was surprised to meet no one except for three Hitler Youth on bicycles armed with *Panzerfausts*. He observed that, 'The big bridges across the Havel on the strategic Berlin-Spandau Road were barricaded but unguarded!'[15] Soviet artillery was shelling the area but failed to hit the Pichelsdorf bridge. A lone Soviet aircraft appeared and attempted to bomb it without success either.

Krukenberg's men camped overnight in the trees near the Reich Sports Field Stadium while he went into the city to receive orders.

Krukenberg was to assume control of Defence Sector C and replace SS-Brigadier Joachim Ziegler as commander of the 11th SS Panzergrenadier Division Nordland. Ziegler seems to have lost his nerve; according to Krukenberg, he had requested to be relieved. However, General Weidling had no confidence in Ziegler and wanted him removed. Krukenberg was somewhat dismayed to learn from General Krebs that although numerous units outside the city had been summoned, the French SS were the only ones to answer the call.

On 25 April, the Red Army overran Zehlendorf almost immediately. The Hitler Youth and Volkssturm units tried to stage their last defence around the town hall. They were blasted by Soviet artillery and tanks at close range. The mayor attempted to stop the butchery by hanging out a white flag. He then took his own life. Soviet riflemen marching through Schöneberg avoided the blocked streets by entering the neighbouring buildings to emerge behind the defenders. About 400 Hitler Youth were cornered and gunned down. They did not have the skill or experience to be able to save themselves. 'There is only one way in which I can describe the mood of the Volkssturm,' said Marshal Konev, among whom he included the boy soldiers, 'in the decisive fighting for Berlin – hysterical self-sacrifice.'[16] Konev and Zhukov's forces linked up on 25 April to the west of Berlin and Potsdam at Ketzin on the Havel. Contact had been made southeast of Berlin the previous day.

Soviet troops attempted to cut between the Havel bridges and the Reich Sports Field Stadium on 27 April. They pushed towards the Charlottenburger Chaussee to the north of the stadium. This area was held by about 1,000 troops forced back from the Siemensstadt district, who were hastily reinforced by 2,000 new Hitler Youth recruits. These

Hitler was so short of troops he had to employ the Hitler Youth to defend Berlin.

boys had been rounded up from their homes and as no weapons were available, they were told to pick them up off the battlefield. Although the Soviets were driven back, their attackers were caught in a deadly crossfire with predictably horrific results.

By 30 April, the Hitler Youth units at Pichelsdorf bridge and along the Heerstrasse were still holding out despite the presence of the Soviet 47th Army, as were those on the Spandau bridge. War correspondent William Shirer later wrote, 'Artur Axmann ... had deserted his battalion of boys at Pichelsdorf Bridge to save his neck.'[17] That day, the Soviet 125th Rifle Division set about ending German resistance at Kladow, southwest of Gatow, and at Pichelsdorf. Axmann, hoping to help Hitler escape Berlin, gathered 200 Hitler Youth at the Reich Chancellery. When Hitler refused to go, Axmann kept them as a personal bodyguard.

Major Bernd Freytag von Loringhoven, General Guderian's aide-de-camp, Lieutenant Colonel Rudolf Weiss, General Burgdorf's aide-de-camp and Captain Gerhard Boldt were given permission by Hitler to escape down the Havel. After leaving the Führerbunker on 29 April, they made their way through the Tiergarten to the zoo. Reaching Charlottenburg, they were given a ride in an armoured car to the stadium.

When von Loringhoven and his companions reached Pichelsdorf at dawn on 30 April they crossed the bridge despite the presence of three Soviet tanks on the far bank. Mercifully, these did not open fire because their crews were still sound asleep. 'On the other side,' noted von Loringhoven, 'the Hitler Youth in position with their rocket-launchers had not budged.'[18] The Hitler Youth, Volkssturm and regular soldiers had bravely weathered five days of constant artillery and tank fire defending Pichelsdorf. 'Inadequately equipped with only rifles and *Panzerfausts*, the boys have suffered terribly from the effects of the Russian shelling,' their commander told Captain Boldt. 'Of the original 5,000 only 500 are still fit for combat.'[19] Pichelsdorf bridge was then severed after the Soviets hit the German demolition charges.

In Spandau, the streets echoed to the sound of Soviet propaganda broadcasts in German as loudspeaker trucks drove up and down exhorting the defenders to surrender. The latter responded by shelling the areas held by the Soviets. In the meantime, von Loringhoven and the others found a boat and paddled down to Wannsee. Weiss was subsequently captured by the Soviets and von Loringhoven taken by the Americans.

On 1 May, frightened Berliners and exhausted troops also tried to use Hitler's so-called relief route to escape. Just before midnight, the survivors of the Müncheberg Panzer Division, the 18th Panzergrenadier Division and the 1st Flak Division, using the last of their half-tracks and panzers, headed westwards from the Tiergarten. These ragged formations were divisions in name only. Their objective was the Charlotten bridge and Spandau. Rumour had it that trains would take them to Hamburg.

They were soon joined by a horde of hangers-on, both military and civilian, in buses, delivery vans and even fire engines. Among them was Heinrich Himmler's brother Ernst. 'Mothers with prams were hoisted on trucks, whose wood gas generators burned smokily,' recalled Lothar Loewe. 'Elegant ladies slung rucksacks over fur coats.' Looking down the column he noted, 'Paymasters, army veterinary surgeons ... paratroopers and the remainders of still passably organized units, set off.'[20] This mass exodus involved up to 10,000 people. Charlotten bridge had changed hands three times, which meant it would have to be secured again to facilitate the breakout.

The Hitler Youth at Charlotten were under a deluge of shellfire from Perkhorovich's 47th Army. When the column of escapees arrived, they deployed 20-mm quad self-propelled flak guns along the eastern bank to provide covering fire. This did not have the desired effect. Major Horst Zobel with the Müncheberg Panzer Division decided to press on regardless. Clambering into his armoured personnel carrier, he led the last of their tanks across the bridge.

The first wave of people and vehicles was met by a hail of bullets, bombs and shells and few survived. Some in desperation threw themselves into the river. Human remains and wreckage were strewn along the entire length of the bridge. From the second wave, some managed to reach the shelter of the houses on the far bank. Anyone wounded on the bridge was left behind and many were crushed by the successive waves of frightened humanity. Among the dead was Ernst Himmler. The German flak guns kept firing until they ran out of ammunition or were silenced by Soviet mortar bombs dropped from the surrounding neighbourhoods.

Numbers counted in favour of the escapees and the Soviets were eventually forced from the river. Under fire from Soviet machine guns in the tower of Spandau town hall, the Germans fought back. A detachment from the 9th Parachute Division supported by a Tiger tank stormed the building. The greatly reduced column drove on westwards with ever decreasing numbers. At every turn, they were decimated and very few ever reached the Elbe. About 5,000 got as far as the village of Tremmen, but having run out of ammunition and fuel they had little option but to surrender. Zhukov, fearful that Hitler and other senior Nazis might be among the carnage on Charlotten bridge, ordered every dead body and abandoned vehicle to be checked. It was a grim task as most had been so badly burned that they were beyond recognition.

That day, Soviet tanks supported by the 350th Rifle Division overcame German resistance on Wannsee Island, which was held by the remains of the 20th Panzergrenadier Division. They attempted to break out southwards. Only about 2,000 made it, but they were eventually cornered by Soviet fighters and tanks supported by infantry. When the shooting stopped, just 187 remained, including a few frightened Hitler Youth. By this stage, continued resistance by the teenagers on the bridges had become pointless. 'It was a crime that children should have had to be used – abused is perhaps the better word – in such a way,' wrote historian James Lucas, 'and the crime must be laid at the door of Hitler and his associates.'[21]

General Perkhorovich was reluctant to storm the remaining German defences, especially Spandau Citadel. He decided to send Major Grishin and Captain Gall from his propaganda department to negotiate with the Citadel garrison. They approached the brick bridge under a white flag and were greeted by a rope ladder. Once inside, they were met by Colonel Jung and Lieutenant Colonel Koch. The latter noted that Hitler's orders stated that any fortress commander who attempted to surrender was to be executed immediately, along with their family. Grishin and Gall did not know that Hitler was dead by this stage so were unable to point out that his orders no longer stood.

Captain Gall, who could speak German, explained that Berlin had been overrun and that the Red Army had linked up with the Americans on the Elbe. He offered immediate medical assistance, food and no reprisals if they surrendered. The alternative would result in no mercy being shown. 'We are all soldiers and we all know that a great deal of blood would be shed,' said Gall firmly. 'And if many of our soldiers die in the process, I cannot answer for the consequences.'[22] He then told them they had until 1500 hours to make up their minds. The two Soviet officers then returned to their own lines. At the allotted hour, two German lieutenants emerged from the Citadel to say their commandant had accepted the terms of surrender but would need them in writing.

Later, when the garrison was being marched out by Soviet riflemen, Lieutenant Colonel Koch approached Grishin and Gall. 'We are about to say goodbye to you,' he said in fluent Russian. 'Yes, I speak a little Russian. I lived in Petersburg as a child.'[23] The Soviets later discovered that the two German commanders were doctors responsible for Germany's chemical weapons programme. The Red Army also captured at Spandau doctors Schulte-Overberg and Stuhldreher. All four men had been involved in developing and testing sarin and tabun nerve agents. They were sent to the Soviet Union but declined to divulge their secrets.

Chapter 7

This Attack is Murder

While events were playing out at Pichelsdorf and Spandau on 21 April, Hitler ordered an all-out counterattack on the Soviet armies surrounding Berlin. In particular, he hoped that Himmler's Waffen-SS would ride to the rescue as it had done so many times before. The Führerbunker staff were alarmed by the sight of Hitler leaning over his map repeatedly muttering 'Steiner, Steiner.'[1] All became clear when he ordered SS-General Felix Steiner's forces some 40 km (25 miles) to the north of Berlin to march on the city. Steiner would cut through Zhukov's spearhead and cover the withdrawal of von Manteuffel's 3rd Panzer Army. Hitler placed his faith in Steiner because he was a tough Eastern Front veteran who had served with the Waffen-SS from the very start. Most notably, he had helped organize the evacuation of

80,000 soldiers and civilians from Tallinn and successfully withdrawn from Courland.

More recently, Steiner had commanded the short-lived 11th SS Panzer Army in Pomerania, which had rescued the German garrison trapped at Arnswalde. Afterwards, Steiner withdrew with his 3rd SS Panzer Corps to the Stargard and Stettin area on the northern Oder. In Hitler's fevered mind, this SS army still existed, which he inflated to the status of Army Group Steiner, whereas in reality it had been stripped of its divisions for use elsewhere. Steiner stood slack-jawed as he listened to the Führer on the telephone. Hitler informed him that Reichsmarschall Göring was to place his private army at Steiner's disposal. Furthermore, all the forces between the capital and the Baltic were to be involved in the attack. 'When I asked precisely where the attack was to take place,' recalled a bemused Steiner, 'the Führer gave me no answer. He simply hung up. I had no idea where or when or with what I was to attack.'[2]

In a state of confusion, Steiner called General Krebs, the army's chief of the general staff, to explain his situation. It was clear that Hitler had no idea of the realities of the Eastern Front. Even if he wanted to attack towards Berlin, he simply did not have the troops for such an operation. He had lost three entire divisions trying to stop the Red Army and two fresh divisions promised by Army Group Vistula never materialized. His forces comprised the battered remains of 4th SS Police Division, which had escaped from Danzig without its equipment, amounting to just two battalions and a division of sailors. The latter was needed to relieve two of his other divisions that were tied down holding defensive positions. Steiner argued that the sailors were only good for guard duties and could not be expected to fight as regular infantry.

Before Steiner could finish, Krebs handed him over to Hitler. 'You will see,' said the Führer, 'the Russians will suffer their greatest defeat, the bloodiest defeat of their history, before the gates of Berlin.'[3] Steiner rubbed his stubbled chin with his free hand and rolled his eyes. 'Upon the successful conclusion of your mission,' concluded the Führer, 'depends the fate of the German capital.'[4] When Steiner's orders arrived, they stated everyone was under pain of death not to withdraw and if they did not carry out the Führer's wishes. 'Officers who do not comply unconditionally with this order are to be arrested and shot immediately,' Hitler warned the hapless SS-general. 'You, Steiner, are answerable with your head for the execution of this order.'[5] Steiner realized that further argument with Hitler or Krebs was a waste of time.

Hitler then personally called General Karl Koller, the Luftwaffe's chief-of-staff, at Wildpark-Werder on the outskirts of Berlin. 'All Air Force personnel in the northern zone who can be made available are to be placed at the disposal of Steiner and brought to him,'[6] he instructed. As usual, he was not taking 'no' for an answer. 'Any commander who holds back his troops,' Hitler warned Koller, 'will forfeit his life in five hours.' After Koller looked aghast, Hitler said, 'You yourself will guarantee with your head that the last man is thrown in.'[7] In a panic, the unfortunate Koller phoned the army High Command to find out who or what was Steiner. When General Heinrici heard of Hitler's mad plan, he was appalled. He called Krebs to denounce it and demand the withdrawal of the 9th Army. Krebs responded that the decision was not Heinrici's to make and, 'That responsibility is borne by the Führer.'[8] Nor would Krebs let Heinrici talk to Hitler, on the grounds that the Führer was very tired. What he really meant was that the Führer was tired of arguing with his recalcitrant generals.

At most, Steiner could muster about 11,000 soldiers with hardly any artillery, anti-tank guns or panzers. He had fewer than 50 tanks and even then, he only had enough fuel for about half of them. This equated to barely a division, hardly the powerful army or army group that Hitler envisaged. Steiner anticipated there would be at least 100,000 well-equipped Soviet troops blocking his way. Hitler's attack would result in nothing but a massacre. When 5,000 reinforcements did turn up, they consisted mainly of Luftwaffe ground personnel who, like the sailors, were barely suitable as infantry. Steiner refused to use them on the grounds that he would be signing their death warrants.

'The Navy men I can forget about,' said Steiner angrily. 'I bet they're great on ships, but they've never been trained for this kind of fighting.'[9] He later admitted, 'I did not want to lose a single man in an enterprise which was doomed to crushing disaster from the beginning.'[10] Furthermore, he was not going to start executing his officers for failing to carry out such a ridiculous task. 'The plan of attack was based on facts that had no basis in reality,' explained Steiner, 'but only in the fantasies of the Chancellery.'[11] His best hope was to reach the Elbe and surrender to the Americans. Hitler's northern pincer would be heading west, not south.

Hitler kept pestering General Krebs on the morning of 22 April about the progress of Steiner's attack. Krebs' response was that there was nothing to report as yet. Hitler then asked General Koller to send out reconnaissance aircraft to see how Steiner was doing, but they could not find him. By the afternoon, at the daily military conference, after hearing that Berlin was almost completely surrounded, Hitler demanded to know what was going on. Reluctantly, Krebs admitted that Steiner had not attacked as he was still gathering his forces. Hitler went quiet, then ordered everyone out of the room except for his senior commanders, Burgdorf, Jodl, Keitel and Krebs. He then flew into an absolutely monumental rage, accusing everyone of betrayal, corruption and cowardice. 'The war is lost!'[12] he screamed in fury. Then, in despair, he added, 'It's all finished, everything, everything…'[13] Looking round the room, having calmed down slightly, he said, 'Gentlemen, it's over. I shall stay here in Berlin and shoot myself when the moment comes.' His generals stirred uneasily, wondering if they were expected to die alongside him. 'Anyone who wants can go now,' he said. 'Everyone is free to do so.'[14]

When asked how he could continue to command without his staff, Hitler retorted that Reichsmarschall Göring could take over the leadership. He had been named as Hitler's official successor in 1941. Hitler's generals tried to placate him and suggested that he evacuate south. After all, they reasoned, Field Marshal Schörner's Army Group Centre remained fully intact in Czechoslovakia, as did Field Marshal Kesselring's two armies in northern Italy. Likewise, Admiral Dönitz had headed for northwest Germany to take command of the armies still fighting there. Hitler, though, would not be dissuaded from his chosen course of action.

While Krebs and Burgdorf opted to remain in the Führerbunker, Keitel and Jodl, having lost their headquarters at Zossen, moved to Krampnitz between Berlin and Potsdam. Keitel did not want to abandon the Führer, but Hitler responded, 'You will follow my orders.'[15] Major Bernd von Loringhoven recalled Hitler said, he would 'stay in Berlin to direct the defence of the city and end his life rather than fall into enemy hands.'[16] Hitler summoned Joseph Goebbels, his wife and their six children from their bomb-damaged house in Wilhelmstrasse to join him.

General Koller had not attended the briefing and sensibly remained out of the way at Luftwaffe headquarters. 'I should never had been able to tolerate being insulted all day,' he noted in his diary. At 1815 hours, General Eckhard Christian, the Luftwaffe liaison officer at the Führerbunker, arrived to brief Koller about Hitler's complete meltdown. Koller was so amazed that he headed to Krampnitz, where Jodl told him that Hitler wanted Göring to negotiate with the Allies. Koller flew to Munich to inform his boss of this on 23 April. The dithering Göring feared that if he took power, he could be branded a traitor and that if he did not act, he would be perceived as weak. Foolishly, he sent Hitler a message saying that if he did not hear back by 2200 hours he would automatically assume the leadership of Germany. Presenting Hitler with such an ultimatum was immediately seen as a deliberate provocation. Hitler's response was to accuse him of high treason and order that to avoid the death penalty he must resign all his official posts with immediate effect. For good measure, Göring was arrested by the SS.

On 23 April, Hitler sent SS-Lieutenant General Hermann Fegelein to personally deliver his orders to Steiner. Fegelein was Himmler's liaison officer in the Führerbunker so carried not only the authority of the Führer but also the Reichsführer, the commander of the SS. The ambitious and legendary playboy had married Gretl, Eva Braun's sister, the previous summer. In light of Eva being Hitler's long-term mistress, this made Fegelein the Führer's de facto brother-in-law. Steiner still refused to comply and told Fegelein he could not act until he had gathered sufficient troops. Empty-handed, Fegelein returned to Hitler the following day. 'Steiner must attack tomorrow,' yelled Hitler. 'He must be in Berlin by the evening!'[17] Hitler then ordered Fegelein to go back to Steiner.

In the meantime, Jodl pointlessly went to see Steiner to order him to get started. Steiner made his position perfectly clear: 'I don't want to do it.'[18] Jodl said that he should deploy his fresh reinforcements. 'Yes, all those pilots with little iron crosses dangling from their collars,' Steiner replied sarcastically. 'No! They are all untrained. They'll be slaughtered by the Ivans.'[19] An exasperated Jodl returned to his headquarters. When General Heinrici arrived, he got a similar response from Steiner when he enquired about his forces. 'I'll tell you what I have,' said Steiner, 'a completely mixed-up heap that will never reach Spandau from Germendorf.'[20]

Steiner had been promised the 3rd Naval Division, 7th Panzer Division and the 25th Panzergrenadier Division to strengthen an attack from his bridgehead at Kremmen, south of the Ruppiner Canal. In theory, this meant he could strike southeast to Spandau and southwest to Nauen. Two full-strength armoured units might have done the trick, but the truth was both divisions were emaciated. Furthermore, these three divisions had yet to materialize. General Heinrici requested that they be sent to bolster the 3rd Panzer Army instead, but General Jodl refused. This did not stop Heinrici ordering the 7th Panzer Division not to move.

Shortly after, Field Marshal Keitel arrived at Steiner's headquarters and ordered him to move on Nauen. He promised him the Schlageter Infantry Division, despite the fact that it had ceased to exist a week before on the west banks of the Elbe. Keitel was at a loss regarding the whereabouts of the 7th Panzer Division. Unknown to him, Colonel Hans Christern, its commander, was intent on withdrawing westwards to surrender to the British. Brandishing his field marshal's baton, he tried to bully Steiner into launching an attack. 'History and the German people will despise everyone who does not do his utmost to save the situation and the Führer,'[21] he warned. 'No, I won't do it,' replied Steiner. 'This attack is murder. Do what you want with me.'[22] Keitel and Jodl had to accept that Hitler's elite Waffen-SS commander was now fighting for one thing and one thing only – survival. Once again, the 3rd SS Panzer Corps failed to obey.

According to most accounts, Steiner's attack never took place. However, on 24 April, von Loringhoven noted, 'With his three divisions almost out of steam, Steiner's group eventually launched their attack, but given the Russian superiority, it came to nothing.'[23] Once again, Hitler was furious and von Loringhoven adds, 'Steiner was dismissed and replaced by General Holste, but made a pact with the latter to retain his command.'[24] Steiner no doubt informed his successor that his so-called army group was a figment of Hitler's deluded imagination. That day, Soviet tanks captured Nauen and began pushing south towards Potsdam.

General Rudolf Holste was in command of the 41st Panzer Corps that formed part of General Wenck's 12th Army. This comprised just three weak infantry divisions. Holste had his hands full as Keitel had ordered him to ignore the Elbe and protect Wenck's northern flank and march on Berlin. However, Holste knew he was not going anywhere in a hurry as his corps not only lacked tanks but also transport. He requested 48 hours to prepare for redeployment. He then telephoned his wife to prepare for their escape westwards.

Hitler learnt that von Manteuffel's 3rd Panzer Army had been forced back by a Soviet breakthrough north of Prenzlau, which exposed Steiner's rear. Ironically, it was the redeployment of troops to support Steiner that had facilitated the Red Army's latest success. The unfortunate 3rd Naval Division was swiftly destroyed during the withdrawal. This breakthrough forced Keitel to release the 7th Panzer and 25th Panzergrenadier Divisions to Heinrici and not Steiner. It meant that Steiner's northern pincer was finally written off. Although ordered to counterattack, Heinrici instructed his men to hold the line Neubrandenburg–Neustrelitz north of Berlin to cover the retreat.

Hitler's reaction as normal was to blame his commanders. 'In view of the broad natural barrier formed by the Oder,' he said, 'the Russian success against the 3rd Panzer Army can only be attributed to the incompetence of the German military leaders there!'[25] Krebs leapt to the defence of von Manteuffel, but this simply reminded Hitler of Steiner's failure. Looking at the map, Hitler resumed his demand for a counterattack north of Berlin. 'The 3rd [Panzer] Army will make use of all available forces for this assault, ruthlessly depleting those sections of our frontline which are not under attack,'[26] he instructed.

Hitler chose to ignore the fact that the Eastern Front had long ceased to exist and that he had no reserves because he refused earlier in the year to withdraw his numerous divisions from the occupied territories. Looking at his generals, he added, 'It is imperative that the link to Berlin from the north be restored tomorrow evening.' When Steiner's name was mentioned, Hitler cried, 'Those arrogant, tedious, indecisive SS leaders are no good to me anymore.'[27] The relief of Berlin would have to be conducted by somebody else. The question though was who?

After Fegelein saw Steiner for the second time, he visited Himmler in his personal train west of Hohenlychen. When he told the Reichsführer that Steiner was repeatedly refusing to obey orders, Himmler revealed he had instructed Steiner not to act so as to force Hitler to leave Berlin as soon as possible. There was, he said, no chance of Steiner breaking through the Soviet ring round the city. This, however, was only part of the picture; Himmler had opened negotiations to surrender. Fegelein flew back to the capital, landing on the East–West Axis. He dared not tell the Führer what Himmler had told him because he was loyal to the Reichsführer and likewise wanted Hitler to leave Berlin.

Chapter 8

Where is Wenck?

The only other forces potentially available to try to save Berlin were General Wenck's 12th Army to the southwest, holding the Elbe on the Western Front. He was instructed to leave a rearguard to face the Americans and march on the capital at once. On paper, his army numbered seven divisions, but in practice, manpower-wise these amounted to just three infantry divisions with no panzers or air support. Wenck's forces numbered at most about 45,000 men. Field Marshal Keitel drove to Alte Hölle to personally order Wenck to save Berlin and link up with Busse's 9th Army. Wenck wisely responded by saying what Keitel wanted to hear, 'Of course, Field Marshal, we will do what you order.'[1] At the same time, Busse was told to pull his strongest division out of the line and send it west to link up with Wenck. However, Busse knew that such a move would simply weaken his already crumbling defences. Wenck, assessing what intelligence he had, realized that rescuing the troops of Busse and Reymann was the real priority, not Berlin.

Encouragingly, reports soon began to come in that Wenck was indeed marching on Berlin. In reality, only limited elements of his 20th Corps, with four 'divisions', was pushing north with the sole goal of getting as far as Potsdam and no further. Once at Potsdam, it was hoped to rescue General Reymann's 20,000-strong garrison. Just one division was involved in this northern thrust while the rest were battling eastwards in a desperate bid to save Busse's 9th Army from being slaughtered. Busse, after being driven from the Seelow Heights, had delayed withdrawing his forces because of Hitler's demands that he defend Berlin. He and his men were therefore trapped once Marshal Konev had rolled past Zossen and reached the Teltow Canal in southern Berlin.

Wenck struck east between Beelitz and Treuenbrietzen on 24 April using elements of three divisions. His aim was to reach Luckenwalde to the southwest of Kummersdorf. His men immediately ran into the Soviet 5th Guards Mechanized Corps and elements of the 13th Army. In anticipation of this attack, Major General Yermakov commanding the 5th Mechanized had moved to set up ambush positions with his artillery and tanks. He also established a mobile reserve using a tank company from the 51st Guards Tank Regiment, whose job was to seal any German breakthroughs.

At Treuenbrietzen, the Germans attacked day and night but the Soviet 10th Guards Mechanized Brigade refused to give ground. The following day, units from two of Wenck's divisions, supported by assault guns, renewed the attack but were bombed by the Red Air Force. 'They came in, wave after wave, at hedge-hopping altitudes,' said Konev, 'showering the attacking German tanks with small anti-tank bombs.'[2]

The Soviet 13th Army then moved to reinforce the beleaguered defenders of Treuenbrietzen and reinforce the left flank of the 5th Guards Mechanized Corps.

Not all the fighting was going the Soviets' way. Notably, the 10th Mechanized Corps was almost surrounded and in danger of being overrun. The Soviet 30th Army quickly sent help in the form of the 147th Rifle Division. On the afternoon of 25 April, the 15th Rifle Regiment moved into southern Treuenbrietzen to reach 10th Mechanized. The rest of the 147th Division then linked up with 5th Mechanized. 'The fresh attempts by Wenck's army on April 25 in the Beelitz-Treuenbrietzen area proved to be just as futile as the preceding ones,' reported Konev with satisfaction. 'The attacks were fierce, but we beat them back successfully and our losses were minimal.'[3]

That day, Hitler nonetheless continued to indulge his optimistic delusion that the capital would be saved by a three-pronged attack. 'The situation will improve! The 9th Army will approach Berlin and hit the enemy together with the 12th Army,' he reassured General Weidling, the military commandant of Berlin. 'This attack will be inflicted along the Russian southern front. Steiner's troops will advance from the north and hit the northern wing.'[4]

'All these plans were the fantasies of Hitler and his entourage,' said Zhukov dismissively, 'who had lost the capacity of thinking realistically.'[5] This was especially true once Konev and Zhukov's forces that circled to the west of Berlin had linked up. On 25 April, the 328th Rifle Division belonging to the 47th Army and the 65th Tank Brigade from the 1st Guards Tank Army, forming the spearhead of Zhukov's 1st Belorussian Front, met with the 6th Guards Mechanized Corps from the 4th Guards Tank Army with Konev's 1st Ukrainian Front in the Ketzin area. Thereby, the more than 400,000-strong Berlin enemy force was cut into two isolated groups,' reported Zhukov, 'the Berlin and the Frankfurt-Guben group.'[6]

The 35th Guards Mechanized Brigade from General Lelyushenko's 4th Guards Tank Army was tasked with taking Ketzin. However, two of its battalions were sent to Brandenburg, leaving just an infantry and artillery battalion and some tanks. At Ketzin, with no sign of the Germans, three or four volunteers swam the Havel channel to retrieve the local ferry. Although a company of riflemen successfully crossed, four panzers prevented the supporting armour from joining them after one tank was damaged and another knocked out. Rather than wait for their artillery to destroy the panzers, the Soviet riflemen circling round them tried to assault the town. They were confronted by a lone German armoured personnel carrier armed with a flamethrower. It incinerated a handful of exposed Soviet soldiers before it was silenced by accurate artillery fire. Passing the burnt and twisted bodies, Lieutenant Evgeni Bessonov recalled, 'It was an awful sight.'[7] Afterwards, the panzers withdrew and the Soviet riflemen stormed into Ketzin to find it undefended except for the odd sniper. 'The town was captured by practically a single company without tanks,' observed Bessonov with pride, 'because they were only just starting to cross the channel on the ferries that were brought up.'[8] Late that evening, he and his men met with Zhukov's tanks. 'Thus, Berlin was fully encircled by Soviet troops,'[9] said Bessonov.

The Germans responded to the loss of Ketzin by shelling it. Bessonov was in conference with his company commander, Senior Lieutenant Nikolai Chernyshov, when the building they were standing beneath was hit. Several men from their communications platoon were killed and several wounded. Bessonov's belt buckle saved his life by catching a piece of shrapnel, though it still gashed his stomach. A second splinter hit him in the leg while a third almost severed three fingers on his left hand. He was bandaged and evacuated to a captured German hospital in Luckenwalde. His journey was dangerous as bands of German soldiers kept emerging from the forest to shoot at passing Soviet lorries. Bessonov heard rumours that they had executed Soviet wounded on the open road, but he reached Luckenwalde without incident.

Busse at 0800 hours on 26 April attempted to cut a path through to Wenck. He knew it was an all-or-nothing mission. The very survival of his command rested on its success. Instead of using a single division as instructed, he employed the remains of three. His spearhead was created with units from the 21st Panzer, Kurmark Panzergrenadier and 712th Infantry Divisions. The Luftwaffe tried to drop ammunition and fuel to the 9th Army but most of it failed to reach them thanks to marauding enemy fighters. Instead, the panzers were fuelled using petrol syphoned from abandoned and wrecked vehicles. The battle group was first preceded by a German barrage that fired off the last of their artillery ammunition. Once they reached Halbe, they were to push on to Baruth to the southwest, which would put them on the road to Luckenwalde.

Konev had foreseen this breakout attempt and ordered the 38th Guards Rifle Corps with three divisions from the 28th Army to deploy into blocking positions in the Baruth area. The 3rd Guards Army was also instructed to create two defensive lines and reserve positions were formed using three divisions from the 13th Army. Notably, the 395th Rifle Division from the latter was tasked with holding Baruth. General Gordov, commanding the 3rd Guards, was told to keep a division in reserve at Teupitz, block the roads through the woods and create defences along the Berlin–Cottbus Road. All these forces were backed by the 4th Bomber Corps with three divisions of bombers from the 2nd Air Army. Soviet pilots were ordered to pound anything that moved, though trying

Soviet artillery inflicted terrible casualties on the Germans trapped in the Halbe pocket.

to pick out targets among the trees would prove a challenge. Nonetheless, Soviet bombs and shells inevitably inflicted terrible injuries upon those showered in both metal and wooden splinters.

Martin Kleint and his fellow Kurmark Panzergrenadiers were grateful for the support of the remains of the 502nd SS Heavy Tank Battalion equipped with massive 68-ton Tiger IIs. 'I sat relatively safely in my seat on the fourth tank, my machine gun ready,' he recalled. 'Each tank resembled a colony of ants weaving its way forward.'[10] Unfortunately, he was knocked off by the dense foliage suddenly snagging his weapon and fell into the road. Narrowly avoiding being run over by the following tank, he ran after his ride and clambered back on feeling embarrassed by such a silly accident. First, they had to get over the Dahme river at Märkisch Buchholz in order to reach Halbe. On the way, they passed through Kehrigk, where an improvised air strip was established in the hope of flying in supplies and flying out the more seriously wounded.

Soviet anti-tank gunners were waiting for them at Halbe. Three panzers were instantly knocked out. Kleint watched as, 'Crews squeezed themselves out of their narrow hatches completely wrapped in flames.'[11] Soviet riflemen in the surrounding buildings opened fire and shells began to land on the German column. The main road rapidly became strewn with dead and wounded German soldiers. One helpless man who had lost a leg was run over by a panzer and crushed to death before his comrades could rescue him.

Soviet riflemen had barricaded themselves in Halbe railway station, the signal box and the nearby forester's house. These strongpoints enabled them to dominate the railway crossing and the area became the scene of fierce fighting. Likewise, Halbe's main crossroads for Teupitz and Teurow became a battlefield. Kleint and his comrades, after briefly sheltering in a cellar, made their way into the nearby forest. 'Exhausted, we simply stumbled on with only one goal in mind,' he said, 'to get away from the burning inferno, to flee this doomed town.'[12]

The fighting was fierce but despite the intervention of Soviet bombers, they failed to halt the German push. By 1000 hours, Busse's escaping battle group had cut the Baruth–Zossen road, thereby severing the supply lines to the 3rd Guards Tank and 28th Armies. However, at Baruth, the 395th Division stood its ground, while the 50th and 96th Guards Rifle Divisions from the 38th Guards Rifle Corps counterattacked from the south. Desperately, the Germans continued to press forwards, knowing they could not retreat. Although the battle group had forced its way between the Soviet 3rd Guards and 28th Armies, it was trapped in the woods northeast of Baruth and broken up into smaller groups. Soviet aircraft flew 2,500 ground attack sorties and 1,700 bombing missions against the German breakout. Captivity or a miserable death awaited those isolated among the trees.

In Berlin, the Red Army shelled the Chancellery on the night of 26 April. The Führerbunker vibrated with the concussion and Hitler was increasingly desperate for news of outside help. The following day, a signal from Wenck indicated that he was several miles from Potsdam. If that was the case, it offered the hope that he could move up the Havel and into the capital. In truth, Wenck was still 40 km (25 miles) away. Major von Loringhoven recalled how the news of Wenck's progress lifted spirits in the Führerbunker. 'Again I saw happy looks on faces…' he noted. 'But the euphoria did not last long.'[13] Hitler's valet, SS-Lieutenant Colonel Heinz Linge, echoed von Loringhoven's sentiments. 'Walter Wenck's army broke through to Potsdam,' he noted with enthusiasm. 'The Russian encirclement of Berlin seemed threatened from the north. Hitler radiated confidence. But it was only a brief flare.'[14] Once reality set in, Linge observed, 'Apathy followed the short period of euphoria.'[15]

Goebbels leapt at this news. 'The Wenck Army is coming closer and will liberate us,' he told his staff enthusiastically. 'I must now spread the word!'[16] His Propaganda Ministry broadcast that Wenck was in Potsdam and was about to reach Berlin. 'The situation has changed decisively in our favour,' claimed the radio announcement. 'Berlin must be held till Army Wenck arrives, no matter what the costs!'[17] It also divulged Wenck's position, 'In their attack to liberate Berlin, the young divisions of Wenck's Army have reached the region south of Ferch.'[18] When Wenck heard this, he was flabbergasted as the Red Army would now do everything in its power to stop him. 'We won't be able to move tomorrow,' Wenck told Colonel Günther Reichhelm, his chief-of-staff.[19]

General Lelyushenko's 4th Guards Tank Army ensured that Wenck would never reach Berlin. His 10th Guards Tank Corps, supported by a rifle division from the 13th Army, had forced their way on to the southern part of Wannsee Island, containing the German troops there.

Potsdam was taken on 27 April and Lelyushenko sent his 6th Guards Mechanized Corps west towards Brandenburg. It ran into the lead elements of Wenck's northern thrust.

General Weidling, the ill-fated military commandant of Berlin, on the evening of 27 April tried to get Hitler to acknowledge that all was lost. The city was completely surrounded, their defensive perimeter was rapidly shrinking, and the Luftwaffe was unable to deliver any further supplies. Hitler, though, kept blaming disloyalty for the situation and began fretting about being captured by the Red Army. Weidling knew that within three days they would be out of ammunition and that their only hope was to launch a breakout to try to reach General Wenck. Wenck was of the same opinion when he radioed Berlin to say, 'Counterattack of the Twelfth Army is stalled south of Potsdam. Troops are engaged in very heavy defensive fighting. Suggest breakthrough to us.'[20] He got no response.

By this stage, General Krebs was increasingly desperate, warning Field Marshal Keitel that 'the Führer expects help immediately; at most there are only forty-eight hours left. If no help arrives by then, it will be too late! The Führer asked me to reiterate this.'[21] Hitler also took matters into his own hands. 'I expect the relief of Berlin,' he signalled Keitel on 28 April. 'What is Heinrici's army doing?' he demanded to know. 'Where is Wenck? What is happening to the Ninth Army? When will Wenck and Ninth Army join us?'[22] Keitel reported, 'The offensive of the Ninth and Twelfth armies had been halted by a strong counterattack … rendering continuation of the offensive impossible.' To the north of Berlin, the news was no better either as Keitel added, 'The army group of SS-General Steiner had still not yet arrived.'[23] Morale in the Führerbunker plummeted once more. 'By evening, the intelligence left no doubt that the attack had failed,' wrote von Loringhoven. 'The defeat of Wenck's Army had sounded the death knell for all military hope.'[24]

Nonetheless, Martin Bormann and General Krebs issued one last plea to Wenck. They knew from Reuters that Himmler had approached Britain and America seeking a separate peace deal. On 29 April, they signalled Wenck pointing out that only Hitler had the authority to broker such a deal. They added that, 'A condition precedent to this is the immediate establishment of contact between your army and us, so as to give the Führer intra- and extra-political freedom for conducting talks.'[25] Their real, selfish, motive for sending this message was the fear of being abandoned to the Red Army. Only Wenck could open a corridor to the Elbe but it was too late.

Chapter 9

Northwest Frontier

At this 11th hour, one way that Berlin could have been reinforced was using Göring's numerous parachute divisions. By the end of the war, he had almost a dozen of these fighting as infantry on the Eastern and Western Fronts as well as in Italy. Getting them into Berlin, however, was almost impossible. The problem was that these divisions were not jump trained so could only be air landed. An operation to drop 1,500 parachutists at night in the winter of 1944 during Hitler's Ardennes offensive ended in complete disaster with the inexperienced paratroopers and their weapons scattered over a wide area. In late February 1945, the Luftwaffe had attempted to deliver reinforcements from the 25th Parachute Regiment, 9th Parachute Division to the besieged city of Breslau. This mission had ended in failure despite two attempts because the transport aircraft could find nowhere to land in the dark. At least two aircraft were shot down and a third crashed before they gave up. Only a small parachute battle group ended up fighting on the streets. The rest of the division was committed as infantry to the defence of the Oder instead.

While to the south of Berlin the Soviet and American armies were thrusting towards the Elbe, to the north, the Soviets were pushing on Rostock on the Baltic coast. German military forces to the northwest of the capital comprised Army Group Northwest commanded by Field Marshal Ernst Busch. This consisted of the weak 25th Army, which was largely trapped in the Netherlands, and the 1st Parachute Army, which had been pushed back towards Bremen by the British. These forces included three parachute divisions, which in theory could have been redeployed to defend Berlin just as the 9th Parachute Division had been. In practice, none of these units comprising former Luftwaffe ground personnel had received parachute training.

Around 120,000 Germans under General Johannes Blaskowitz were tied down in the western Netherlands, including one of the parachute divisions. The latter was reliant on horse-drawn transport and bicycles so was hardly mobile. Notably, the 25th Army only had three infantry divisions under its control, which meant the rest of these forces consisted of rear echelon personnel and Luftwaffe staff. In contrast, the 1st Parachute Army comprised a dozen or so very depleted divisions.

Busch could have readily employed some of the 350,00 German troops needlessly left in Norway. They could have been shipped south from Oslo across the Skagerrak and down to Kiel. Likewise, German troops deployed around Copenhagen could have been sent to Rostock to help slow the Soviet advance. An entire division was pointlessly occupying the Danish island of Bornholm in the western Baltic. Even if Busch had been given permission to redeploy some of the occupation forces in Denmark, they were needed to protect 250,000 German refugees who had been evacuated there on Hitler's orders by sea and rail since early February 1945. This included everyone who had been evacuated to Stettin and Swinemünde. Hitler had insisted, 'The armed forces will afford all possible assistance in this respect.'[1]

Field Marshal Bernard Montgomery, to prevent Busch from moving reinforcements south from occupied Denmark or Norway, planned to sweep northeast to Hamburg on to Lübeck and north to Flensburg and the Baltic Sea. Churchill and Eisenhower had another goal in mind. 'My object was to get there in time to be able to offer a firm front to the Russian endeavours to get up into Denmark,' noted Montgomery, 'and thus control the entrance to the Baltic.'[2] Eisenhower had ordered as early as mid-September 1944, 'Should the Russians beat us to Berlin, the Northern Group of Armies would seize the Hanover area and the Hamburg group of ports.'[3] Crucially, Hanover was on the road to Berlin.

'May I point out that Berlin itself is no longer a particularly important objective,' acknowledged Eisenhower after the Rhine crossing in March 1945. 'Its usefulness to the German has been largely destroyed and even his government is preparing to move to another area.'[4] Nonetheless, he still wanted the western Allies to play their part, adding, 'What is now important is to gather up our forces for a single drive and this will more quickly bring about the fall of Berlin.'[5] To achieve this, Eisenhower wanted to overrun Hitler's weapons factories in the Ruhr while Montgomery cleared German forces from Lübeck and Kiel. Beyond that, his biggest concern was not Berlin but preventing Hitler from creating a Nazi fortress in southern Germany.

Field Marshal Busch was in an impossible position. He did not have the forces to fend off the advancing British and Canadian armies let alone send reinforcements to Berlin. His area of responsibility covered those parts of the Netherlands still under occupation, the North Sea coast and Schleswig-Holstein. The only unit he could have conceivably deployed to Berlin was the 7th Parachute Division. However, following Montgomery's Rhine crossing, it had been reduced to 4,000 men and even if they had reached one of Bremen's two airfields there were no transport aircraft to carry them. General Blaskowitz reported in early April that the fighting strength of the 7th and 8th Parachute Divisions was just 200 men, each supported by a dozen assault guns. Hitler's paratroops were going nowhere. The Luftwaffe's very first parachute training school at Stendal west of the Elbe could have provided a cadre of men for Berlin, but all the staff and instructors had already been sent west to fight.

Nor were Hitler's special forces in a position to come to his rescue. The once elite commando Brandenburg Division had been scattered to the four winds. In the closing months of the war, Hitler's highly trained commandos had been consigned to fighting as infantry or sent on desperate bridge demolition operations. SS-Lieutenant Colonel Otto Skorzeny, who had once commanded Hitler's special forces, was in Vienna and only just escaped before it fell to the Red Army. His tough SS parachute battalion had been lost defending the Oder and the survivors ordered to head for the Alps along with Skorzeny to help establish a Nazi redoubt. Even had Skorzeny wanted to go to Berlin to serve the Führer one last time, he had neither troops nor any means of reaching the city.

The Kriegsmarine or German navy had surplus manpower in the ports of Schleswig-Holstein but no one really wanted them. Admiral Dönitz had offered Hitler 12,000 sailors for the defence of the Oder. However, General Heinrici refused to deploy them on the grounds that they lacked combat experience. This had led to a row between him and the admiral. 'Don't you think there's a big difference between fighting at sea and fighting on land?' demanded Heinrici. 'I tell you, all these men will be slaughtered at the front! Slaughtered!'[6] Reluctantly, Hitler had agreed to keep Dönitz's sailors in reserve. Only the ill-fated 3rd Naval Division was sent to join Steiner but he also refused to use them for offensive operations.

Things were moving too fast for Busch to have time to worry about what was happening in Berlin. Nonetheless, a defensive line anchored on Hamburg, Bremen and Hanover could screen the western approaches to the Nazi capital. The crude oil refineries around the three cities had made them regular targets for the Allied bomber fleets. 'Nearly all the roads and important rail junctions had been smashed by our bombers,' noted General Brian Horrocks, commander of the British 30th Corps, 'and cities like Hanover, Bremen and Hamburg were just a shambles.'[7] To defend them, Busch had to resort to using a completely rag-tag collection of units.

To slow the British advance towards Hanover, the Germans anchored their defence west of Osnabruck on the tree-lined Ibbenbüren ridge. This was held by seven companies of cadets from Hanover's non-commissioned officers' school. After some hard fighting, the British 11th Armoured Division took Osnabruck on 4 April and continued to press eastwards. They captured only 450 prisoners, showing just how weak the garrison was. Six days later, the US 84th Infantry Division, belonging to General Simpson's US 9th Army, rolled into Hanover having circled around the city's main defences.

On 8 April, Eisenhower informed Montgomery that if he got an opportunity to capture Berlin cheaply, he would take it. Certainly, General Bradley commanding the US 12th Army Group had the forces to cut western Germany in half. The Americans between Hanover and Coburg fielded some 27 divisions. Hitler, fearing that communication between northern and southern Germany might be cut, announced that in the event of this happening, Admiral Dönitz would become commander-in-chief of the Northern area. This would include Army Groups Northwest and Vistula as well as those forces in Denmark and Norway. Field Marshal Kesselring in Italy would assume full control of the Southern area. These appointments, however, would only be made if the Führer was unavailable in either of the areas. Such a division of command would have no impact on the defence of Berlin. All it did was convince Admiral Dönitz that he, not Göring, would become Hitler's successor. Dönitz was amused when Hitler added that separated commanders would have to rely on local 'supply, transport, communications and armament organizations.'[8] This was a complete fantasy as Germany's logistical infrastructure had collapsed.

German forces were so weak that defending Bremen and the river Weser from attack was an impossible task. One of the city's better-equipped battalions had already been sent to the Eastern Front to fight on the Oder. In early April, southwest of Bremen, the 20th SS Training Division was driven back by the British 7th Armoured Division. At Rethem, southeast of Bremen and east of the Weser, the German 2nd Marine Division from Hamburg held out for just four days. West of Bremen near Brinkum in mid-April, a fanatical battalion of SS held up the British advance until they were all dead or captured. Busch knew after the surrender of Field Marshal Model's Army Group B in the Ruhr that Army Group Northwest was on its own. The capitulation of Model's men signalled the loss of forces that were almost twice the strength of Busch's command.

In the face of this continuing if chaotic resistance it was clear that General Brian Horrocks' British 30th Corps would have to take Bremen by force. By this stage, Zhukov had commenced his assault on the Seelow Heights, sealing the fate of Berlin. Way to the southeast on Montgomery's right flank, General Simpson's US 9th Army had reached Magdeburg and the Elbe. Hitler had no idea of the precarious state of his forces in northwestern Germany. On 21 April, when he ordered Army Group Steiner to counterattack the Red Army north of Berlin, he instructed, 'Every available man between Berlin and the Baltic Sea up to Stettin and Hamburg is to be drawn into this attack.'[9] Major von Loringhoven, one of Hitler's staff officers in the Führerbunker, also recalled, 'All units stationed between the Elbe and the Oder were to march on Berlin.'[10] There were no available men, as Steiner discovered.

General Fritz Becker endeavoured to hold the British west of Bremen and the Weser. The defenders consisted of elements of the SS, Hitler Youth and members of the Volkssturm as well as Luftwaffe personnel, police and sailors fighting as foot soldiers. By this stage of the war, the German police had lost all its more able-bodied officers, who had been recruited into military field police units or one of Himmler's two SS police divisions. On 22 April and 24 April, the defenders were heavily bombed by the Royal Air Force as a prelude to Horrocks' attack. However, much of Bremen and indeed Hamburg and Hanover already lay in ruins thanks to the earlier raids. Bremen's industrial area along the river had been flattened and parts of the city were flooded. A number of prominent industrial brick chimneys remained standing, though, which would make ideal observation posts for German artillery spotters.

Publicly, General Becker was hopeful that Bremen would act as a bulwark, at least temporarily. West and southwest of the town, the extensive flood waters were about 1.2 m (4 ft) deep. This posed a challenge for the British attack. Even the British Buffalo amphibious assault vehicle was hampered, as the water in many places was not deep enough for it to float, but too deep for it to get traction on the bottom. All this greatly helped Becker's defence of the gasworks and docks on the southern bank of the river, which were held by a mix of SS, Hitler Youth, Volkssturm and police. The key bridge over the canal at Kattenturn to the south was rigged for demolition with 227 kg (500 lb) bombs and protected by 88-mm and 40-mm flak guns. Becker was confident that the British would pay a heavy price for any further push into Germany.

The British 3rd Division struck from the south while the 43rd Wessex Division and the 52nd Lowland Division come in from the north. The 51st Highland Division conducted a feint to the southwest to lure out Becker's reserves. Montgomery was delighted at the presence of the latter unit. 'I have a very great affection for the Highland Division,' he later wrote. 'It was the only Infantry Division in the armies of the British Empire that accompanied me during the whole long march from Alamein to Berlin.'[11]

In the event, the waterlogged ground proved more of a hindrance than an effective obstacle. The 3rd Division riding in the Buffaloes penetrated the southern part of the city, catching Becker's men by surprise. Resistance along the railway embankment proved initially tenacious, but the defenders soon surrendered after Crocodile flame-thrower tanks appeared on the scene. When the 43rd Division attacked Burgher Park on the eastern side of the city, it captured Becker. He later complained, 'You put your soldiers into the Verdammte Schwimmen Panzer and came up behind us – it is not fair!'[12]

Two days later, the remains of the garrison surrendered, with 6,000 men including two generals and an admiral having been taken. The British also discovered 16 new submarines and two destroyers in the dockyards. 'It was in Bremen that I realised for the first time just what the Germans must have suffered as a result of our bombing,' observed

General Horrocks. 'It was a shambles; there didn't seem to be a single house intact in this huge seaport.'[13] In the meantime, the 51st Highland Division headed north to Bremerhaven and Bremervörde.

In Berlin, Hitler was probably completely unaware that Bremen had been lost. In the Führerbunker, he was almost completely cut off from the outside world. Just as Horrocks' attack was commencing on 24 April, the German High Command headquarters was relocating from Krampnitz to Rheinsberg so were largely out of touch. Their subsequent communication with the Führerbunker was poor and very intermittent. 'We didn't know much about what was happening,' said Major von Loringhoven. He resorted to relying on Reuters news bulletins broadcast from London. There was, he said, 'an atmosphere of chaotic improvisation'[14] in the Führerbunker. Hitler's press secretary, Heinz Lorenz, transcribed these, which were then presented as intelligence. 'We found ourselves in a grotesque position,' confessed von Loringhoven, 'whereby any situation report given to Hitler was based largely on information derived from enemy radio.'[15] SS-Senior Squad Leader Rochus Misch, Hitler's bodyguard, admitted, 'I regularly listened to BBC London.'[16] Hitler had decreed that anyone caught listening to foreign radio stations be imprisoned, but there was simply no other source of information to be had.

The only last-minute reinforcements Hitler received from north-western Germany were around 200 sailors sent by Dönitz. They bravely landed on a makeshift airstrip on the Charlottenburger Chaussee following the loss of the airfields at Gatow and Tempelhof. As Misch observed, they landed 'in the middle of the inferno.'[17] It was a futile and senseless sacrifice of young naval ratings. To the very end, though, Dönitz was determined to prove that 'the crews of warships are every bit as good'[18] as Heinrici's soldiers.

Busch's position disintegrated with the loss of Bremen. He had no reserves and could do nothing. The remains of the 7th Parachute Division were trapped in the Oldenburg area west of Bremen, while the 8th Parachute Division was also caught near Bremen. The 6th Parachute Division remained trapped at Zutphen, northeast of Arnhem in the Netherlands. Once Montgomery's forces were over the Elbe, Major General Alwin Wolz, the commandant of Hamburg, knew it would not be long before he had to surrender. However, he had to play for time, for the surrender of Hamburg would mean the loss of Schleswig-Holstein and those Baltic ports still conducting last-minute evacuations in the face of the advancing Red Army. There was also confusion among the SS, as some units were under the impression that rather than rally to Berlin they were to withdraw to Schleswig-Holstein.

Wolz's garrison consisted of the usual dregs drawn from the Hitler Youth, Volkssturm, sailors who were former U-boat crews and a miscellaneous mix of SS, including elements from the 12th SS Training Battalion. In the face of unexpectedly fierce resistance from these forces, the British 7th Armoured Division began to prepare for an all-out assault. In the meantime, the remnants of the 1st Parachute Army were still desperately trying to escape over the Elbe using the surviving bridges and ferries. After striking northeast of the city, the British 11th Armoured Division arrived at Lübeck on 2 May – a mere 48 km (30 miles) from the Soviets at Rostock. Hamburg surrendered to the British the following day. This completed the wider encirclement of Berlin to the northwest, but by that stage the city was lost and beyond help.

Chapter 10

Alpine Fortress

While the battle for Berlin was at its height, Eisenhower and his generals continued to fret about Hitler creating a 'National Redoubt'[1] from which to conduct a last stand. The mounting concern was that the capture of Berlin might not signal the end of German resistance. This in part dissuaded Eisenhower from making a bid for the Nazi capital. 'For many weeks we had been receiving reports that the Nazi intention, in extremity,' noted Eisenhower, 'was to withdraw the cream of the SS, Gestapo, and other organizations fanatically devoted to Hitler, into the mountains of southern Bavaria, western Austria, and northern Italy.'[2] Certainly, by fortifying the Alpine passes, the Germans could potentially hold out indefinitely until such time as they were blasted or starved into submission. Eisenhower foresaw this would result in 'a costly siege' or prolonged guerrilla warfare.[3] There was every reason to suppose that if Hitler decamped to Bavaria, his followers there would fight to the death.

It seemed quite plausible that Hitler would choose his Berghof residence at Berchtesgaden, south of Salzburg, on Obersalzberg mountain as a centre for continued resistance. Obsersalzberg was covered in holiday homes of senior Nazis and riddled with tunnels. Munich just to the northwest of Berchtesgaden was Germany's third city after Berlin and Hamburg. Munich not Nuremberg had been the location for Hitler's very first massed rally back in the early 1920s. It was there in the hands of his storm troopers that the Nazi swastika and red, white and black flag made their public debut. It was only in later years that his rallies had moved north to Nuremberg. Munich was also the scene of Hitler's failed *coup d'état* in 1923 in which he had hoped to emulate Mussolini's rapid rise to power. Instead, it took him a decade. Ever since, though, the region had been a staunch Nazi heartland.

In addition to the last of his armed forces, Hitler could direct the clandestine Werewolf organization from Berchtesgaden. This had been set up by SS-Lieutenant General Hans Prützmann in the summer of 1944 to conduct partisan warfare behind enemy lines on both the Eastern and Western Fronts. Prützmann was a tough veteran who had seen action against Soviet partisans and studied their tactics closely. Werewolf recruited volunteers, largely employing Austrian soldiers, Hitler Youth and Nazi Party officials. It established its own bases, but the rapidity of the Allied advance greatly curtailed its training programme. Hidden supply and weapons depots were set up in Austria and Germany, though these could only sustain operations for a limited period. In Austria, their headquarters was based in Passau. Werewolves were to operate in civilian clothing, which meant that they were not protected by the Geneva Conventions.

Prützmann found trying to form Werewolf a difficult task in the face of competing Nazi interests. For a start, the Hitler Youth did not want to give up its remaining personnel, the bulk of whom had already been taken into the Waffen-SS or the Volkssturm. Furthermore, Goebbels had announced in March 1945 the formation of the Adolf Hitler Freikorps under the control of Robert Ley, head of the German Labour Front. This meant mobilizing yet more factory workers. It was to consist of ardent Nazis mounted on bicycles whose task was to tackle enemy tanks. Like the Volkssturm and Werewolves, the Freikorps would not wear uniforms or if they did, they were to remove any rank badges and party armbands. Goebbels claimed that a 2,000-strong Adolf Hitler Freikorps was rallying to Berlin from across Germany along with the Mohnke Freikorps. Both organizations were a propaganda fantasy. The creation of yet another militia was simply a waste of time and effort that needlessly competed not only with the Hitler Youth and Volkssturm but also Werewolf. Any units that were ever raised by the regional governors quickly vanished, either overrun by the Soviets or subsumed into the Volkssturm. When it came to equipment, Prützmann found that the military had very little to spare and what it did hand over was dated.

Nonetheless, Goebbels grandly claimed in a public radio broadcast that Werewolf would 'drown the enemy in a sea of blood.'[4] Werewolves would not only attack Allied targets behind the lines but also punish anyone caught collaborating or showing defeatism. German citizens within Allied-occupied areas were not to co-operate or they would face assassination. By early 1945, about 5,000 volunteers had received some form of training, but such small numbers hardly constituted an effective partisan army. At best, they could function as small stay-behind units to gather intelligence and carry out limited terror attacks. Once the

Red Army crossed into Austria, the German military released Austrian troops to join Werewolf, in the hope they would fight fanatically against the occupation of their homeland.

Some terror attacks were launched on British and American forces, but it is hard to gauge whether these were premeditated by Werewolf or simply spontaneous action by armed civilians. Notably, though, on 24 March 1945, the American-appointed mayor of Aachen was murdered by Werewolf agents. Foolishly, Goebbels gloated over this killing on the radio on 1 April and called for a national rising. 'Every means is justified if it helps to damage the enemy...' stated the Werewolf charter. 'Hate is our prayer. Revenge is our battle cry.'[5] This immediately tipped the Allies off about Werewolf's existence.

When Werewolf agents killed General Maurice Rose, commander of the US 3rd Armored Division, on 8 April, the Americans resolved to use extreme force against all civilians resisting them. The net result was that Werewolf consigned yet more German children to death or imprisonment. That same month, Colonel Robert Allen and a number of other officers from Patton's US 3rd Army staff were ambushed and captured by civilians. Allen was wounded in the right arm, part of which had to be amputated in a German hospital. Patton was furious and noted with satisfaction in his diary, 'The town where it took place has been removed, together with, I hope a number of civilians.'[6] Fearing he might be targeted for assassination, Patton took to sleeping with a loaded carbine beneath his bed.

'The purpose of the Werewolf organization,' noted Eisenhower, 'which was to be composed only of loyal followers of Hitler, was murder and terrorism.'[7] Understandably, he feared that Werewolves would be used to impede his advance on the National Redoubt. 'The way to stop this project...' adds Eisenhower, 'was to overrun the entire national territory before its organization could be affected.'[8] Allied intelligence failed to highlight just how weak Werewolf was and its inability to sustain prolonged operations. Soviet intelligence was also aware of it and was convinced female operatives were deliberately infecting Soviet soldiers with venereal disease.

Optimistically, Hitler hoped that when the time came the regular armed forces would join Werewolf. When Model's Army Group B surrendered in the Ruhr in mid-April, its soldiers were expected to take to the hills. 'The code word "Werewolf" had been sent out by Hitler's command post,' said Lieutenant Günther Materne, who was caught in the pocket with his unit. 'This meant that we were all supposed to divide up into small groups and head east.'[9] Few if any followed this order. Instead, demoralized by the war, they waited to be taken into captivity.

Hitler, according to Albert Speer, had indeed planned to move to Berchtesgaden to take command in southern Germany. Speer noted in early April 1945, 'At that time he still intended to lead the final struggle in the so-called Alpine Redoubt.'[10] However, just before Hitler's birthday on 20 April, Speer recalled, 'The night before the idea had been bandied about of not defending the metropolis and, instead, transferring to the Alpine Redoubt. But overnight, Hitler had decided to fight for the city in the streets of Berlin.'[11] Efforts by those around Hitler to get him to move his headquarters to Obersalzberg all failed. 'We all attempted to dissuade him,' said General Jodl. 'We even proposed bringing troops from the West to fight in the East. The Führer's answer to this was that everything was falling apart now, anyway, and he was no longer able to continue.'[12]

Hermann Göring warned the Führer that only one north–south road through the Bavarian forest remained open and that it could be cut at any moment. 'How can I call on the troops to undertake this decisive battle for Berlin,' responded Hitler angrily, 'if at the same moment I myself withdraw to safety?'[13] Göring was at a loss what to say when Hitler added, 'I shall leave it to fate whether I die in the capital or fly to Obersalzberg at the last moment.'[14] Both Speer and Göring knew that it was the last moment. Martin Bormann, who had been making preparations for their departure, was dismayed. However, Goebbels, in typical fashion, declared Hitler's decision a historic act. Only Göring fled to Bavaria, hoping to take power. Dönitz, Himmler, Jodl and Keitel were all eventually to make their way to Schleswig-Holstein.

On the night of his birthday, Hitler summoned two of his secretaries, Christa Schroeder and Johanna Wolf, and informed them that a car would take them to Munich. Schroeder asked to stay but Hitler said he was going to form a resistance movement and would later need their help. He smiled sadly at the pair and said, 'I will join you as soon as possible.'[15] They were busy packing when Hitler personally telephoned them to announce that the road south had been cut and they would have to fly out. Schroeder was surprised because during her 12 years of service with Hitler, he had never called her before. Just after midnight, he rang again and instructed, 'Children, make ready, hurry, the machine will take off soon as it is warmed up.'[16]

In the event, they flew from Tempelhof in the early hours of 21 April to Salzburg with a group of soldiers. They then bussed to Berchtesgaden and reported to the Berghof. 'Besides Hitler's naval adjutant [Admiral] Jesko von Puttkamer,' noted Schroeder, 'some of the SS-Begleitkommando had moved into quarters at the Berghof, proof that Hitler had at least given some thought to coming to the Alpine Redoubt.'[17] Another reason why Hitler may have decided not to go was that should Göring or any other members of his inner circle attempt a coup, he would be easily isolated.

Schroeder and Wolf had a very narrow escape as they were supposed to have flown from Staaken. When they did not turn up, their seats were given to two other women who were both killed when the aircraft crashed near Dresden. The plane is believed to have been intercepted by the RAF, who demanded it make for Cologne. When the pilot refused to comply, the aircraft was shot down. As Schroeder's luggage was on board, one of the dead females was initially identified as her. The other woman was thought to be Martin Bormann's secretary, Else Krüger, but she was not on the flight either. Among the dead was Wilhelm Arndt, Hitler's favourite manservant. He was carrying secret documents for the Führer, which were never recovered.

'Two days later on the afternoon of 22 April, Hitler stated during a situation conference that he was going to remain in Berlin,' recalled Heinz Linge, Hitler's other valet. 'We, who until then had been hoping that he would soon transfer his HQ to the so-called Alpine Redoubt, were one disappointment richer.'[18] Later, Hitler turned to Linge and said, 'Now I shall remain in Berlin and die here. As I am too infirm to carry a weapon I shall take my own life, as is fitting for the commandant of a redoubt.'[19] As far as Linge was concerned, it was the wrong redoubt.

'I am obliged to demand that you fly to Berchtesgaden this very night,' General Keitel told Hitler, 'to ensure the continuity of command over the Reich and the armed forces, which cannot be guaranteed in Berlin.'[20] However, Hitler remained adamant that he was staying. 'There is nothing to stop you flying to Berchtesgaden at once,' he replied. 'In fact, I order you to do so. But I myself am going to remain in Berlin.'[21] He instructed Bormann, Jodl and Keitel to fly out, but they would not go. 'In seven years,' said Keitel, 'I have never refused to obey an order from you, but this order I shall never carry out.' Looking at the three

Soviet tanks pushing into Berlin's suburbs. Once the city was surrounded, there was no hope for the garrison.

men, Hitler concluded the meeting by saying, 'Either I fight and win the battle of Berlin – or I am killed in Berlin.'[22] It was clear that he had completely abandoned the idea of an Alpine Redoubt.

Although Hitler had never shown any great interest in Werewolf, on 22 April, he ordered a belated call to arms. 'We have to adopt the same method which was shown and taught to us by the Russians,' he instructed. 'Our men have to infiltrate through the lines by ones or in small groups … and must attack if they reach the rear areas.'[23] He was clearly in a state of denial or ignorance when he said German guerrillas were to be 'supplied with sufficient ammunition, petrol and other materials.'[24] Lieutenant General Prützmann had already singularly failed with such an endeavour.

Christa Schroeder thought the Führer might be about to join them when Hitler's personal physician, Dr Theodor Morell, arrived at the Berghof on 24 April. However, Morell, in a state of despair, announced that he had been sacked and banished. The pair had fallen out after Morell tried to give Hitler an energy-boosting injection. Hitler accused his doctor of trying to drug him with morphine in order for his generals to get him on a plane to Salzburg. Before his departure, Hitler ordered Morell to remove his uniform, 'And act as if you've never seen me.'[25] Morell's medical colleagues were glad to see the back of him as they thought he was a charlatan who had slowly been poisoning Hitler for years. Schroeder observed, 'He was very distressed and bitter... It had hit him hard.'[26]

The Allies, though, had no way of knowing about this turn of events. 'As regards Berlin,' stated Eisenhower, 'I am quite ready to admit it has political and psychological significance, but of far greater importance will be the location of the remaining German forces in relation to Berlin.'[27] At the end of March, General Alexander Patch's US 7th Army intelligence warned that the Alpine or National Redoubt could be defended by 'an elite force, predominantly SS and mountain troops, of between 200,000 and 300,000 men.'[28] In other words, an entire German army group. Quite where they thought these forces were going to come from is hard to fathom. On all fronts, Hitler had exhausted the last of his manpower reserves.

The loss of Vienna to the Red Army in mid-April had seen the greatly depleted Army Group South driven back into western Austria. During their month-long Vienna offensive, the Soviets claimed to have destroyed 32 German divisions, captured 130,000 prisoners and destroyed 1,300 panzers and assault guns as well as 2,250 field guns. At the end of April, they reached Brno, putting them firmly on the road to Prague, which Hitler was determined to hold. This meant that Field Marshal Schörner's Army Group Centre fighting in western Czechoslovakia was hardly in a position to send troops either. This was especially the case once it was trapped east of Prague. Likewise, the German armies conducting desperate fighting withdrawals in Italy and

Yugoslavia were barely keeping their enemies at bay and were unable to spare any forces.

Nonetheless, Allied intelligence suggested that Hitler planned to make a last stand in southern Germany and western Austria with about 20 SS divisions. It also claimed, 'here armaments will be manufactured in bomb-proof factories, food and equipment will be stored in vast underground caverns and specially selected corps of young men will be trained in guerrilla warfare.'[29] Apart from the existence of Werewolf, there was absolutely no evidence to support this assessment. Neither the Nazi Party nor the German armed forces had made any real preparations for such an eventuality. Any plans that did exist were quickly overturned by the speed with which the Americans reached the Elbe. 'It grew into so exaggerated a scheme that I am astonished that we could have believed it as innocently as we did,'[30] General Bradley later confessed.

The Soviets did their bit to fuel the grand delusion thanks to intelligence coming out of Czechoslovakia. This was fed to Brigadier General Heliodor Pika, head of the Czechoslovak military mission in Moscow. He in turn shared it with the Red Army's chief of operations, General Shtemenko. 'We began to get reliable reports,' said Shtemenko, 'that Hitler was building an "Alpine Redoubt".'[31] Pika's intelligence adds that Shtemenko 'reported concentrations of German troops and matériel in the mountains.'[32] It also spoke of train and truck loads of building materials and workmen. Whether these alleged preparations were an attempt to build an Alpine Redoubt or simply efforts to slow the Red Army's advance through Czechoslovakia is unclear. It is quite possible that the Czechoslovaks deliberately exaggerated the situation in a desperate bid to speed up the liberation of their country. 'The location of the "Alpine Redoubt" – on the boundary between Germany and Austria … corresponded perfectly to our conclusions,'[33] claimed Shtemenko.

All this unsubstantiated intelligence was certainly enough to persuade Eisenhower to act the way he did in trying to prevent a last stand. 'The evidence was clear that the Nazi intended to make an attempt,' said Eisenhower with conviction, 'and I decided to give him no opportunity to carry it out.'[34] Even after General Bradley cut communications between northern and southern Germany, thereby forcing Hitler to stay in Berlin, Eisenhower continued to worry about the threat of a southern Nazi fortress. 'The strong possibility still existed that the fanatical Nazis would attempt to establish themselves in the National Redoubt,' he said, 'and the early overrunning of that area remained important to us.'[35] Such an operation would inevitably tie up the US 3rd and US 7th Armies as well as the French 1st Army. Churchill was not happy about this. He wanted the Allies to press forwards towards Berlin and felt that by concentrating in the south Eisenhower would weaken Montgomery's efforts to liberate Denmark before the Red Army.

To facilitate Eisenhower's plans, on 22 April, General Patch's US 7th Army advanced down the Danube and turned south towards Munich. 'Whether Hitler ever intended to fortify the Bavarian Alps was anyone's guess,' said Major Dick Winters with the US 101st Airborne Division, 'but Eisenhower wasn't taking any chances.'[36] To the west of the city lay Augsburg, which the Americans would have to take first. The core of the garrison there was thought to number only around 1,000 men supported by 88-mm flak guns. The Augsburg commandant, General Franz Fehn, soon began to find his soldiers deserting when the US 3rd and 4th Infantry Divisions supported by armour approached. The recruits of the German 27th Artillery Replacement Regiment rapidly fled their posts, leaving roadblocks unguarded. The demolition teams working on the bridges did not complete their jobs either. Furthermore, although some of the Luftwaffe's flak batteries continued to resist, some began to sport white handkerchiefs and pillowcases dangling from their gun barrels. The Americans took this as a good sign. 'I don't want you to fire into Augsburg at all unless it is actually observed firing,' instructed Major General John O'Daniel, commander of the US 3rd Division. 'Keep your eyes open for white flags or other signs of surrender.'[37]

Morale was not good in the city as its hospitals were crammed with German wounded and the Messerschmitt factories in the southern suburbs had been reduced to rubble by Allied bombers. Augsburg had last been attacked by the RAF in February 1944, whereas neighbouring Munich had first been hit in September 1942, enduring a total of nine major raids, the last of which had occurred in January 1945. General Fehn, lacking authorization to do so, refused to surrender after he was visited by a civilian delegation, so the Freedom Party of Augsburg took matters into their own hands. On 27 April, two German businessmen sought out Brigadier General Harold Blakeley, commander of the US 4th Division, with a view to handing over the city.

Fehn was in a ridiculous situation as by early next morning he only had 80 men left under his command. Major General O'Daniel sent his soldiers on to the streets. They were greeted by some civilians, who led them to General Fehn's command post in a pillbox. The Americans gave Fehn five minutes to surrender. To the amusement of his captors, when they entered, he tried to telephone for SS reinforcements before he was marched out as a prisoner of war. The group were confronted by a large white flag that had been hoisted high above St Ulric's, the city's 15th-century Benedictine abbey. The deputy gauleiter of Augsburg chose to shoot himself rather than be captured.

Eisenhower and Bradley remained convinced the German armed forces were intending to conduct a last stand in southern Germany. They also felt the only way to get German troops in Denmark and Norway to surrender was to overrun the area of the National Redoubt. Once this was captured along with Berlin, it would make continued German resistance pointless. Therefore, US 42nd and 45th Infantry Divisions spearheaded the immediate drive on Munich. In front of them, the remains of the German 2nd Mountain Division and some SS units conducted a fighting retreat. En route, the Americans liberated Dachau concentration camp, where they killed 300 SS guards in a firefight, and were confronted by the most appalling scenes of human suffering. 'The impact of seeing those people behind that fence,' recalled Major Winters, 'left me saying, if only to myself, "Now I know why I am here!"'[38] West of Munich, the Americans rounded up 2,500 German prisoners of war. 'It was an enchanting time,' adds Winters, 'watching Hitler's Third Reich crumble before our eyes.'[39]

Munich, although it had taken a pounding in the air raids, was still functioning, unlike ruined Dresden. Nonetheless, key landmarks had been hit. The cathedral was destroyed, as was the university, and the city gates had been damaged. 'The more we got to see of Munich,' recalled Victor Klemperer, who visited the city in early April, 'the more evident was the dreadful destruction. Whole fields of rubble and great buildings and palazzi in ruins.'[40] The citizens of Munich soon found three US infantry and two armoured divisions bearing down on them as the Americans vied for position to be first into the city. Some of the inhabitants, realizing the war was over, secured the bridges across the Isar river and welcomed the Americans in on 30 April. However, in the suburb of Hauptstadt der Bewegung, an SS battalion barricaded itself in and around its barracks and delayed the Americans until 1500 hours. It eventually took artillery to subdue them.

Insurgents from Action for Freedom of Bavaria seized Munich's radio station, the city hall and local newspaper offices. They prematurely announced the end of Nazi rule, encouraged German troops to desert and urged people to hang out white flags ready to greet their liberators. The group also claimed that the Nazi Governor of Bavaria, General Ritter von Epp, was negotiating with the Americans so continued fighting was now pointless. However, Paul Giesler, the gauleiter of Upper Bavaria, employing SS units, quickly crushed the rising. Some 40 rebels were rounded up and needlessly executed in the closing days of the war. Epp, although he claimed he was not involved, was arrested for treason. It would take until 3 May for the US 3rd and 42nd Divisions to finally secure the city centre.

In the meantime, the US 10th Armored and 44th Infantry Divisions crossed into Austria on 29 April. Although Patton's US 3rd Army was instructed to take Salzburg and block the passes from the city into the Austrian Tyrol, the honour fell to General O'Daniel. On the road to the city, the Americans met almost no resistance. Local German forces were only equipped with small arms and their roadblocks along the *Autobahn* did little to slow the enemy advance. American shelling of Salzburg quickly convinced the garrison commander to surrender on 4 May. That same day O'Daniel's division arrived at Berchtesgaden, though the US 101st Airborne Division contended they were the first to secure it. The latter took the surrender of General Theodor Tolsdorff, commander of 82nd Corps, but they did not locate any of the top Nazis.

The presence of American and French forces at Obersalzberg ended any German hopes of a National Redoubt. It soon became evident, however, that this was simply a Nazi deception plan. The Allies found little sign of serious preparations for prolonged resistance in the Alps. The Germans had intended to make their last stand in Berlin all along. Three entire Allied armies had been sent chasing shadows. Stalin was happy because this strategic distraction had given him a completely free hand with Berlin. 'Not until after the campaign ended,' General Bradley later admitted, 'were we to learn that this Redoubt existed largely in the imaginations of a few fanatic Nazis.'[41] The German military agreed with his prognosis. 'A great deal has been written about the Alpine Fortress, mostly nonsense,'[42] said Field Marshal Kesselring after the war. Nonetheless, the Allies' fear of Werewolf did not go away. Major von Loringhoven was interrogated extensively by the British on the subject. He recalled, 'They feared especially that the Werwolf [sic.] organisation … might trigger off clandestine resistance to the occupying forces.'[43]

British intelligence, thanks to Bletchley Park signals intercepts, had quite an accurate picture of the movement of senior Nazis in both Germany and the occupied territories. On 22 April, Göring was known to be in Obersalzberg and that he had fallen from favour with Hitler after he suggested he should take control of the country as Berlin was under siege. Between 19 and 26 April, British intelligence on the basis of German radio traffic anticipated Himmler would arrive in Salzburg, though he never did. Instead, he went to Hohenlychen sanatorium at Lychen, north of Berlin, and then to Schwerin. This and Göring's arrest discredited British and American concerns about the creation of an Alpine fortress. It was not until the evening of 28 April that intelligence indicated that SS-Lieutenant General Gottlob Berger was gathering SS units in Austria for some purpose. Intelligence also picked up on the row between Berger and SS-Lieutenant General Ernst Kaltenbrunner about surrendering in Italy, which the latter vehemently opposed. Kaltenbrunner was head of security in the southern region of the Reich. It was also known, according to General Krebs, that Hitler at 0600 hours on 27 April was still very much in command of the defence of Berlin.

Chapter 11

Pinned Down

Eisenhower's fears that Hitler might create an Alpine fortress were in part fuelled by what was happening in Italy and Yugoslavia. By April 1945, the Allies' 5th and 8th Armies, having pushed up the Italian peninsula, were poised to break through into northern Italy. The concern was that the Germans might stage a last-ditch rearguard action on the river Po while their 10th and 14th Armies withdrew across the mountains into Austria and towards Munich. Notably, there were two German parachute divisions fighting in Italy that could conceivably be redeployed by air. Similarly, in Yugoslavia, the German army might escape north towards the mountains. Therefore, it was vital that the Allies pinned down these troops. Eisenhower needed his forces to trap the Germans as quickly as possible.

However, Eisenhower lost the opportunity to end the war in Italy before Berlin was taken. SS-General Karl Wolff, the senior SS commander in Italy, secretly promised the Americans that Army Group C in Italy would not move to defend the Alpine Redoubt if his surrender terms were met. Wolff was well connected as he had previously served as the head of Himmler's staff and as a Waffen-SS liaison officer with Hitler's forward headquarters. SS-Senior Squad Leader Rochus Misch, Hitler's bodyguard, recalled, 'He did not seem to be an unpleasant type. He was also very calm and objective.'[1] Wolff briefed Hitler in Berlin on 6 February 1945 about the Allies' initial approaches via Switzerland. Hitler seems to have taken little interest but acquiesced to talks as part of his unfounded hope that the British and the Americans would come to Berlin's rescue.

Wolff in early March met with American representatives in Switzerland with the full knowledge of Hitler and Field Marshal Kesselring, who had been Commander-in-Chief Italy. Wolff proposed German units would surrender on the northern Italian plain after offering token resistance in the Po valley and once Berlin had fallen. This would prevent German forces in Italy withdrawing into the Alps. In return, Wolff wanted the Allies to cancel their pending spring offensive, stop bombing targets in Italy and, crucially, grant immunity from prosecution for the German negotiators. Wolff had every reason to seek immunity as he was complicit in the deaths of 300,000 people sent to the Treblinka extermination camp. Ridiculously, Wolff also wanted Army Group C to retain control of its areas of occupation. It is highly unlikely that he informed Hitler of the exact details of these proposals. Hitler would never have agreed to them and most likely would have thrown Wolff in prison or had him shot for treason.

Kesselring knew there was little point in trying to get their troops into the Alpine Redoubt because it was complete 'make-believe'.[2] He was aware that the defences on the southern edge of the Bavarian Alps stretching to Switzerland were still under construction, while to the north and northeast there were no fortifications, and none had been begun. Once Kesselring was appointed Commander-in-Chief West, he became less keen on the idea of surrendering in Italy as it would expose Germany's southern flank. Army Group G, fighting against the Americans and French north of the Alps and east of the Rhine, would either have to give ground or surrender as well. Likewise, it would imperil the German position in Yugoslavia.

General Heinrich von Vietinghoff, Kesselring's successor in Italy, wanted to withdraw behind the Po and use it as a natural defensive barrier. He reasoned that if they acted quickly, they could ferry all their heavy weapons and equipment across and be ready to meet the Allies' spring offensive. 'The retirement of the main forces of Army Group E in the Balkans through a narrow bottleneck required time,' warned Kesselring, 'and might become impossible if ... a gap be torn open by the recoil of Army Group C in Italy.'[3] Hitler refused, insisting that Army Group C fight where it stood. This lack of flexibility consigned von Vietinghoff's armies to their fate. Without an authorized withdrawal and prepared crossings, Army Group C would struggle to reach the Po before being outrun by Allied armour. Not only would von Vietinghoff's men never reach the Alps, but they would be trapped in Italy.

When Stalin heard of the negotiations, he accused the British and Americans of trying to orchestrate a separate peace deal. The talks ground to a swift halt and Himmler ordered Wolff not to return to Switzerland. Stalin also suspected that Hitler was holding on to Yugoslavia to enable the British to consolidate their position in Greece following the German withdrawal in October 1944. Stalin's plan was that all of the Balkans should fall under communist rule once he had taken Berlin. The British military intervention in Athens against Greek communists was an unwelcome complication. The presence of the Red Army in Bulgaria, Romania and Hungary threatened Hitler's lines of communication through Yugoslavia and he had little choice but to abandon the occupation of Greece.

Early in 1945, it certainly looked as if General Alexander Löhr's Army Group E might escape from Yugoslavia. It had scored a number of successes against Josip Broz Tito's communist Yugoslav partisans. Although Tito's four armies numbered 800,000 men, fortunately for Löhr's forces, they were ill-prepared and short of heavy equipment otherwise the Germans would have been very quickly overwhelmed. General Koča Popović, the commander of Tito's 2nd Army, called his men, 'Untrained youths and schoolboys!'[4] Löhr's so-called army group was really only a single army in strength. When it retreated from Greece it absorbed the remnants of Army Group F, which had previously been responsible for the Balkans until it was disbanded in March 1945. It was at that point Tito launched a general offensive with his 4th Army moving up the Dalmatian coast, while his 1st and 2nd Armies pushed through central Yugoslavia. His 3rd Army, supporting the Soviets and Bulgarians, cut along the border with Hungary and headed for Slovenia.

Löhr's response was calm and measured. The German 21st and 91st Corps in Montenegro withdrew along the Lim valley to reach the river Drina in Bosnia. These two corps had previously been operating in Albania and Kosovo. They were regularly harried by partisans and Allied aircraft and were greeted by devastation and demolished bridges. 'Their fuel ran out, their motorized equipment gave out and was destroyed,' said Milovan Djilas, one of Tito's commanders, 'everywhere along the road there were charred and overturned trucks.'[5] When they ran out of food, they took local farm animals and civilian clothing to keep warm in the mountains. Despite this, the Germans did not stop, and broke through into Bosnia.

'The German units, not fully manned and certainly less confident than before,' observed Djilas, 'nevertheless successfully resisted our inexperienced army.'[6] Limited German counterattacks made inroads into the 1st Army and scored a success against the 2nd Army in northern Bosnia. They also forced the 3rd Army over the river Drava into Hungary. German fire was much more accurate and deadly than the Yugoslavs'. 'One German mortar is more effective than two of my batteries!' grumbled General Peko Dapčević, commander of the 1st Army.[7] By April, Army Group E was holding on in Croatia with its Croatian allies. Tito was determined to liberate Croatia because he had intelligence indicating that its pro-Nazi fascist puppet government was planning to ask for the protection of the Allies. The Croatians had 17 divisions fighting alongside the Germans, none of which wanted a return to Serbian rule.

On 12 April, General Dapčević's 1st Army broke through the Syrmian Front and into eastern Croatia, forcing Army Group E northwards. 'This was the greatest and bloodiest battle our army ever fought,'[8] said Djilas proudly. One unit that was desperate to escape Tito's clutches was the 7th SS Division Prinz Eugen, defending the Vukovar area. This had been recruited in the Balkans in 1942 and used extensively for brutal anti-partisan operations. As far as Tito was concerned, these men were traitors and each deserved a bullet to the head. Their commander, SS-Colonel August Schmidhuber, was understandably keen to withdraw into Slovenia and then disappear into the Alps. Army Group E continued resisting at every step. Reaching Zagreb, the Croatian capital, cost Dapčević about 36,000 dead. Even then, two German infantry divisions continued to hold out in the city until the end of the war.

At the head of the Adriatic, the wholly inadequate German 97th Corps tried to stop Tito's 4th Army. 'By the end of April our forces were dangerously overstretched,' noted Major Erich Körner, 'and Corps Order of Battle included units whose men could not be considered as reliable soldiers.'[9] Its 41st Infantry Division was a penal unit made up of deserters and those guilty of other military offences. The 188th Mountain Division was not at divisional strength, nor had it received any mountain warfare training and was made up of ad hoc units. The 237th Infantry Division comprised older soldiers well over military age. 'How could one repose confidence in such men?'[10] asked Körner. Surprisingly, 97th Corps held its ground, but the Yugoslavs simply bypassed it and headed for Trieste. The 97th Corps then fought its way towards Austria until it was finally forced to surrender on 6 May. The rest of Löhr's troops, including the 7th SS Division, were herded into the Slovenian–Austrian border area. There, they were trapped against the Alps, with little prospect of reaching southern Germany. Army Group E would render no assistance to Austria or Bavaria.

In Italy, in accordance with Eisenhower's wishes, the Allies piled on the pressure to tie down Army Group C. At 0945 hours on 14 April 1945, the US 5th Army launched an offensive about 32 km (20 miles) southwest of Bologna, west of Highway 64. Despite its US title, it included British and Commonwealth, Brazilian, French and Italian forces. German positions were pounded by bombers and fighter bombers followed by a barrage of 75,000 shells. The ground assault was opened by the US 4th Corps with US 2nd Corps committed the following day. By 17 April, the US 10th Mountain Division was 18 km (11 miles) southwest of Bologna. The South African 6th Armoured

Division was tasked with taking Finale Emilia on the Panaro river, a southern tributary of the Po. This would cut off four German divisions, the 65th and 39th Infantry and 1st and 4th Parachute, that were trying to withdraw through a gap between the US 5th Army and the British 8th Army. The latter to the east had forced the Argenta Gap, between the marshes of the Reno river and Lake Comacchio and was also pushing for the Po. Its offensive strength in armour was 3:1, artillery 2:1 and infantry 1.6:1. The Allies were supported by thousands of Italian partisans who were resisting the German occupation by attacking their lines of communication and supply depots.

The US 5th Army cut Highway 9 west of Bologna on 18 April. This forced the German 65th and 305th Infantry Divisions, which were also caught between the Allied advance, to hastily retreat north. The Allies entered Bologna unopposed on the morning of 21 April. Once the 8th Army had overcome the German defences on the Reno river it was hoped to turn the German retreat into a rout. It was intended that the 8th Army would cross the Po north of Ferrara. Units of the latter had reached Bondeno west of Ferrara by 22 April, leaving the bridge over the Panaro at Finale Emilia to the southwest of Bondeno the main German escape route towards the Po.

Rocket battery commander Lieutenant Hans Golda, with the German 278th Infantry Division, was instructed to cross the Panaro at Bondeno, but they soon learnt it was in enemy hands. Instead, they headed for Finale Emilia. Some 3.2 km (2 miles) short of the bridge, they joined an enormous traffic jam. 'In the direction of Finale we could hear the sounds of battle,'[11] said Golda. Local partisans were blocking the bridge. In response, Golda deployed his rocket launchers, which drove them away. To the west of the town, the South Africans captured the Foscaglia Canal bridge, but the Germans blew up the Finale Road bridge at 0200 hours on 23 April. This left large numbers of Germans trapped south of the river.

At Ro, northwest of Ferrara, the German 21st and 98th Infantry Divisions took three days to get over the Po using a homemade pontoon bridge. This could only be employed at night because of unrelenting attacks by enemy fighter-bombers during the day. Both divisions were forced to leave much of their heavy equipment behind. Lieutenant Golda and his battery reached the Po on 22 April. There was no way to get his rocket launchers over the river, so they were abandoned. Golda, after deploying a rearguard, led his men along the river and by good fortune found a ferry still operating.

Also on 22 April, General von Vietinghoff, the German command-in-chief in Italy, met with SS-General Wolff, who had just returned from seeing Hitler. Wolff knew any talk of withdrawing forces to defend Obersalzburg was complete and utter nonsense. Hitler had claimed that German forces could continue resisting for another two months on a front stretching from Prague to Berlin. Wolff, who had seen what was happening in Berlin and with the Red Army poised to launch its attack on the city, did not believe him. Rather than fighting his way back to Bavaria, von Vietinghoff hoped to surrender as soon as possible, but Wolff received no authorization from Hitler. 'Time is running out,' he warned Wolff. 'Hundreds of thousands of German soldiers are waiting for the words from me that will save their lives.'[12] Wolff agreed that they needed to resume negotiations with the Americans as soon as possible and volunteered to return to Switzerland.

The remains of the 26th Panzer and 29th Panzergrenadier Divisions were by now in a desperate situation. The former was planning to cross the Po north of Bondeno but as it was occupied, attempted to cross east of Ferrara. Both divisions came under attack from the British 78th Infantry

Division, while the 8th Indian Division, having taken Ferrara, crossed to the northern bank. Under constant attack, the Germans' chain of command collapsed along the Po, heralding the end of organized resistance. General von Schwerin, in charge of the 76th Corps, surrendered on 25 April. The remains of his forces lay strewn along the southern banks of the Po. These included thousands of vehicles, almost 300 artillery pieces and 80 panzers. The British 5th Corps took 14,000 prisoners.

By nightfall on 24 April, the US 5th Army had secured the southern bank of the Po stretching some 97 km (60 miles) from the Taro river west of Parma to the boundary with the British 8th Army at Felonica. It had covered 64 km (40 miles) since 21 April and captured 30,000 German prisoners. The Germans had also lost 32,000 killed or wounded reaching the Po. The US 10th Mountain Division was already over the river and heading north. It was ordered to make for Verona to cut Highway 11 and sever the German escape route to the Brenner Pass between Verona and Lake Garda. Everywhere, German divisions were in a state of chaos and near collapse.

From their Felonica bridgehead, the men of General Richard Heidrich's 1st Parachute Corps, consisting of the 1st and 4th Parachute Divisions, were ordered to swim across the Po using tyres or rafts on the night of 24 April. The ferries were reserved for the ambulances carrying the seriously wounded and those vehicles left behind were set on fire. The bridgehead defences were held by the paras and members of the 994th Grenadier Regiment supported by an anti-tank gun detachment and a few panzers. Late in the afternoon, a heavy mist descended, and the evacuation commenced early under the cover of this. 'The crossing was a well-conducted exercise,' recalled one of the survivors, '... with guides on the far bank and a hot meal before the march to defensive positions behind the river.'[13]

Towards evening, the rearguard came under attack by tanks but these were driven off by the anti-tank guns and artillery firing from the northern bank. At 0400 hours, the last company withdrew after it had blown up the surviving panzers and anti-tank guns. 'Now we had a wide river as defence in front of us,' recalled one German para. 'We could hold such a position for a long time – or so we thought.'[14] Instead, they were ordered to march north towards Verona in a desperate bid to outrun the enemy. The remaining elements of General Heidrich's two parachute divisions reached Verona but by the end of 25 April it was in American hands. The US 88th Infantry Division just swept through their positions.

Wolff and two members of Vietinghoff's staff flew to Switzerland on 25 April. The staff officers were then flown to the Allies' headquarters at Caserta. By this stage, though, they were not in a position to ask for terms, nor were the Allies prepared to offer any. It was unconditional surrender or nothing. A frustrated Wolff returned to his headquarters knowing full well that he was in danger should Himmler turn on him for not countenancing a last heroic stand.

By the following day, the German forces in northern Italy had been cut in half. The roads to the Brenner Pass had been blocked by the Americans. The US 4th Corps was instructed to make sure that no German forces could reach the Alpine Redoubt. In response, it sent a division east of Lake Garda to the Brenner Pass. The US 2nd Corps was to move east of Verona to Vicenza to block the roads from the Adriatic. The speed of the US 5th Army's advance ensured that von Vietinghoff was unable to consolidate his forces or co-ordinate an orderly withdrawal. The Germans hoped that once the Allies reached the Po, they would pause, thereby giving them some breathing space. However, there was no pause.

The British 8th Army crossed the river Adige north of the Po on 27 April and swung east towards Trieste to link up with Tito's 4th Army, thereby cutting the Germans' line of retreat into Austria from Yugoslavia via Italy. To the west, the US 5th Army took Genoa. That day, Field Marshal Kesselring met with von Vietinghoff and Dr Rudolf Rahn, the German ambassador to Italy, at Innsbruck to discuss the desperate situation. SS-General Wolff was also supposed to be in attendance but was held up by Italian partisans. There was a brief discussion of the latest political developments. 'Vietinghoff next reported on the military situation,' recalled Kesselring, 'which had deteriorated alarmingly and must lead to a debacle.'[15] Vietinghoff also said a definitive decision needed to be taken about surrendering in Italy. Kesselring decided against this, as such a move would expose German forces north of the Alps. He also warned of 'the psychological effect ... on the officers and men fighting around and in Berlin.'[16]

Nonetheless, German commanders, knowing full well they would never reach the Alps, began to take matters into their own hands. On 29 April, the German 148th Infantry Division and the German-trained Italian Fascist Bersaglieri Division, which had been caught by the Americans south of the Po, surrendered. General Otto Fretter-Pico, commander of the 148th Division, and about 15,000 troops found themselves capitulating to the Brazilian Division. The German/Italian Army of Liguria also gave up. This consisted of three other German-trained Italian divisions. The Germans never fully trusted these units and had restricted them to anti-partisan operations. The same day, the US 92nd Infantry Division reached the French–Italian border at Menton, France.

General Hans Schlemmer in northwestern Italy gathered his 75th Corps, consisting of two divisions, northeast of Turin ready to make a last stand. When news of Hitler's death reached him on 1 May, he agreed to surrender. The following day, General von Vietinghoff, with Kesselring's authorization, finally signed the unconditional surrender in Italy at Caserta. Eisenhower was relieved because there were still 230,000 German troops in northern Italy and Austria's neighbouring provinces. Well over 100,000 Germans were also captured in Yugoslavia. This included the remains of the 7th SS Division, which surrendered at Celje in Slovenia. Significantly, in Eisenhower's mind, all these troops had been prevented from reaching Hitler's Bavarian stronghold. In the meantime, the bloody battle for Berlin was reaching its terrible climax.

Part 3

The Last-ditch Defence

Chapter 12

Escape from Halbe

To the southeast of Berlin by late April, General Busse's 9th Army and elements of General Gräser's 4th Panzer Army, numbering perhaps around 200,000 men with 2,000 guns and 300 panzers, were trapped in the Spree forest near Halbe. Between them, Zhukov and Konev had half a dozen armies encircling the region. Zhukov's 3rd Shock, 69th and 33rd Armies were pushing in from the northeast and east respectively. Konev's 3rd Guards, 13th and 28th Armies had swung in from the southwest and headed north. Zhukov's men contacted Konev's right flank on the Dahme river near Königs Wusterhausen on 24 April. Two days later, the German pocket was considerably reduced when the Soviets overran Storkow and Beeskow in the north and Lieberose in the south. This left those trapped holding out in the Schwielochsee area. It was the junction of the 28th and 3rd Shock Armies to the northwest of the pocket that had sealed the Germans' fate.

'By 27 April ...,' observed Konev, 'the battle to liquidate the German Frankfurt-Guben grouping was progressing. The Germans were being hit from all sides by five armies.'[1] Nonetheless, the Red Army was having an equally tough time of it. Yermakov's battered 5th Guards Mechanized Corps found itself fighting on two fronts. The bulk of his men were fending off Wenck's attack to the west, but part of his corps was also facing east and Busse's troops. To strengthen the Soviet position at Luckenwalde, General Lelyushenko, despite having to take Wannsee, sent not only the 63rd and 68th Guards Tank Brigades but also the 72nd Guards Heavy Tank Regiment from the 10th Guards Tank Corps. In the face of all this armour, it seemed as if a German breakthrough was impossible.

Busse's men and the thousands of civilians sheltering with them had one thought: escape westwards to reach the Elbe and the Americans. The presence of refugees carrying all their worldly possessions in hand- and horse-drawn carts made it almost impossible to conduct an organized fighting withdrawal. On paper, the 11th SS Panzer Corps was supposed to be leading the breakout and protecting the northern flank. The 5th Corps was supporting it and covering the southern flank, while it fell to the 5th SS Mountain Corps to provide the rearguard. This left the 32nd, 35th and 36th SS divisions belonging to the latter in the unenviable position of trailing along behind. However, it was really a case of every unit for itself.

The forest roads were choked with people and vehicles, greatly slowing down movement and offering easy meat for the prowling Red Air Force, Soviet artillery and Katyusha rocket launchers. 'In turn,' said Konev, 'the German troops brought pressure to bear on the armies of our army group which blocked their way to the southwest.'[2] However, at every turn, the Soviets seemed to be waiting for the 9th Army. Twice it tried to break free and twice it was foiled. 'They were consolidating their battle formations and striking at us with increasing force,' noted Konev, 'What else could they do? Apart from surrender, they could do nothing but try to get through our formations and join up with Wenck.'[3]

'If the first attempts to break out through the encirclement succeeded,' said SS-Major Diehl with the remains of the ad hoc 35th SS Police Grenadier Division, 'they were immediately destroyed by Russian aircraft and artillery.'[4] Diehl's unit was formed using police training school instructors from Dresden. Although called a division, it was only ever of regimental strength and had fought on the Neisse front before withdrawing. Now the survivors clung to each other as they desperately sought to get out of the Halbe pocket.

In the face of the encroaching Red Army, many of the police grenadiers were understandably suffering from poor morale. On the Neisse, they had endured heavy casualties at the hands of Konev's men and the survivors had no desire to be captured by the Soviets. Furthermore, they were only too aware of the terrible firebombing of their home city earlier in the year. The ease with which the RAF had incinerated some 25,000 people had clearly signalled that the war was all but lost. The German authorities claimed that 200,000 people were killed in Dresden. Inevitably, some of the police grenadiers had lost friends and family consumed in the flames.

The 32nd SS Grenadier Division had almost reached Halbe when its right flank came under fire. Although the division technically consisted of three grenadier regiments, like the 35th SS, manpower-wise it only amounted to a single regiment or three battalions. Men of the 1st Battalion, 86th SS Volunteer Grenadier Regiment caught

Busse's 9th Army breakout, 26 April–1 May 1935.

Encirclements

0   10 miles
0   10 kilometres

TWELFTH ARMY

Heilstätten

Beelitz

Ferch

STRASSE 2

Treuenbritzen

Elsholz

Nieplitz

Jüterbog

STRASSE 101

Luckenwalde

Kummersdorf

Zossen

STRASSE 96

Baruth

Mark

Radeland

Zesch am See

Teupitz

Halbe

Dahme

BERLIN–DRESDEN AUTOBAHN

Märkisch Buchholz

Ninth Army rear-guard

the Soviets by surprise and with the support of three panzers pushed through the town. They passed an abandoned Soviet field kitchen with the food still bubbling in the pots, but they could not stop to taste it. SS-Grenadier Alfred Blombach and his comrades fought to keep the road from Halbe to the *Autobahn* open. In response, the Soviets heavily shelled the *Autobahn* and launched continual attacks. Blombach was hit by shrapnel in the head, the back and lower right arm and knocked unconscious. When he woke up, he found himself in a ditch on his own apart from some corpses. At some point, a passing medic had bandaged his head and moved him from the road, which had prevented him from being crushed or hit by more shrapnel. Hailing down a passing *Kübelwagen* staff car, he was picked up. Blombach was later transferred to an ambulance and was subsequently captured.

One unit among the SS that was particularly desperate to escape was the 36th Waffen Grenadier Division der SS. This had been formed using a brigade of German criminals as well as Ukrainian and Russian deserters. During its time on the Eastern Front and the Warsaw Uprising it had committed the most unspeakable atrocities, making it one of the worst German units ever to wear a uniform. Rape, torture and murder had been its calling card. Its commander, convicted rapist SS-Colonel Oskar Dirlewanger, was wounded on 17 April and replaced by SS-Brigadier Fritz Schmedes. The men of the 36th SS knew they could expect no mercy if they fell into the hands of the Red Army. Discipline was such that on 28 April, members of its 73rd Waffen Grenadier Regiment hanged their own commanding officer. Schmedes, who was a former commander of the 4th SS Police Panzergrenadier Division, and his staff were determined to surrender to the Americans. The Soviets were aware of their presence in the pocket and had every intention of massacring them wholesale. There were also 5,000 Russian auxiliaries serving with the 9th Army and they knew exactly what fate awaited them if caught.

That same day, large groups of demoralized German soldiers began to surrender, with the Red Army rounding up 14,000 prisoners. SS-Chief Gunner Hans Schaller recalled 'it was on the evening of 28 April that our army became a leaderless horde.'[5] He was with the 506th Nebelwerfer Battalion, but they had already destroyed and abandoned their rocket launchers. 'Resembling a swollen grey inchworm,' wrote SS-Senior Staff Sergeant Horst Woycinick in his diary on 29 April, 'we're marching on a forest lane leading to what will be the break-through battle.'[6] He was with the remains of the 32nd SS Grenadier Division, who were constantly shelled and bombed as they sought to break out westwards. Successfully driving the Soviets from Halbe, they headed for Baruth. SS-Sergeant Haufschildt, with a group of panzers and tank destroyers, led a column of up to 20 vehicles and 2,000 soldiers and civilians towards Baruth. After coming across a field covered in 300 corpses, they knew they could expect no mercy.

Otto Boomgard was a flak gunner with the 32nd SS Division whose unit had discarded their 37-mm anti-aircraft guns. On foot, he followed two halftracks through Halbe. Once on the other side, they passed through some woods, where they were shelled. 'I got a splinter in the knee making it impossible for me to move,'[7] he recalled. Boomgard was hoisted into one of the vehicles, which he discovered was already packed with casualties. They made good progress until they ran into Soviet anti-tank guns and machine guns. An armoured car in front suffered a direct hit and had its turret blown off, killing the crew. Boomgard's vehicle escaped through the woods and across an open space. Once back in the trees, the exhausted crew and passengers dismounted to take a breather. Suddenly, Soviet troops were on them. 'All I remember was running for a few hundred metres,' said Boomgard, 'before hiding underneath some brush wood. A little later on I made my way through Russian lines in the dark.'[8]

SS-Colonel Hans Kempin, the last commander of the 32nd SS Division, was ordered to take charge of the remains of the rearguard. His instructions stated: 'Consider the situation and then break out of the pocket, deciding whether to head for Berlin or the Elbe.'[9] Although his party was caught by air attack, they reached Halbe and got through. SS-Corporal Eberhard Baumgart, who was wounded, managed to hitch a lift with some others on the back of an armoured car. 'I registered the fact that the sounds of battle were fading,' he recalled with relief. 'The driver slowed down and I dared to lift my head. We'd made it! We'd broken through!'[10]

It fell to SS Captain Horst Mathiebe's battalion to cover the 32nd SS Division's withdrawal. At Streganz, his grenadiers counterattacked Soviet troops attempting to cut them off and fighting took place around the brickworks, which was being used as a French prisoner of war camp. 'Had the Ivans succeeded in breaking through,' noted Mathiebe, 'the division would have been stuck in the pocket without any escape route.'[11] He was thankful that his men were prepared and successfully drove the enemy off. 'Kempin radioed me,' recalled Mathiebe, 'with his compliments for this brave operation.'[12] His men then covered the retreat over the Dahme but lost radio contact with the rest of the division. Feeling abandoned, they reached the bridge near the Klein-Hammer forest warden's lodge and crossed just before German sappers blew it up. They then headed for Halbe and safety.

On this third attempt, some 25,000 men managed to slip the Red Army's noose. They were, however, in a terrible condition. 'The physical state and morale of the officers and men … permit neither a new attack nor long resistance,' Busse warned Wenck on 29 April. 'The fighting capacity of the 9th Army is obviously at an end.'[13] This gave Wenck the opportunity he needed when he informed the German High Command, 'This means that an attack on Berlin is now impossible, having ascertained that we can no longer rely on the fighting capacity of the 9th Army.'[14] During that day, the Soviets took 30,000 prisoners.

Not all the SS caught by the Soviets were necessarily combatants. Dutch volunteer Joost van Ketel was serving as a dentist with the 23rd SS Panzergrenadier Division Nederland when he was captured in the woods. His only hope of escape was to bluff his captors into believing he was a forced labourer. 'Not SS,' he had said firmly, adding 'Russian comrade – Holland.'[15] He then brandished a striped pass in the tricolours of the Dutch flag. His baffled captors sent him on his way. He performed the same trick with an American patrol when he reached Dessau on the Elbe. The rest of his division under SS-Brigadier Jurgen Wagner were not so fortunate and were surrounded by the Red Army at Fürstenwalde and wiped out.

In the meantime, Hitler signalled Jodl demanding, 'Inform me immediately: 1. Where are Wenck's spearheads? 2. When will they attack? 3. Where is the Ninth Army? 4. Where is Ninth Army going to break through? 5. Where are Holste's spearheads?'[16] At 0300 hours on 30 April, Keitel and Jodl plucked up the courage to reply, '1. Wenck's spearhead is stuck south of Schwielow Lake. 2. Consequently, the Twelfth Army cannot continue its attack on Berlin. 3. The Ninth Army is fully encircled. 4. Holste's Corps had been forced into a defensive position.' They then admitted, 'Attacks on Berlin have not advanced anywhere.'[17]

One group of about 4,000 soldiers and civilians reached the *Autobahn* west of Halbe but ran into an ambush on the night of 29

April. The column did not have any cover and many were instantly killed or wounded. In a desperate bid to escape the shelling, some fled in all directions only to be shot or captured. In a state of terror, many civilians killed themselves. Just as Keitel and Jodl were signalling Hitler, those remaining were being rounded up by the Red Army. 'What followed was an example of how Russians have fun,' noted Major Brand from the 2nd Panzer Division, who was taken along with Lieutenant Melzer. 'We were stood against a wall along with some SS officers; the SS officers were shot. Melzer and I were spared.'[18]

Busse and his exhausted survivors reached Kummersdorf, to the northeast of Luckenwalde, on 30 April and prepared to fight their way through the Soviet 5th Guards Mechanized Corps. He was fortunate that he avoided the Baruth–Luckenwalde road or he would have run straight into the armour of the 10th Guards Tank Corps that was massed in the area. Busse was also fortunate that the heavily forested landscape was not good tank country. He appreciated that his men were tired and hungry but exhorted them to one last effort. 'On your feet! Keep moving! Only a few more miles to go!'[19] he urged. They were almost out of ammunition, with few remaining guns and mortars to blast the Soviets out of the way. Their last panzer was sent forwards to the sound of gunfire coming from behind the Soviet positions. Mercifully, the firing was coming from the 12th Army. Busse linked up with Wenck at Beelitz, southwest of Berlin, on 1 May. When they met, Wenck grabbed his colleague by the hand and said simply 'Thank God you're here.'[20] Busse reckoned he had led about 40,000 to safety, whereas Konev later claimed only 4,000 got through.[21]

Colonel Reichhelm, Wenck's chief-of-staff, was disappointed to come across General Holste minus his men. 'Why aren't you with your troops?'[22] Reichhelm asked accusingly. Holste looked uneasy for a moment, then replied, 'I do not have any any more.'[23] Reichhelm knew that this was not true and woke Wenck, insisting Holste be immediately arrested. Wenck was too tired to make a decision, furthermore there was little point in punishing Holste when the German army had collapsed. Holste continued on his way with his wife to the Elbe.

Everywhere, Busse's forces had left behind a trail of devastation. 'All around in the woods there [are] dead, dead and yet more dead,' observed Soviet war correspondent Konstantin Simonov, 'the corpses of those who fell while running under fire.'[24] Some 22,000 German soldiers were later buried at Halbe, along with 2,000 civilians. The rest of the 9th Army was captured. The Soviets claimed they had killed 60,000 Germans troops and taken 120,000 prisoners. There is of course no way to verify these figures.

Both Busse and Wenck knew they would have little option but to surrender their surviving 100,000 troops and hangers-on to the Americans. Their best hope was to skirt south of Brandenburg through Genthin to reach the German bridgehead on the eastern bank of the Elbe between Ferchland and Schönhausen. There, they would be able to establish a defensive perimeter against the Red Army. Key to their escape would be the damaged road bridge at Tangermünde in the middle of the bridgehead, the ferry at Ferchland and the railway bridge at Schönhausen. On 1 May, Rochus Misch listened in on a phone call between Busse and General Burgdorf. He recalled, 'Busse said it looked bad – there would probably be nothing for it but to accept captivity.'[25]

However, the withdrawal over the Elbe was reliant on the good will of General Simpson's US 9th Army on the west bank. Busse and Wenck agreed that the 9th Army would cross first while the 12th Army held the perimeter. In the meantime, they would have to endure five days of Soviet attacks and shelling before Simpson agreed to take German

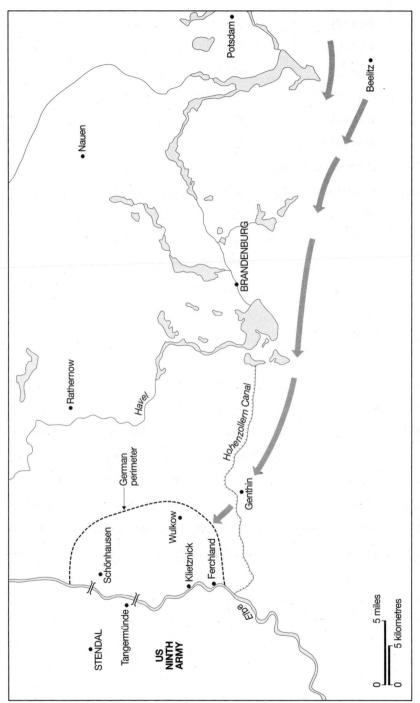

The 9th and 12th Armies' withdrawal, 1–8 May 1945.

wounded and unarmed troops. He was not permitted to accept civilian refugees. Crucially, Simpson also refused to let the Germans repair the bridge to speed up the evacuation. Once the Soviets closed in, the river would become a scene of death and mayhem as desperate people tried to swim or paddle across. After his fighting withdrawal from Halbe, Busse's army would descend into chaos in the closing days of the war.

One of the few units to get over the river at Tangermünde with any semblance of discipline was Major General Heinrich Götz's Infantry Division Scharnhorst. This unit had only come into being in Dessau at the end of March using the remains of two other divisions and local high school students. It fought with Wenck against the Americans at Barby and then the Soviets at Beelitz. Battalion commander Captain Peter Rettich noted that the division was likely 'the last formation of the Wehrmacht still in battle order in northern Germany.'[26]

Afterwards, many blamed Busse for not acting sooner to save the bulk of his command. While he could certainly have taken a unilateral decision, he was not officially authorized by Hitler to retreat westwards until 27 April, by which time it was far too late. Konev was of the view that the 9th Army fought well, whereas he felt that Wenck was just 'going through the motions.'[27] This was a little harsh in light of the 12th Army being so weak. Nonetheless, the upshot was that all Hitler's attempts to relieve Berlin ended in miserable failure. Steiner, Holste, Wenck and Busse had not tried to save Berlin, nor could they.

Chapter 13

Death in the Tiergarten

As the fighting progressed in late April, the western defences of Berlin's government district, including the Reichstag, Propaganda Ministry, Reich Chancellery and Air Ministry, were anchored on the Tiergarten. This vast 2.5 sq km (630 acre) parkland was divided by the East–West Axis that passed through the Brandenburg Gate to Unter den Linden. To the north, it was bordered by the river Spree and to the south by the Tiergartenstrasse. Most of the park's trees had been shredded by the bombing and shelling. Any that survived were carted off by Berliners for firewood. The barren grounds were now covered in entrenchments, minefields and barbed wire. The park had also become the repository for hidden emergency gasoline stocks. About 40,000 litres (8,800 gallons) had been buried in the Tiergarten.[1] There were also several thousand litres buried in the zoo bunker.[2]

In the southwestern corner of the Tiergarten lay Berlin's famous zoo and two massive concrete flak towers. These edifices would severely slow the Soviet advance from the west. The larger of the two was technically called a G Tower but was better known as the 'zoo tower' or 'bunker'. At over 40 m (130 ft) high, it covered a city block and housed not only flak guns but also an enormous air raid shelter, hospital and warehousing. It had its own independent water and power supply and accommodation for a hundred-strong garrison. It was so well protected and provisioned that it was believed the tower could hold out for up to a year on its own.

Luftwaffe doctor Captain Walter Hagedorn, working in the tower's 95-bed hospital, recalled people saying, 'We can stick it out until either [General] Wenck or the Americans get here.'[3] From the roof, Colonel Wöhlermann, General Weidling's artillery commander, noted, 'One had a panoramic view of the burning, smouldering and smoking great city, a scene which again and again shook one to the core.'[4] The tower's guns when used in a ground role could fire into all the surrounding city districts and could provide welcome support for the troops defending the Tiergarten. The smaller neighbouring building, called an L Tower, was a command and communications centre, which provided targeting data. It also relayed by radio Hitler's increasingly desperate orders when telephone lines were not available.

The sprawling zoo had only closed to the public on 20 April 1945 after the electricity supply was cut and the staff could no longer pump water. The keepers were struggling to keep their remaining animals alive. Many of these were dehydrated and malnourished. They were regularly driven to a state of nervous panic by the constant explosions. At the start of the Second World War, the collection numbered some 14,000 animals, birds, fish and reptiles; by 1945, just 1,600 remained. The zoo had been hit over a hundred times by Allied bombers and many of the survivors had been evacuated to other zoos around Germany. Some of the rare cattle had vanished, stolen by hungry Berliners. Of the larger animals, all that remained were five lions, ten bison, a single male elephant, a female hippopotamus and her baby, a baboon and a gorilla. The zoo was about to become a battlefield because the grounds were held by 5,000 well-dug-in German soldiers.

At the eastern end of the Tiergarten to the north of the Brandenburg Gate was the Reichstag, while to the south were the ministries along with the Chancellery.

To the northwest and northeast of the Reichstag it was vital to hold the Moltke and Weidendamm bridges over the river Spree as well as the Alexanderplatz. The Moltke bridge offered the most direct route to the Königsplatz and the Reichstag. To the south, the defenders of the Landwehr Canal were preventing the Red Army from reaching Belle-Alliance-Platz and moving up Friedrichstrasse. In response, the Soviets exerted relentless pressure on the defenders. From the north, General Vasily Kuznetsov's 3rd Shock Army was pushing south towards the Tiergarten. From the east, Lieutenant General Nikolai Bezarin's 5th Shock Army was pushing inwards. Bezarin was operating on a front just over 400 m (440 yards) wide using two corps.

To the south of the city, four Soviet armies fought their way over the Teltow Canal. The defence line on the northern bank was considerable and, according to Konev, 'It consisted of trenches, reinforced concrete pillboxes, and dug-in tanks and self-propelled guns.'[5] The Germans had also fortified the surrounding houses, which had walls up to 1 m (3.3 ft) thick, and the local factory buildings. The latter, noted Konev, 'formed a kind of medieval rampart running down to the water's edge.'[6] According to Soviet intelligence, these defences were held by 15,000 troops with 500 machine guns, 250 guns and mortars and 130 tanks and armoured cars. This force sounded more impressive than it really was. 'What a motley crowd it was that gathered along the Teltow Canal,' observed Konev,'especially in the Volkssturm battalions, where seasoned soldiers served alongside old men and weeping teenagers.'[7] Although the defenders had blown up some of the canal bridges and mined the others, they could not stop the inevitable.

Once they were across the canal, Soviet troops were able to clear the suburbs of Steglitz and Schmargendorf as well as reaching the southern reaches of Grunewald. When they swung north to Pichelsdorf this cut the lines of communication between Berlin and those forces holding Potsdam and the Island of Wannsee. To the southwest, another Soviet army had cut its way to Babelsberg and Potsdam. This trapped 20,000 German troops on Wannsee just to the north of Babelsberg. North of the Teltow Canal, one of the Red Army's key objectives was the Tempelhof airport. The fear was that Hitler and the senior Nazi leadership might try to use it to fly out. The 39th and 79th Guards Rifle Divisions were given the task of overwhelming the airport's defences. These were held by SS troops, dug-in panzers and flak guns. By noon on 26 April, the airport buildings and the runways had been captured.

The taking of Tempelhof airport permitted the riflemen of Chuikov's 8th Guards Army to force their way over the Landwehr Canal. Their goal was the Tiergarten, which they found they could penetrate via the underground railway tunnels. What Chuikov really needed was the bridge on the Potsdamerstrasse as that would make it possible to push his tanks through to the Tiergarten. The Soviets decided to use a ruse to take the bridge. A tank was covered in sandbags doused in fuel and when it reached the crossing, it burst into flames. The SS troops fell back in the face of the advancing blaze and other Soviet tanks rumbled over the bridge.

Despite this subterfuge, on the whole there was nothing subtle about the Red Army's advance. 'A battle in a city is a battle of firepower, a battle at close quarters, in which close-range firing is carried out not by automatic weapons only,' Chuikov explained to his commanders, 'but by powerful artillery systems and tank armaments, all firing over a few score metres only.'[8] The drawback with this tactic was that the rounds tended to pass right through the building, leaving it standing.

German troops with a Panzerfaust *anti-tank weapon prepare for the final onslaught.*

North of the Tiergarten, General Perevertkin's 79th Rifle Corps from the 3rd Shock Army captured the district of Alt-Moabit or Old Moabit. On 28 April, Major General Shatilov's 150th Rifle Division, which formed part of 79th Corps, took the factory district to the south of the Kleiner Tiergarten. Their next objective was the imposing Moabit Prison. Rumour had it that Joseph Goebbels was in charge of its defence. This spurred on the attackers, keen to lay their hands on a senior Nazi. Colonel Zinchenko's 756th Rifle Regiment stormed the prison and released 7,000 men but disappointingly discovered no sign of Goebbels. Many of them were Soviet prisoners of war who immediately found themselves being recruited as combat replacements for 79th Corps.

The defenders of the Tiergarten now endured Kuznetsov's 3rd Shock Army bearing down on them from the northwest, Bezarin's 5th Shock Army with 11th Tank Corps pushing in from the east and Chuikov's 8th Guards Army striking from the south. Marshal Konev, not wanting to be outdone by Zhukov, ordered General Rybalko's 3rd Guards Army to clear southeastern Berlin. His intention was that by the close of 28 April, the 7th Guards Tank Corps and the 20th Rifle Division would be deployed on the western edge of the Tiergarten. However, in light of Chuikov's progress on the Landwehr Canal there was every chance of him and Rybalko becoming tangled up. Reluctantly, Konev instructed Rybalko to veer west once he reached the canal and to abandon his line of advance on the Schöneberg district. This meant that he would not take part in the fighting for the Tiergarten and indeed the central district.

In the meantime, the 10th Guards Tank Corps, part of Lelyushenko's 4th Guards Tank Army and the 350th Rifle Division from the 13th Army, fought their way on to the southern shores of Wannsee. Escape was almost impossible with Soviet troops in Babelsberg and the Grunewald. Despite this, German civilians and soldiers desperately tried to get over the Havel before the Red Army overran the island. Some paddled across using anything that floated.

Rybalko's 3rd Guards drove their way into Charlottenburg to the west of the Tiergarten on 28 April. At the same time, Bogdanov's 2nd Guards Tank Army fought to clear the southeastern area of Charlottenburg and the western defences of the Tiergarten. Chuikov's 8th Guards Army also cut into the Tiergarten. The 28th Guards Rifle Corps on his left gained the edge of the zoo by Budapesterstrasse and was within hailing distance of the 2nd Guards Tank Army. On his right, the 4th Guards Rifle Corps took Potsdamer station just to the south of the Reich Chancellery.

Soviet troops fought their way into the grounds of the zoo on 29 April and the hippo called Rosa was killed by artillery fire. The zoo director, Lutz Heck, had already shot the lions and the baboon. The flak tower commander insisted the latter be destroyed after its cage had been damaged and he was worried about the animal escaping. From the Hippopotamus House, the Soviets were able to fire up at the flak towers. Shells began to pound at G Tower's impenetrable concrete walls, forcing the inhabitants to lower the 10 cm (4 in)-thick steel shutters protecting the firing apertures. It was designed to house up to 15,000 people during air raids, but Doctor Hagedorn estimated there were up to 30,000 civilians crammed in the installation as well as the troops defending it. Hagedorn, working in the hospital, had 1,500 wounded on his hands as well as 500 dead. 'In between lulls,' he said, 'we tried to take out the bodies and the amputated limbs for burial, but it was almost impossible.'[9]

In the Tiergarten and the grounds of the zoo, the fighting intensified. Soviet tanks were able to advance along the East–West Axis and Tiergartenstrasse heading for the Unter den Linden. Soviet artillery was also deployed on the East–West Axis in order to shell the Tiergarten and the government district. Once Kuznetsov's 3rd Shock Army had reached the Reichstag it was only a matter of time before he linked up with Chuikov. The defenders would be trapped in an area of about a thousand yards that was dominated by Soviet artillery. The Soviets had almost completely overrun the Tiergarten by the late morning of 30 April and most of its defenders were either dead or captured.

The 79th Guards Rifle Division deployed two regiments to cover the zoo flak tower. Their commander, Colonel Gerasimenko, knew that gaining entry was almost impossible. Several German prisoners were rounded up and sent late on 30 April with a message asking the garrison to capitulate. 'We propose that you surrender the fortress without further fighting,' it read. 'We guarantee that no troops, including SS and SA men will be executed.'[10] The garrison, playing for time, did not reply until the following morning. Colonel Haller, claiming to be the commandant, sent a note saying they would surrender at midnight. This delay of a whole day was intended to gain time for the garrison to escape.

By 1 May, Chuikov's men were fighting for final control of the central area of the Tiergarten. Bogdanov's 2nd Guards Tank Army had reached the eastern edge of Charlottenburg to link up with the 8th Guards units in the zoo. That evening, the 3rd Shock Army met the 8th Guards just south of the Reichstag, while the 2nd Guards Tank Army linked up with the 8th Guards and the 1st Guards Tank Army in the Tiergarten. The last of the resistance in the Tiergarten had been overcome. This left those in the flak tower cut off and on their own.

Chapter 14

Avalanche of Fire

In the city centre, the massive Adlon Hotel between the Reichstag and the Reich Chancellery inevitably became a scene of German resistance. Located on the junction of Unter den Linden and Wilhelmstrasse to the east of the Brandenburg Gate, the Adlon dominated the exit from the East–West Axis. In particular, it overlooked the wide-open space of the Pariser Platz. Part of the surrounding area was a diplomatic district that included the former British, French and Soviet embassies, so it had been a popular haunt of foreign diplomats. Years earlier, partygoers had been photographed happily clasping champagne glasses at its tables; now the remaining staff skulked along the Adlon's empty corridors serving disillusioned SS officers with fine wines and brandy.

The hotel had opened in 1907 and incorporated the neighbouring Reichshof Hotel, though the latter had become the headquarters for the

Ministry of Food and Agriculture in 1938. It was once one of the world's most luxurious hotels and was popular with revellers seeing in the New Year. The Adlon had been a favourite haunt of the aristocracy and wealthy upper-middle class, though it had not always been to the tastes of the senior Nazi Party officials; Hitler had stopped the Adlon and every other venue from playing jazz. As the war progressed, many of the city's bars, cafes and restaurants closed but the Adlon remained defiantly open.

To offer the building some protection, a high brick wall was built around the ground floor, giving it a rather fortress-like appearance. Although part of the hotel was requisitioned as a military hospital and its windows filled with sandbags, its bars were available to those seeking solace in alcohol. 'The Hotel Adlon was still in operation, despite the bombs and grenades that were already landing in the street,' recalled SS-Colonel Léon Degrelle. 'In the brightly lit dining hall waiters in tuxedos went on solemnly and unflappably serving people.'[1]

Eva Braun, before finally joining Hitler in the Führerbunker, had booked a guest into the hotel. Eva's older sister, Ilse, who had escaped from Breslau by train, met her at the Adlon on 21 January 1945. 'I'm sorry not to be able to put you up at the Chancellery,' said Eva, 'but it's full of soldiers and we're rather short of space.'[2] Ilse was shocked by the Adlon's continuing opulence despite the war. The pair had almost fallen out that night when dining alone in the library of the Chancellery, since Ilse blamed Hitler for leading the country to destruction, after seeing thousands of wretched refugees fleeing Breslau. 'Your Führer is a fiend,' said Ilse, 'he's dragging you into the abyss with him, and all of us along with you!'[3] In the past, Ilse's greatest crime had been to criticise the Führer's dress sense.

A shocked Eva was taken aback and angrily responded, 'You deserve to be stood up against a wall and shot.'[4] Ilse did not press the point further, knowing full well that Hitler had driven Eva to attempt suicide twice during the 1930s. Furthermore, Ilse recalled her sister's chilling words when Hitler had announced the outbreak of war: 'If something happens to him, I will die too.'[5] In despair, Ilse fled Berlin to Bavaria. Eva, following their sour meeting, sought sanctuary in Munich only to return to Berlin to be at Hitler's side in mid-March.

The Adlon became a sanctuary for some of Hitler's few remaining allies. On the orders of Foreign Minister Joachim von Ribbentrop, the cellar bar was made available to diplomats from Mussolini's puppet Italian republic and Japan as well as the survivors from Hitler's fallen eastern European allies and Vichy French, who did not want to or simply could not go home. At night, many of them slept there as their embassies had been damaged in the bombing. Von Ribbentrop hoped the Japanese ambassador could put out peace feelers via the Japanese embassy in Stockholm, but nothing came of it. On 7 April, he had told the Japanese ambassador that the military situation could, 'Necessitate the temporary transfer of the German Government to south Germany.'[6] This seemed to substantiate reports that Hitler was preparing an Alpine Redoubt on the border between Germany and Austria.

The Royal Air Force bombed the city centre on 12 April and both the Adlon and the Chancellery caught fire. Once the Red Army had penetrated Berlin's defences, the Adlon's cellars were used as a dressing station for wounded soldiers, overseen by SS-Colonel Dr Zimmermann. The SS had another hospital to the south in the Reich Chancellery cellars. In late April, the adjacent diplomatic area was assaulted by the Soviet 32nd Rifle Corps, consisting of three rifle divisions supported by the 11th Guards Tank Brigade. Some of the abandoned embassies had been fortified as strongpoints. These were stormed by the 60th Guards, 295th and 416th Rifle Divisions. Japanese diplomats, whose country was not at war with the Soviet Union, sent a delegation to the Red Army to demand the return of three cars and other stolen property. Soviet riflemen had little regard for diplomatic niceties in the heat of battle.

To the east of the hotel, Major-General Firsov's 26th Guards Rifle Corps forced its way towards the cathedral and the sprawling Royal Palace on Museum Island as well as the Rotes Rathaus or Red City Hall on the far bank of the Spree. The latter, held by members of the 11th SS Panzergrenadier Division, was attacked by two regiments from General Fomichenko's 266th Rifle Division on 29 April. Spearheading the assault with armour support were two battalions under Major Alexeyev and Captain Bobylev. The 11th SS comprised of recruits from Denmark and Norway, who like the Frenchmen of the 33rd SS Division had volunteered to defend Berlin to the last. Before the Soviet riflemen could even reach the heavy wrought-iron gates of the Rotes Rathaus, they were mown down by machine-gun fire. Sappers had to be called up to blast holes in the walls of the neighbouring buildings so they could be cleared.

Zhukov recalled, 'Our men were met by such a strong avalanche of fire that further advance along the street was simply impossible.'[7] Instead, Soviet riflemen after capturing the surrounding buildings breached the Rotes Rathaus interior walls using explosives. Out in the street, tanks and self-propelled guns were employed to destroy the gates. 'They used hand-grenades to clear the lobby and halls,' reported Zhukov. 'Every room was fought for.'[8] Among those who entered the building was Junior Lieutenant Konstantin Gromov. He made his way to the roof, where he threw the Nazi flag down into the street and hoisted the Red Banner. For the men of the 266th Rifle Division, this triumph felt like some recompense for being hit by their own artillery on 16 April. Very few of the 11th SS in the building survived to go into captivity.

The shelling of Berlin's streets during the battle was relentless.

By 30 April, the badly damaged Adlon was also in Soviet hands. A Red Army photographer was waiting to record the moment when German walking wounded and their female nurses emerged from the building. One young nurse looked apprehensively into the camera, fearful of the uncertain fate she now faced at the hands of Soviet soldiers. Outside, the Pariser Platz was covered in debris, including burnt-out vehicles. Soviet troops proceeded to loot the hotel's well-stocked wine cellars and got very drunk. On the night of 2 May, the building caught fire and burned down.

Meanwhile, the 26th Guards Rifle Corps set about overcoming the German strongpoint in the ruins of the Börse building, which had been home to the Berlin stock exchange until it was burned down following an air raid in 1944. Using a tunnel, Soviet riflemen were able to get in behind the defenders. To the southwest of the Börse, the 32nd Rifle Corps crossed the Spree to Museum Island to attack the royal palace and the cathedral. Somewhat confusingly for the attackers, the southern portion of the island was known as Fisherman's Island. While units of the 60th Guards and 416th Rifle Divisions pushed on the palace, the 295th Rifle Division struck towards the Reichsbank. Everywhere, Berlin's defence disintegrated into pockets of men fighting desperately for their lives, notably in the Armoury, Prussian State Library and State Opera buildings.

The Soviet 32nd Rifle Corps and the 26th Guards Rifle Corps were ordered to push forwards as far as the Pariser Platz. The 94th and 266th Rifle Divisions still had to overcome the defenders of the Armoury known as the Zeughaus, which traditionally served as the Berlin garrison headquarters. 'We looked inside through window grilles. There were so many weapons!' recalled Soviet war correspondent Vassili Subbotin afterwards. 'Cannon, mortars and muskets stemming from past days and centuries.'[9] He and his companion, Kirill Jegorovitch, were struck by the irony of the situation. 'We were standing in front of the Zeughaus,' adds Subbotin, 'the museum of military history.'[10] This along with the Prussian State Library was on the northern side of the Unter den Linden. Over two thirds of the library's 3 million books had been evacuated after the building was hit by Allied bombers. Under Nazi rule, its librarians were instructed to inform on anyone conducting research on Germany's anti-Semitism. The librarians were long gone.

The 416th and 295th Rifle Divisions were tasked with taking the State Opera across the road as well as the Reichsbank. It fell to the 301st and 248th Rifle Divisions to secure the Gestapo and Reich's Main Security Office buildings. The Opera House, like many other buildings, was a ruin, having burned down in February 1945. However, its cellars had been used as the headquarters for the 11th SS Division until 27 April. SS-Captain Henri Fenet recalled that day: 'All morning the shells continued to crash down on the Opera House, Schloss Berlin and the surrounding area with such violence that the headquarters moved to a less unpleasant place as soon as there was a gap in the shelling.'[11] A company of engineers had been left behind to hold out for as long as they could.

Stalin was determined to get recompense for all the appalling damage Hitler's armies had wrought on the Soviet Union. Likewise, ordinary Soviet riflemen were eager to go on a treasure hunt. The Soviets hoped the Reichsbank still held some of Germany's gold, silver and money reserves, much of which had been looted from the occupied territories. It had gained the gold reserves of Austria, Belgium, dismembered Czechoslovakia, Danzig, Italy, Luxembourg and the Netherlands, which had a wartime value of $621 million.[12] Hitler, following Austria's Anschluss with Germany in 1938, had seized 100 tons of gold bullion belonging to the Austrian Central Bank. A further 14 tons were confiscated from Austria's Jews. After Hitler's conquest of western Europe, the Reichsbank had been left controlling 30 per cent of the world's finances and its reserves had swelled to 10 billion Reichsmarks.[13] Several million of this made its way into the account of Hermann Göring courtesy of the mentally unstable vice president of the Reichsbank. Soviet intelligence had accounted for 2,389 kg (2.35 tons) of gold, 12 tons of silver and millions in paper money seized by Axis forces in the occupied territories.[14]

The Soviets may have also hoped that the bank's vaults contained some of the 21,903 treasures, including 10,890 paintings, which had been stolen from western Europe by mid-1944.[15] Göring alone amassed an illegal art collection that included 2,000 looted paintings. In total, the art stolen by the Nazis was worth in excess of $200 million.[16] Göring's self-indulgent extravagance knew no limits. According to

Albert Speer, Göring's birthday gifts the previous year had included 'cigars from Holland, gold bars from the Balkans, valuable paintings and sculptures.'[17]

The Soviets, though, were to discover empty Reichsbank vaults since Walther Funk, the Nazi finance minister, had spirited away the last of the reserves to Bavaria. These went missing in the wake of the US Army. Ironically, Funk's predecessor, Dr Hjalmar Schacht, had been sacked in 1939 for opposing the cost of Germany's rearmament and from that point on the Reichsbank had come under the direct control of the Führer. Hitler's credit had become limitless. The unfortunate Schacht was subsequently sent to a concentration camp after the attempt on Hitler's life after 1944.

Some of the Reichsbank's gold was later retrieved from a mine at Merkers in Thuringia. General Eisenhower in mid-April witnessed first-hand how the US 3rd Army had discovered an estimated $250 million worth of gold bars concealed in a salt mine as well as countless works of art.[18] This was not all the mine contained. 'Crammed into suitcases and trunks and other containers,' recalled Eisenhower, 'was a great amount of gold and silver plate ornament obviously looted from private dwellings throughout Europe.'[19]

In contrast, the only thing the Soviets did find in the deep cellars of the Reichsbank were the remains of a first-aid post belonging to the 24th SS-Panzergrenadier Regiment. It once formed part of the 11th SS Division. SS-Captain Fenet had been treated there after being shot in the foot, before moving on to the Opera House. All the Reichsbank contained in abundance was fresh Nazi blood.

Chapter 15

Storming the Reichstag

For the Red Army, the most symbolic objective was the imposing Reichstag, Germany's former parliament building on the eastern side of the vast square known as the Königsplatz. Stalin himself had chosen this as their main goal rather than the Reich Chancellery. It had suffered an arson attack just four weeks after Hitler came to power in 1933, which damaged the Deputies Chamber. From then on, parliamentary business was conducted in the Kroll Opera House. Hitler blamed communist troublemakers and used the fire as an excuse to clamp down on civil liberties, paving the way for total Nazi rule. During the war, the Reichstag was employed as a hospital. By 1945, with all the windows bricked up, it had been turned into a forbidding-looking fortress.

When the Red Army launched its assault on the city on 21 April, the artillery bombardment further damaged the building. Shells dropped through the enormous cupola, bringing down some of the girders supporting it. Six days later, at 1400 hours, it was shelled by the 347th Guards Heavy Self-Propelled Artillery Regiment deployed in Charlottenburg. This unit, under the command of Colonel Wenjamin Mironov, was equipped with 152-mm howitzers. 'A long, fiery-red flame shot from Shevtshuk's gun,' recalled Mironov. 'The shell went howling towards the Reichstag and exploded short of its target. The second shot went too far.'[1] Having found the range, one of his companies fired several salvoes. 'The first salvo cracked,' said Mironov. 'I looked through the periscope. The dome of the Reichstag had disappeared behind thick smoke.'[2]

As far as the Soviets were concerned, the raising of their hammer and sickle flag over the Reichstag would signal an end to the battle. Whoever was first to get the 'Victory Banner'[3] in place would become a hero of the Soviet Union. As an incentive, nine of these banners were issued to the assault divisions of the 3rd Shock Army. The honour of storming what Zhukov's planners had dubbed 'Objective 105'[4] was assigned to Major General Perevertkin's 79th Rifle Corps. His command, formed in October 1943, consisted of the 150th, 171st and 207th Rifle Divisions, each with three rifle regiments. The western section of the Reichstag was to be stormed by Major General Shatilov's 150th Division, while Colonel Negoda's 171st Division assaulted the eastern part. It would be no easy task and Perevertkin was reinforced with artillery, self-propelled guns and tanks. First, though, his men had to get over the Spree, which was about 45 m (150 ft) wide, in the face of determined German opposition.

Colonel Negoda's division was instructed to seize the massive Moltke bridge, which gave access to the Königsplatz via Moltkestrasse. They were then to clear the German strongpoint on the corner of Moltkestrasse and Kronprinzenufer, the latter road running eastwards along the southern bank of the Spree past the diplomatic quarter. This strongpoint dominated the approaches to the bridge. Afterwards, Negoda's men were to join Major General Shatilov's 150th Rifle Division in taking 'Objective 107' – the vast Ministry of Internal Affairs known as 'Himmler's House'. This was located on the southern side of Moltkestrasse and its capture would put Soviet troops in position to directly assault the Reichstag itself across the open reaches of the Königsplatz. They were supported by the 23rd Tank Brigade commanded by Lieutenant Colonel Morozov, from Lieutenant General Kirichenko's 9th Tank Corps, and the 10th Independent Flamethrower Battalion. Shatilov's men on Negoda's right flank first had to clear the defenders from the Custom Yard to the west of the bridge before they could cross. On Negoda's left flank, Colonel Asafov's 207th Division was to clear the imposing Lehrter railway station.

The Germans were expecting the Soviets to force a crossing so the Moltke bridge was predictably well defended. On the northern bank, they had built extensive barricades around it along the Alt-Moabitstrasse. They had also barricaded themselves in the Customs Yard and the Lehrter station. The latter was held by some of the survivors of the 9th Parachute Division who had escaped the Seelow Heights. The bridge itself was covered in barbed wire and mines. The southern exit was blocked by heaped rubble and steel girders and the southern bank had been fortified with pillboxes. 'Himmler's House' was held by a mixture of SS units under the command of a police colonel, while two infantry companies from the SS Anhalt Regiment were deployed either side, supported by 250 sailors. SS-Colonel Günther Anhalt had been killed by Soviet shellfire on 25 April and his regiment was now fighting piecemeal.

SS-Sergeant Major Willi Rogmann, in the stronghold on the corner of Alt-Moabit and Kronprinzenufer, set up an observation post for his mortar platoon, as did Sergeant Major Kurt Abicht for his artillery battery. Their weaponry comprised just two mortars and two guns, which were deployed to cover the bridge. German troops in the buildings lining Schlieffenufer, which ran along the southern bank west of the bridge, were able to support the Customs Yard and fire on the northern approaches to the bridge. The defenders of the bridge could also call on support from the Luftwaffe's heavy guns on the zoo flak tower and guns in the Tiergarten. Perevertkin's intelligence estimated that there were about 5,000 German troops on the far side of the river. This seems wildly inflated.

German forces to the east of the Reichstag had no idea of what was going on. 'I had the guns deployed behind our Sector at the entrance of streets leading on to Unter den Linden,' recalled SS-Major General Krukenberg, 'so that they could at least check any tanks surging in from the north, from the Reichstag or Schlossplatz because, despite repeated enquiries, the situation remained obscure for us.'[5] Furthermore, his main line of defence was anchored on Leipziger Strasse facing south so he was not in a position to help the defenders of the Reichstag.

On the evening of 28 April, Soviet tanks stormed the northern barricades protecting the Moltke bridge thrusting along Alt-Moabit and towards the Customs Yard. The supporting riflemen were driven back when they came in range of the pillboxes' machine guns. Just after midnight, two battalions from the 380th Rifle and the 756th Rifle Regiments from the 171st and 150th Divisions stormed over the bridge. However, the Germans remained holding the fortified corner buildings and these had to be cleared before the Spree could be forced in strength. Zhukov recalled, 'In the Reichstag district the enemy resisted desperately our advancing troops having turned every building, stairway, room, cellar into strongpoints and defensive positions.'[6] Once the 380th and 756th Regiments were over the river they were followed by the 171st Division's 525th Regiment, which moved northeast into the Diplomatic Quarter.

On the northern bank, elements of the 9th Parachute Division launched a surprise counterattack. Remarkably, in the confusion, 100 Germans were able to fight their way over the bridge. This, combined with a German counterattack on the southern bank, briefly threw the Soviet bridgehead into chaos. Now that the Soviet assault groups were overwhelming the northern perimeter, the Germans attempted to drop the bridge into the Spree. They had rigged it with explosives and when these were detonated the entire area vanished into a cloud of dust and smoke. When it cleared, it showed that the bridge, although damaged, was still standing and passable to vehicles.

'Himmler's House' was bombarded for ten minutes from 0700 hours on 29 April and was soon in flames. After capturing the corner of Alt-Moabit and Kronprinzenufer, the Soviets hauled mortars up on to the second floor and also fired at the ministry from there. The blaze caused a great pall of smoke, which obscured the Soviets' view down Moltkestrasse towards the Reichstag. From 0830 hours, for the next 90 minutes, Soviet guns and rocket launchers deluged the defensive positions around the Reichstag. In retaliation, Soviet artillery and self-propelled guns firing across the river from the captured Customs Yard were hit by the zoo flak tower's guns. However, the Soviets quickly brought forward replacements.

Heavy fighting followed and by noon the Soviet 380th and 756th Regiments had forced their way into the courtyard of the Ministry of Internal Affairs. The Germans continued resisting on the first floor, where Soviet riflemen secured a few rooms. Shatilov had to deploy reinforcements in the shape of the 674th Rifle Regiment to take the southwestern corner of the ministry. It took until 0430 hours to finally overcome the last of the stubborn German defenders. It also took that long for the 171st Division to clear the western half of the Diplomatic Quarter. 'Now we're tightening the circle round the centre of the city,' wrote Vladimir Pereverzev. 'I am just 500 metres from the Reichstag … we'll be in the Reichstag tomorrow.'[7]

In the meantime, Soviet tanks had rolled over the Moltke bridge, some of which stopped on the southern bank to shell German positions still on the other side of the river. The Soviet armour included Stalin heavy tanks armed with a powerful 122-mm gun. These were used to fire into the surrounding buildings at point-blank range. This progress had,

Soviet armour advancing on the Reichstag.

however, come at a price as German anti-tank guns and soldiers armed with *Panzerfausts* had ensured that the Alt-Moabit and Moltkestrasse were left littered in wrecked Soviet tanks. Two T-34 medium tanks reached the end of Moltkestrasse and were in sight of the Reichstag when they were hit and caught fire. The second tank threw its tracks before clattering to a halt. When the crews emerged and tried to escape, they were shot down in the street.

On the morning of 30 April, the 150th and 171st Rifle Divisions made their final preparations to assault the Reichstag. In Moscow, General S.M. Shtemenko, the Red Army's chief of operations, was delighted by the news. 'In Berlin, there was fighting close to the Reichstag and the Reich Chancellery,' he reported, 'which for several days had been under constant and accurate fire from Soviet infantry and artillery.'[8] That day, Zhukov's intelligence assessed, 'The Reichstag ... was defended by crack SS units. In the early hours on April 28, 1945, the enemy parachuted in a battalion of marines to reinforce the defences of the district.' According to Zhukov's intelligence, the Reichstag district was held by almost 6,000 troops, supported by artillery, assault guns and panzers, which suggested the defences had got stronger, not weaker.

After the fall of the Moltke bridge and the Ministry of Internal Affairs, the Germans defending the Reichstag were understandably expecting the Red Army to press home its attack. They had not only fortified the upper storeys but also the basement. Their intention was that every storey would be a killing zone. The Germans had also built a series of defensive positions facing westwards on Königsplatz in front of a collapsed tunnel now full of water, which created a vast moat protecting the Reichstag. These defences consisted of gun emplacements and trenches screened by barbed wire and mines. Further positions had been prepared on the open ground to the northwest of the Reichstag.

A complete mixture of troops was holding the Königsplatz, including a Luftwaffe flak battery that had a few 88-mm guns. One of these had white bands painted round the barrel, indicating it had destroyed 16 aircraft or tanks. This particular gun was positioned to fire up the Moltkestrasse. Although it was screened by a row of abandoned vehicles, it was not dug in, leaving the crew wholly exposed. The Germans also had panzers concealed to the right of the Reichstag. Forces deployed in the surrounding streets were ordered to counterattack at the soonest opportunity.

The towers on each corner of the front of the Reichstag provided good vantage points for German gunners overlooking the Königsplatz. The whole of the Reichstag was one gigantic haven for German snipers. No matter how much firepower the Red Army poured into the Königsplatz it would still be a difficult space to cross without incurring heavy casualties. Soviet war correspondent Vassili Subbotin observed, 'it seemed impassable, covered with shell holes, railway sleepers, pieces of wire and trenches.'[9]

Shatilov, commander of the 150th Division, allotted 'Victory Banner' No.5 to Colonel Zinchenko's 756th Regiment. Zinchenko in turn issued it to Captain Neustroyev's 1st Battalion. Captain Davydov's 1st Battalion, 674th Regiment, Senior Lieutenant Samsonov's 1st Battalion, 380th Regiment and two assault teams from the 79th Rifle Corps command under Major Bondar and Captain Makov were also assigned banners. Everyone was eager to be the first to plant their flag and make history.

'Permission to be the first to break into the Reichstag with my section?' Sergeant Ishchanov asked Captain Neustroyev in 'Himmler's House'.[10] Neustroyev nodded in agreement and at 0600 hours, Ishchanov's men clambered out of a first-floor window and made their way on to the Königsplatz. Vassili Subbotin recalled the first man to leave. 'Suddenly a soldier rose up, unfolded a red flag and charged forward,' noted Subbotin. 'That was Pyotr Pyatnizki.'[11] In the middle, he and the other attackers were impeded by the water obstacle.

German crossfire coming from the Reichstag on the eastern side of the Königsplatz and the Kroll Opera House on the western side swept the square mercilessly. Fresh Soviet troops were ordered to clear the opera house. The German flak guns on the zoo bunker firing from 2 km (1.2 miles) away also added to the carnage. 'Again there was a well-known whizzing sound over us,' said Subbotin, 'and heavy shells ripped up the asphalt.'[12] When the assault battalion from the 380th Regiment reached the northwest corner of the Reichstag they came under immediate counterattack by German tanks. A Soviet anti-tank battalion had to be summoned to deal with them. 'On this day, it was one of the most strenuous days of the war,' said Subbotin, 'there was bitter fighting on the square in front of the Reichstag.'[13]

Meanwhile, the Red Army continued to move artillery, tanks and rocket launchers across the Moltke bridge in growing numbers. However, it was still under fire from German troops in the Schlieffenufer buildings and the Tiergarten. Asafov's 207th Division was ordered to clear the Schlieffenufer before pushing south to take the opera house. Once across the river, the guns of the Soviet 420th Anti-Tank Artillery Division were manhandled on to the roof of 'Himmler's House' while ten rocket launchers were positioned in its courtyard. Tanks and artillery were also gathered at the end of Moltkestrasse opposite the Swiss embassy. In total, the Soviets deployed 89 guns plus Katyusha rocket launchers to pound the defenders of the Reichstag at 1300 hours for 30 minutes. Many of the bricked-up windows at the front of the Reichstag were blasted open by direct fire. Under this covering barrage, the assault battalions crept closer.

Neustroyev's reconnaissance troops with their banner, along with the advanced company, entered the Reichstag via the doors and breaches in the walls. His men were photographed dashing towards the Reichstag but this was probably a re-enactment for the benefit of Soviet cameramen. Reaching the central staircase, they cleared the first floor, but not before the Germans hurled hand grenades down the stairs, showering shrapnel everywhere. When the Soviets reached the second floor, Sergeants Kantaria and Yegorov drove the defenders back using grenades. They prematurely raised their banner No.5 over the ruined staircase at 1425 hours only to be halted on the third floor by intense machine-gun fire. Neustroyev put Lieutenant Berest in charge of the assault group and tasked him with clearing the second floor. Colonel Zinchenko in the meantime greeted Kantaria and Yegorov, who had retrieved their Victory Banner, with a smile. 'Well then, off you go, lads,' he said and then pointing upwards added, 'and stick the Banner up there.'[14] In the meantime, the 171st Rifle Division fought to clear the rest of the Diplomatic Quarter to the north of the Königsplatz. It also moved to secure the Kronprinzen bridge over the Spree to ensure no German reinforcements could reach the Diplomatic Quarter.

Zhukov recalled, 'However, even after the lower storeys of the Reichstag had been taken, the enemy garrison did not surrender. Fierce fighting took place inside the building.'[15] A renewed push to secure the Reichstag was launched at 1800 hours. It took almost four hours of bitter close-quarter combat before the banner was eventually hung above the building. 'At 9.50pm on April 30 Sergeant M.A. Yegorov and Junior Sergeant M.V. Kantaria,' recounted Zhukov, 'hoisted the Victory Flag received from the army Military Council on the main cupola of the Reichstag.'[16] Some Soviet gunners had beaten the two sergeants to it, but as Soviet photographer Yevgeni Khaldei was not ready, their efforts were considered unofficial. Instead, the famous staged photo was taken two days later. 'Not until evening as the sun began to set, lighting up the entire horizon with its red glow,' wrote General Perevertkin, 'did two of our soldiers raise the banner of victory on the burned-out cupola.'[17] General Kuznetsov called Zhukov to report, 'The Red Flag is on the Reichstag! Hurrah, Comrade Marshal!'[18]

'And finally I received the long-awaited call from Kuznetzov,' said Zhukov with satisfaction, 'the Reichstag had been taken; our red banner had been planted on it and was waving from the building.'[19] He was understandably elated and added as an afterthought, 'What a stream of thoughts raced through my mind at that joyous moment!'[20] Nonetheless, even then the Red Army had not overcome all of the garrison. Deep in the hidden bowels of the Reichstag some 300 Soviet riflemen found themselves battling to contain a much larger force of German troops who refused to give up. 'The cellars were full of Fascists,' said Rifleman Pyotr Schtscherbina. 'They threw hand grenades and fired Panzerfausts at us, dust falling from above. But we stood at the cellar entrances and fired back.'[21] Elsewhere in the building, German stragglers prowled along the corridors catching unwary Soviet soldiers. No mercy was shown or expected by either side. Both resorted to pistols and knives. 'The fighting within the main building of the Reichstag,' observed Zhukov, 'repeatedly took the form of hand-to-hand combat.'[22]

While the 674th and 756th Rifle Regiments sought to overcome the last of the Reichstag's defenders, the 380th Rifle Regiment was sent to clear the corner of the Tiergarten by the Brandenburg Gate. Unbeknown to the Soviets, the continuing resistance inside the Reichstag was being directed by SS-Lieutenant Babick from the SS Anhalt Regiment. His command post was concealed in the cellar of a building across the street

Soviet tanks outside the Reichstag.

to the rear of the Reichstag. Both were connected by a tunnel along which Babick could send orders and receive wounded.

'Groups of SS sitting in a building on the banks of the Spree, not far from the Reichstag, refused to surrender,' recalled war correspondent Vasily Grossman. 'Huge guns were blasting yellow, dagger-like fire at the building, and everything was swamped in stone dust and black smoke.' He then walked into the Reichstag and saw, 'Soldiers are making bonfires in the hall.'[23] To celebrate their victory, they were slurping tins of condensed milk, which they opened using their bayonets. 'Our soldiers were wandering around, battered folders of documents were strewn about and there was the smell of burning,' observed interpreter

Yelena Rzhevskaya. 'The Reichstag's documents were being used as cigarette paper.'[24] Everywhere, Soviet troops wrote their names on the columns and walls of the ruined Reichstag. Except, that is, for Major Yury Ryakhovsky. 'I disliked the idea of behaving like a tourist,' he said. 'We were not there as tourists.'[25] Artist Pyotr Krivonogov would later paint a highly dramatic picture of Soviet troops celebrating their victory outside the Reichstag.

Sheltering in the southwestern cellars of the Reichstag were survivors of the Luftwaffe flak battery, who had escaped from their positions on the Königsplatz. They had not been involved in the defence of the building on 30 April, but the following day, they took part in an unsuccessful counterattack. The gunners had been so cocooned that they did not realise the Soviets were above them until ordered into action. The fighting in the cellars continued until the afternoon of 1 May when the Germans announced they wished to lay down their arms. This was prompted by parts of the building being on fire. 'It was hot,' recalled Rifleman Schtscherbina. 'The building filled with smoke. The fire soon reached us and we could no longer stay.'[26] Furthermore, communication with SS-Lieutenant Babick had been cut by this point.

Captain Neustroyev, Lieutenant Berest and a translator went to negotiate. They were greeted by three officers and a female translator. The Germans mistook Berest for a colonel so spoke with him. 'We have not come to Berlin to let you monsters go,' warned Berest. 'If you do not surrender, not one of you here will come out alive.'[27] The Germans wanted the Soviet troops to parade outside in front of the Reichstag so there would be no misunderstanding when they came out. Affronted, Berest refused and left with Neustroyev and their interpreter. The trapped Germans surrendered later that night. The Soviets discovered that the basement held 300 German soldiers, 500 wounded and 200 dead. 'Only individual groups of Nazis in different sections of the Reichstag cellar,' said Zhukov, 'continued to resist until the morning on May 2.'[28] Soviet troops, weary of fighting by torchlight, resorted to using flamethrowers to silence the last of the recalcitrant resistance. Those who refused to give in were simply cremated.

Soviet losses in taking the Reichstag were heavy, amounting to 2,200 dead. Senior Sergeant Ilya Syanov's company after storming the building had been reduced from 83 men to 26. When the survivors emerged, Syanov observed, 'The soldiers looked awful with burns and other wounds. Their coats were torn, their shoes burnt through, and from their boots jutted the rags and tatters of their footcloths.'[29] General Perevertkin claimed his corps had killed 2,500 Germans and captured 2,600; however, such numbers were far greater than the actual garrison of the area. Colonel Zinchenko found himself appointed commandant of the Reichstag and host to a steady stream of sightseers.

Part 4

Armageddon

Chapter 16

Beneath the Reich Chancellery

Despite Stalin's obsession with the Reichstag, the Red Army's ultimate target was the Reich Chancellery and therefore the Führerbunker that lay in its grounds. Sheltering in the latter was not only Adolf Hitler, but also many of his inner circle. Key among them was Joseph Goebbels, the Nazi propaganda minister; Martin Bormann, head of the Nazi Party and Hitler's private secretary; Generals Hans Krebs and Wilhelm Burgdorf; Hitler Youth leader Artur Axmann; and, on occasions, SS-Brigadier Wilhelm Mohnke. Zhukov and the other Soviet commanders knew the location of the Chancellery but did not know the exact whereabouts of Hitler's command bunker. Once the Red Army was clear of the Tiergarten and reached the Potsdamerplatz, nothing could save the defenders of the Reich Chancellery buildings. These included extensive bunkers and underground garages.

The Reich Chancellery complex was built in a U-shape around once landscaped gardens. To the west lay the Chancellery Guards Barracks, while to the east bordering Wilhelmstrasse was the Old Chancellery building. The Führerbunker, consisting of two halves, was under the northwest corner of the latter and the gardens. The eastern half of the bunker beneath the Old Chancellery was a floor higher than the western half under the gardens and the two were linked by a flight of steps. Tunnels connected the upper bunker with the New Chancellery, Ministry of Foreign Affairs and the Propaganda Ministry.

Hitler resided in the lower western section and his personal quarters comprised a conference room, sitting room, study, bedroom and bathroom. Eva Braun had a separate bedroom that was reached from Hitler's sitting room. The only thing visible on the surface in the gardens was an emergency exit housed in a concrete blockhouse and a partially finished short concrete observation tower fitted with steel shutters. To get to the garden exit from the Führerbunker required climbing four flights of very steep stairs. Some of Hitler's staff liked to go up to the surface to get some fresh air and smoke a cigarette. The stairs were not a good place to get caught whenever there was a power cut. A second tower attached to the blockhouse had been started, but this only consisted of the concrete base and the steel reinforcing bar framework.

The New Chancellery on the southern boundary, constructed by Albert Speer in 1938, ran the length of the northern side of Vossstrasse – the equivalent of four city blocks. Underneath it was a whole series of bunkers, including a hospital with surgical and dental rooms as well as accommodation for Hitler's staff. The New Chancellery had received at least a dozen direct hits by Allied bombers by January 1945. All the windows had been taken out by the blasts. However, its lower levels, including the ground floor and the shelter-cellar, remained in use. 'The Chancellery which I had built seven years before,' said Speer on 25 April, 'was already under fire from heavy Soviet artillery, but as yet direct hits were relatively rare.'[1]

The following day, SS-Senior Squad Leader Rochus Misch, Hitler's bodyguard, observed, 'The Reich Chancellery lay under an artillery bombardment all day.'[2] On 27 April, the Red Army pounded the Reich Chancellery or Objective 106 and the Reichstag with an enormous artillery barrage. The ventilators of the Führerbunker soon became fouled by poisonous fumes drawn in from the explosions.'Despite having plenty of filters,' noted Misch, 'occasionally [chief engineer Johannes] Hentschel had to close the fresh air ventilation systems because it was sucking smoke into the interior.'[3]

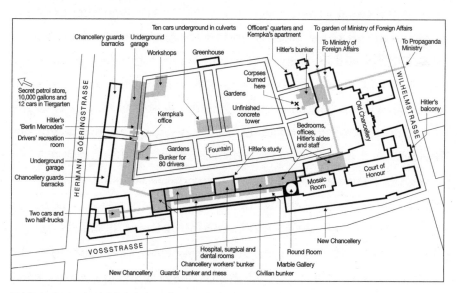

Old and New Reich Chancellery.

General Weidling, the latest battle commandant of Berlin, arrived at the Führerbunker at 2200 hours on 27 April for his evening conference with Hitler. He did nothing to soften the bad news. The remains of Berlin's garrison had been cut off in various pockets and were fighting for their lives. The Red Army had overrun most of their supply depots and at most they had just two days of ammunition left. Food had almost run out and they were unable to treat the masses of wounded crammed into the aid stations and field hospitals.

Weidling recommended attempting an immediate breakout westwards. This would consist of three waves; the first made up of survivors of the 9th Parachute and 18th Motorized Divisions supported by any panzers and artillery they had left; the second, Group Mohnke, would comprise of the SS and Hitler's headquarters staff supported by a navy battalion; while the third would be the remains of the 11th SS Nordland Division and the Müncheberg Panzer Division with a rearguard provided by some of the 9th Parachute Division. Weidling said that the three battle groups, numbering about 30,000 men, could force their way along either side of the East–West Axis across the twin bridges over the Havel at Pichelsdorf, then head northwest via the Heerstrasse. It was therefore vital that the Hitler Youth defending Pichelsdorf hold until the battle groups had crossed the river. Unhelpfully, Hitler's response was that everyone was to remain where they were. No one was to flee Berlin.

'In the concrete block of the Führerbunker we felt the vibrations of the uninterrupted thunder of Russian artillery as it pounded the Chancellery,'[4] recalled Major Bernd von Loringhoven. Conditions in the bunker were exceedingly grim. The lighting flickered on and off as the emergency generator spluttered. As a result, the inhabitants regularly found themselves plunged into complete darkness. The air was full of suffocating dust and smoke. It was also damp as water was seeping in through cracks in the concrete. 'Filth piled up everywhere,' adds von Loringhoven. 'Waste matter was no longer removed.'[5] Many of the staff had been unable to bathe in recent days and the aroma of stale bodies hung in the air.

Hitler was determined to die in Berlin, but he had unfinished business. In the early hours of 29 April, he belatedly married Eva Braun, with Bormann and Goebbels as witnesses. Walter Wagner, the nervous registrar summoned by the Propaganda Ministry, was serving as a member of the Volkssturm. He had been manning a position in an 18th-century wine cellar on Unter den Linden when an armoured vehicle arrived and drove him to the Reich Chancellery. Surrounded by SS guards, his first thought was that he was about to be shot for some petty misdemeanour. Dressed in a Nazi Party uniform and wearing his Volkssturm armband, Wagner looked suitably attired for the occasion. He stood blinking before the bride and groom in the Führerbunker's conference room. Hitler was in a brown uniform adorned with his First World War decorations. Eva wore a black silk dress, which was one of Hitler's favourites. He instructed Wagner, 'in view of the war developments the publication of the banns be done orally and all other delays be avoided.'[6]

It was understandably a sombre and somewhat rushed affair; within just ten minutes, the ceremony was over. When it came to the exchanging of rings it was found they were both too big. These had been provided by the Gestapo and it was best not to dwell on who had previously owned them or their fate. 'At the moment they married they knew that their deaths were imminent,' said Hitler's chauffer, Erich Kempka, who was present in the Führerbunker.[7] Afterwards, they were joined by Burgdorf, Krebs and a few others for drinks. 'No one was in

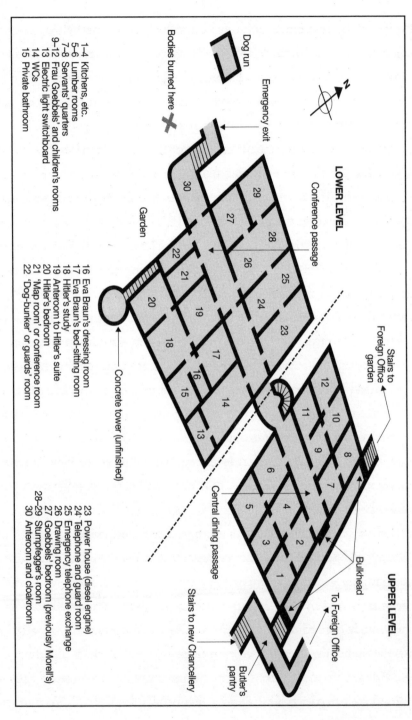

The Führerbunker.

LOWER LEVEL

1–4 Kitchens, etc.
5–6 Lumber rooms
7–8 Servants' quarters
9–12 Frau Goebbels' and children's rooms
13 Electric light switchboard
14 WCs
15 Private bathroom
16 Eva Braun's dressing room
17 Eva Braun's bed-sitting room
18 Hitler's study
19 Anteroom to Hitler's suite
20 Hitler's bedroom
21 'Map room' or conference room
22 'Dog-bunker' or guards' room
23 Power house (diesel engine)
24 Telephone and guard room
25 Emergency telephone exchange
26 Drawing room
27 Goebbels' bedroom (previously Morell's)
28–29 Stumpfegger's room
30 Anteroom and cloakroom

UPPER LEVEL

Bodies burned here
Dog run
Emergency exit
Conference passage
Garden
Concrete tower (unfinished)
Stairs to Foreign Office garden
Central dining passage
Bulkhead
To Foreign Office
Stairs to new Chancellery
Butler's pantry

the mood for rejoicing,'[8] said von Loringhoven. Nonetheless, after the pair retired, according to SS-Lieutenant Colonel Heinz Linge, the Führer's valet, Axmann, Bormann, Burgdorf, the Goebbels family and others celebrated with 'Champagne, sandwiches and tea.'[9]

Walter Wagner was still feeling nervous, especially after he had to correct Eva when she tried to write Braun on the wedding certificate rather than Hitler. However, having got over his surprise, he was in no rush to return to his post. He felt much safer in the Führerbunker. Wagner hung about and drank two glasses of champagne and ate a *Liverwurst* sandwich. This was to be his last meal. Twenty minutes later, he was escorted out of the bunker, but he never made it back to his position as he was killed on Wilhelmstrasse. Walter Wagner would forever be remembered as the person who married Mr and Mrs Hitler.

One man who was very conspicuous by his absence from the wedding was SS-Lieutenant General Fegelein, Himmler's liaison officer and Eva's brother-in-law. Implicated in Himmler's unauthorized peace negotiations, he had abandoned his post. Fegelein on 24 April told SS-General Hans Jüttner, 'I certainly do not intend to die in Berlin.'[10] He disappeared two days later after delivering his final report on Steiner. His plan was to escape through Soviet lines disguised as a civilian and reach Himmler. He telephoned Eva and pleaded with her to go with him. Hitler, noting Fegelein's absence, ordered his arrest.

Fegelein had not got far. He was found intoxicated in the arms of an unknown woman in his Charlottenburg apartment. SS-Major Otto Günsche, one of Hitler's adjutants, claimed, 'His sister-in-law refused to intercede on his behalf.'[11] This seems unlikely as Gretl Fegelein was pregnant. Furthermore, the penalty for desertion was death, but initially Hitler was prepared to strip Fegelein of his rank and assign him to Mohnke's battle group as a punishment. However, Günsche went to Hitler and warned him that Fegelein would desert again. Notably, when Günsche arrived, Eva was crying, and immediately left the room. Fegelein sealed his fate by refusing to recognize any authority but Himmler's. The discovery of incriminating documents regarding the peace talks in his office was the final insult to Hitler.

Fegelein, although not fit to stand trial, was taken to the Chancellery, court-martialled, and shot in the back of the head in the gardens late on 28 April. 'I had seen him pass by my open door in the corridor,' recalled von Loringhoven, 'accompanied by four SS men, dishevelled in appearance, epaulettes and decorations torn from his uniform.'[12] Hitler, according to Misch, delayed his marriage by about 20 minutes so he could check 'to make sure Fegelein was dead.'[13] Fegelein's actions are hard to fathom. Despite saying he did not want to die in Berlin, he foolishly lingered in the city. If he had left immediately, he might have survived, but it is likely that he knew his association with Hitler was ultimately a death warrant. Hitler's actions were less to do with Fegelein's numerous shortcomings, but rather his inability to lash out against Himmler. Fegelein happened to be in the wrong place at the wrong time.

There was nothing Eva could have done to save her sister's wayward husband. 'Hitler had ended his wedding night by taking revenge on his brother-in-law,'[14] noted von Loringhoven. Eva tried to console Hitler saying, 'Poor, poor Adolf. They have all deserted you; they have all betrayed you.'[15] After her wedding, she seemed unmoved by the death of her traitorous brother-in-law. Gerda Christian, one of Hitler's secretaries, observed, 'There were tears in her blue eyes, but they were tears of radiant joy.'[16]

Now that the Red Army was firmly in the city centre, time was rapidly running out. Soviet gains had made it completely impossible to continue ruling Germany from Berlin. This was a reality that even

Hitler was finally prepared to accept. Later in the morning of 29 April, he announced a successor government. It would be headed by Admiral Dönitz in the role of president and minister of war rather than Führer. Dönitz's government would be set up in northern Germany. Hitler also disowned Göring and Himmler, declaring them traitors and expelling them from the Nazi Party. Although Goebbels was appointed chancellor, he refused to leave Hitler's side, saying, 'I should appear for the rest of my life as a dishonourable traitor and common scoundrel.'[17] Goebbels and his wife Magda were adamant they would stay in the Führerbunker.

While Dönitz remained in charge of the navy, newly promoted Field Marshal Schörner would command the army and, it has been suggested, the Alpine Fortress. Schörner, though, was trapped in Czechoslovakia with Army Group Centre so was hardly in a position to exercise effective control. Hitler seemed to have an inflated impression of Schörner's abilities, claiming quite ridiculously that he was 'the only man to shine as a real warlord on the entire Eastern Front.'[18] Likewise, Paul Giesler, gauleiter of Bavaria, appointed interior minister, was in Tegernsee in Upper Bavaria. This meant that Germany's new government was scattered from the very start.

Hitler's actions were cruel, spiteful and deliberately callous. He could have authorized the German armed forces to lay down its arms. Instead, his dying wish was that Germany fight on despite what he had already heaped upon it.

That evening, Hitler held his final battle conference in the Führer-bunker. General Weidling assessed that his men would last another 24 hours at most then they would be out of ammunition. Hitler, after conferring with Krebs and Mohnke, said that there was to be no surrender; however, he would permit small groups to break out.

Weidling knew the only way to stop the bloodletting was to surrender immediately.

Hitler also heard the news that Italian partisans had executed Benito Mussolini and his mistress Clara Petacci without trial the previous day. Their bodies had been driven to Milan, where they were strung up at a petrol station in Piazzale Loreto to be abused and photographed. It was just as well that Hitler did not see the photographs. The angry crowd smashed in Mussolini's face and fired gunshots into his corpse. Clara was left barely clothed when she was hoisted into the air. Hitler knew he and Eva could expect similar treatment if they were captured. Even if they were not shot out of hand, they would be separated and put on trial to face a similar outcome. Death was their fate one way or another. 'I will not fall into the hands of an enemy who requires a new spectacle to divert his hysterical masses,'[19] declared Hitler indignantly. Hermann Göring later claimed that Hitler did see the photographs and had cried, 'This will never happen to me!'[20] This was an outright lie as Göring last saw Hitler eight days before Mussolini's death.

On the surface, the Soviets were creeping ever closer. Colonel Mironov, commander of the 347th Guards Heavy Self-propelled Artillery Regiment, observed, 'Hitler's Reich Chancellery is now only a stone's throw from us.' He instructed Lieutenant Colonel Pashitnov to focus his fire on the building. This was a task he undertook with delight. 'For four years I have dreamed of storming Berlin,' said Pashitnov. 'And now I have been given the task of destroying Hitler's hideout with fire from our SPGs [self-propelled guns], an honourable task.'[21] In response, Martin Bormann was moved to write in his diary, 'Our Imperial Chancellery is turning into ruins.'[22]

Zhukov was under mounting pressure from Stalin to bring the battle for Berlin to an end so that the Red Army's victory would coincide with

Moscow's annual May Day holiday. This would give the celebrations even greater poignancy. 'The battle in Berlin had reached its peak,' acknowledged Zhukov. 'All of us wished to finish off the Berlin group by May 1.'[23] However, last-ditch German resistance in the government district was derailing that goal. 'Although agonized,' he added, 'the enemy continued to fight for every house, for every cellar, for every storey and roof.'[24] The remaining defenders though still found the Red Army's advance relentless. 'Nonetheless,' observed Zhukov, 'Soviet troops took block after block, house after house.'[25]

During these last remaining hours, Hitler may have mourned how his dream of rebuilding Berlin as Germania, the capital of the world, had vanished. Speer recalled how Hitler enjoyed visiting the vast model of Germania in the Berlin Academy of Arts. The scale and attention to detail was incredible. Hitler often bent down in order to imagine himself walking the brand-new streets. A secret pathway had been specially built from the Chancellery so he could easily reach it. 'In no other situation did I see him so lively,' noted Speer, 'so spontaneous, so relaxed.'[26] Now Germania remained just a figment of Hitler's warped imagination. Speer was later to call their plans 'boring,' 'crazy' and 'lifeless.'[27] Ultimately, Speer judged, 'Designs of such a scale naturally indicate a kind of chronic megalomania.'[28] Göring had promised Speer that in the event of Hitler's death he would continue to be the man for the job. There was no chance of that now.

Hitler summoned Mohnke one last time early on 30 April and asked for his honest opinion of the situation. Mohnke informed the Führer that the Red Army was now within about 60 m (200 ft) of the Reich Chancellery. Furthermore, he doubted that his defence could hold more than a day. 'Let me say that your troops have fought splendidly, and I have no complaints,'[29] said Hitler in response. Mohnke was taken aback by this sudden generosity. 'Would that all the others had fought as tenaciously – Heinrici, Holste, Wenck, Busse,' continued Hitler. 'I had hoped to make it until May 5. Beyond that date, I have no desire to live.'[30] Mohnke did not understand the significance of this until Hitler explained that Napoleon Bonaparte died on 5 May 1821. 'Another great career that ended in total disappointment, disillusion, betrayal, despair,' concluded Hitler. 'We were both men born before our times.'[31]

Hitler was now ready to meet his fate in the Führerbunker. 'Arthur Axmann did offer to "bring the Führer out of Berlin" using 200 Hitler Youth volunteers and a panzer,' recalled SS-Lieutenant Colonel Linge, 'but Hitler declined, murmuring quietly, "That is no longer an option, I am remaining here!"'[32] Finally accepting that all was lost, late in the afternoon on 30 April, Hitler and his wife committed suicide. He put a bullet through his brain, and she swallowed cyanide. On his instruction, their bodies were burned in the grounds of the Old Chancellery to try to prevent them falling into Soviet hands. Beforehand, he had said to his staff, 'The time has come, it's all over.'[33]

Rochus Misch watched sadly as Mrs Hitler followed her husband into his study. 'She looked pretty in her dark blue dress with a bright white frilled collar,' he noted. 'For me, she is the only one who went truly nobly to her death.'[34] Speer later regretted advising Hitler to die in Berlin and not Obersalzberg. 'At the time I thought that was a piece of good advice,' he said. 'Actually it was bad, for if he had flown to Obersalzberg the battle for Berlin would probably have been shortened by a week.'[35] This observation, though, was made on the assumption that Hitler would have listened. Despite the Führer's death, Berlin's agony did not immediately end. His suicide and the creation of a new government simply caused yet more confusion and indecision. It also consigned the wretched city to two more days of street fighting.

Chapter 17

Time to Surrender

By the time of Hitler's suicide, the Soviet 4th Guards Rifle Corps was overwhelming the defenders of Potsdamer station and advancing on the Reich Chancellery. In the Führerbunker, Bormann suggested they break out, but Mohnke said it was far too late. Reluctantly, they agreed that General Krebs and General Weidling's chief-of-staff, Colonel Theodor Dufving, would go to Tempelhof to find General Chuikov and seek terms. Before the war, Krebs had served as an assistant military attaché in Moscow and could speak Russian. He also had the dubious accolade of being publicly embraced by Stalin at Moscow railway station just before Hitler invaded the Soviet Union. Krebs wanted an interpreter to accompany them as the translation would slow down the negotiations and give him time to think. A Russian-speaking Latvian by the name of Captain Nailandis was selected for the job. First, a lieutenant colonel under a white flag was sent forward to the positions of the 35th Rifle Division to ask if the Soviets would receive a truce envoy. Lieutenant General Glazunov, commander of 4th Corps, relayed this request to Chuikov. He agreed to a meeting, accompanied by his artillery commander, General Pozharskii, at a forward headquarters.

When Krebs and his little party crossed over into enemy lines, Soviet riflemen tried to disarm them. 'A courageous opponent,' protested Krebs, 'is allowed to keep his weapons during negotiations.'[1] The Soviet soldiers, taken aback by his boldness, allowed the Germans to keep their pistols. They were driven to see Chuikov at 0350 hours on 1 May. He was waiting for them in an apartment on Schulenburgring. Glancing around the roomful of busy Soviet officers, Krebs could not miss the irony of a lithograph of Leonardo da Vinci's *The Last Supper* hanging on one of the walls. He quickly explained what had happened in the Führerbunker. Chuikov understandably knew nothing of the bunker in the grounds of the Chancellery nor the fate of Hitler and his new bride. Indeed, he and his men had never heard of Eva Braun. For all Chuikov knew, this was a ploy and that as they spoke Hitler was escaping from Berlin. Nonetheless, Chuikov lied and said, 'We know that.'[2] Later, he confessed, 'I must admit that Hitler's death was news to me and that I hardly expected to hear anything like that from Krebs.'[3] Chuikov had deliberately masked his surprise as he was determined to remain calm throughout the meeting.

Krebs announced that he wished to negotiate not only on behalf of Berlin but all of Germany. This was backed by letters of introduction from Bormann and Goebbels. Furthermore, said Krebs, Admiral Dönitz, Hitler's successor, needed time to form a new government before talks could commence properly. Chuikov immediately contacted

Zhukov, who in turn called Stalin to tell him that Hitler was dead. 'Now he's done it, the bastard,' said Stalin. 'Too bad he could not have been taken alive.'[4] Zhukov was also disappointed as he had promised Nikita Khrushchev, hero of Stalingrad, he would ship a caged Hitler to Moscow via Kiev 'so you can have a look at him.'[5]

Stalin instructed that the only thing the Red Army was to accept was immediate, unconditional surrender. There were to be no terms. When this was relayed back to Krebs, he said he did not have the authority to agree as it could only be approved by Admiral Dönitz. When asked what Germany would do in the meantime, Krebs responded that they would fight to the last man. 'General,' said Chuikov with an ironic smile, 'what have you got left? What forces would you use to fight with?'[6] He waited for a reaction, then added, 'We are waiting for your unconditional surrender.'[7]

This was the last thing that Dönitz, Goebbels and Krebs wanted if Germany was to salvage any shred of dignity from its catastrophic defeat. 'If we agree to unconditional surrender,' replied Krebs, 'we shall cease to exist as a legal government.'[8] Chuikov, growing impatient with his defeated enemy, then pointed out that Krebs was not in a position to negotiate as German troops were already surrendering everywhere. In a state of denial, Krebs refused to believe this, claiming there were only isolated instances.

Colonel Dufving was sent back to consult with Goebbels. On the way, he was shot at by SS troops and only narrowly missed being killed after a Soviet officer pulled him out of the line of fire. 'Don't shoot! Don't shoot! I'm an official negotiator!'[9] screamed Dufving until the firing stopped. Once in the Führerbunker, he informed Goebbels that the Soviets were demanding unconditional surrender. 'To that I shall never, never agree,'[10] exclaimed Goebbels. He and the other senior

Nazis clung to the delusion that Germany could somehow avoid its final humiliation and occupation. Goebbels seemed to lose his nerve when he asked if it was still possible to break out through Soviet lines. Dufving looked as him incredulously and replied, 'Only singularly and in civilian clothes.'[11] Goebbels, using a specially laid telephone line, ordered Krebs to return to the Führerbunker. Goebbels and Bormann had been given until 1000 hours to comply with Chuikov's ultimatum. When no answer was received, the Red Army continued its assault on the government district.

Chuikov was telling the truth when he said that the Berlin garrison was already surrendering. At 0430 hours, the demoralized German troops in the grounds of the zoo sent a message to Lieutenant General Ryzhov, commander of the 28th Guards Rifle Corps, seeking a truce. Some 30 minutes later, Major Bersenev and his driver made their way to the northeast corner of the zoo. Two German officers bearing a white flag appeared at 0520 hours. However, members of the SS in the zoo had other ideas. The officers were 183 m (600 yards) away from Bersenev when they were shot in the back, and he was wounded. Fortunately, his driver managed to drag him to safety. Fearing Pongo the gorilla might escape, the SS also wanted him dead. Foolishly, three SS men entered his enclosure intent on killing the weakened animal. In order to save ammunition, they drew their knives. All three died but not before they stabbed Pongo to death. The zoo director, Lutz Heck, was ordered to destroy his prize baboon. He shot it with a single bullet, though the act broke his heart.

In the meantime, Chuikov offered Krebs tea and sandwiches. 'We sat down wearily,' said Chuikov, 'feeling the closeness of the end of the war.'[12] He noticed that Krebs' hands were trembling and suggested brandy, which Krebs readily accepted. Outside, the roar of Soviet artillery and rocket launchers was continuous and the German general shrank back with every blast. It was evident that he was exhausted and under a great deal of stress. Afterwards, still refusing to surrender, Krebs left, although Chuikov got the impression the general would have happily accepted being taken prisoner. Chuikov was amused that Krebs returned twice, claiming that he had left behind his gloves and then his briefcase – even though he had not brought one with him as all his documents had been carried in his side pocket. However, Chuikov needed him to return in order to make Germany's position perfectly clear. It was a defeated nation and would be treated as such.

When Krebs finally got back to the Führerbunker he found General Weidling there with Bormann and Goebbels. He repeated Chuikov's insistence on unconditional surrender. Goebbels and Bormann remained adamantly opposed to this. 'The Führer always insisted on carrying on the struggle to the end,' snapped Goebbels, 'and I do not want to surrender.'[13] Weidling pointed out that resistance was almost at an end and that as Hitler was dead there was no point following his orders. Chancellor Goebbels still refused to change his mind.

In a state of exasperation Weidling departed for his headquarters and invited Krebs to join him. 'I shall stay here until the last minute,' said Krebs solemnly, 'then put a bullet through my brain.'[14] To the remaining inhabitants of the Führerbunker it felt as if every Soviet gun was firing on the Reich Chancellery. This caused Colonel von Dufving to wonder if Krebs had given away their location. 'That afternoon the enemy resorted to using flamethrowers to reduce isolated points of resistance,' reported SS-Brigadier Krukenberg, commander of the remnants of the battle group from the 33rd SS Division.[15] When Goebbels and Bormann did finally reply to Chuikov at 1800 hours they once again refused to accept unconditional surrender.

Just 30 minutes later, the Red Army commenced its final attack in the areas around the Chancellery. To the south, the 248th and 301st Rifle Divisions from Bezarin's 5th Shock Army stormed the Gestapo Headquarters and the Air Ministry. The latter was held by Luftwaffe ground personnel and a detachment from the 11th SS Division Nordland. A Soviet self-propelled gun then manoeuvred to fire across the Vossstrasse and knocked the swastika off the front of the Chancellery. At the same time, the 230th Rifle Division took the State Post Office and attacked the Finance Ministry opposite the Chancellery. Slowly but surely, Soviet riflemen and supporting tanks fought their way towards the Chancellery complex and its grounds, which were now defended by less than 800 SS troops, including Hitler's 30-strong bodyguard detachment under SS-Lieutenant Colonel Franz Schädle. Frenchman SS-Captain Henri Fenet was with a group from the 33rd SS Division holding a building just a few hundred metres from the Reich Chancellery. Repeatedly, they beat off Soviet tank attacks, but continual shelling of their stronghold left it in imminent danger of collapsing on them. During a brief lull, he and his men relocated to a more intact building. Despite the end being in sight, Fenet noted, 'The Reich Chancellery is being fiercely defended.'[16] He watched in horror as an enemy tank rolled past his position before it was knocked out by a second *Panzerfaust* shot. 'The fighting at the approaches to and inside the building were especially fierce,'[17] noted Zhukov. However, Krukenberg claimed, 'There was much heavier fighting on Unter den Linden than ever took place near the Reich Chancellery.'[18] Major Anna Nikulina led an assault group on to the roof and unfurled the Red flag.

Goebbels' Ministry of Propaganda continued to spew out lies. 'This afternoon,' announced a solemn German radio broadcast, 'continuing the fight against Bolshevism to his last breath, our Führer, Adolf Hitler, fell in the battle for Germany at his command post in the Reich Chancellery.'[19] It did not inform listeners that he had taken his own life. The German High Command propagated an even bigger lie, signalling the armed forces: 'The Führer died in the heroic battle for Germany in Berlin with his men.' Ridiculously, it then added, 'The battle for our people is being carried on.'[20] Admiral Dönitz, who initially was not informed of Hitler's death, also announced that the Führer had died 'this afternoon' fighting 'at the head of his troops.'[21]

By this stage, continued resistance in Berlin had become utterly pointless. General Weidling on the evening of 1 May instructed the remains of the garrison to cease fighting and to break out in groups. There was to be no rearguard and it would be every man for himself at 2300 hours. Krukenberg was amazed when Mohnke asked him if he would assume responsibility for the defence of the city and all available troops. 'I rejected this stupid idea,'[22] said Krukenberg. Mohnke responded that they had little other option than to follow Weidling's orders. 'In leaving the Chancellery,' said Krukenberg, 'I saw no disorder in the rooms or corridors.'[23] He sent his aide-de-camp, SS-Second Lieutenant Valentin Patzak, to the Air Ministry to give the order, but he was never heard of again.

At the same time in the Führerbunker, Magda Goebbels poisoned her six children. She and her husband then went up to the surface and shot themselves. Their bodies were half-heartedly burned and Joseph Goebbels was left a charred and twisted obscenity. 'They were not burned, only roasted,' recalled Johannes Hentschel, the Führerbunker's chief engineer. 'Goebbels's face was deep purple, like a mummy's. Frau Goebbels's face had been horribly consumed by fire.'[24]

Many of the survivors in the Chancellery and Führerbunker now belatedly fled out into the chaos. Up to 2,000 people had been sheltering in the Chancellery, plus there was a similar number of men with Mohnke's battle group in the surrounding area. Around 1,200 of those in the Chancellery were wounded and the rest were mainly Mohnke's SS troops. The senior officers, including Mohnke, appreciated that there was little chance of such large numbers escaping together. When the German garrison trapped in Budapest tried to break out in February 1945 they were rapidly massacred by the Red Army on the streets and in the nearby woods at very close range.

To try to avoid this, those gathered in the Chancellery were divided up into ten varying sized groups and told to set off as best they could every 20 minutes. They were to run across Wilhelmplatz, then using the subway at Kaiserhof, head for Friedrichstrasse subway station to cross under the Spree to reach the Stettiner Bahnhof station in northern Belin, which was hopefully behind the Red Army. The trouble with this was that the stations and tunnels were crammed with 20,000 civilians. Those groups that made it were to rendezvous near Schwerin about 129 km (80 miles) northwest of Berlin. From there, they would make their way to Schleswig-Holstein to join Dönitz. Armed with just rifles, submachine guns and the odd *Panzerfaust*, they faced little prospect of success against Soviet artillery, rockets and tanks.

'It was hard to calculate our chances,' recalled Mohnke, leading the first group. 'We were quite ignorant of the real military situation from borough to borough ... I was just hoping, somehow, to survive the coming twenty-four hours.'[25] He anticipated that if they got out of the city they could fade into the countryside where no one would know who they were. One officer who declined to go with Mohnke was the head of Hitler's bodyguard. SS-Lieutenant Colonel Schädle had been hit in the leg by shrapnel on 28 April and the wound festered, rapidly going gangrenous. Four of his men volunteered to carry him on a stretcher for the breakout but he did not want to slow them down, nor be taken alive. 'Schädle stated that he would shoot himself in the head after our departure,'[26] said Erich Kempka.

After initially making good progress, Mohnke's party were thwarted in their attempt to get under the Spree by two transport officials who steadfastly refused to open a flood door. Although Mohnke was exhausted, he was almost amused when the railwaymen produced a copy of the 1923 regulations that stated the door must be kept closed once the trains stopped running at the end of the day. For some reason, Mohnke, perhaps impressed by the men's adherence to orders, chose not to force the matter. After this surreal encounter, his group retraced their steps and got over the Spree using a narrow bridge, but became scattered and were eventually captured. Afterwards, Mohnke acknowledged, 'Our chances were always much less than fifty-fifty.'[27]

Bormann was with the third group, which included Artur Axmann, Erich Kempka and Heinz Linge, protected by the last available Hitler Youth and Volkssturm. Their plan was to cross the Spree using the Weidendammer bridge under the cover of darkness, escorted by three panzers and three armoured personnel carriers from the 11th SS Division. The latter forces under the command of SS-Lieutenant Hansen realized that to drive into the waiting arms of the Red Army was suicide. Nonetheless, they obediently followed orders. Gathered around the lead tank, everyone ducked low and hoped for a miracle. Although they barged through the southern barricade and got over the bridge, the noisy armour was swiftly knocked out by waiting Soviet gunners. 'Suddenly the Russians opened up with everything they had,' recalled Kempka. 'A second later, a hellish tongue of flame burst out unexpectedly from the flank of the panzer.'[28] He was knocked unconscious as it exploded and Bormann along with those around him was thrown in the air like a rag doll. After sheltering in a large crater in a state of dazed confusion, they went back the way they had come.

Bormann's much reduced group continued on foot and reached Lehrter station, via the Friedrichstrasse station railway bridge, where they ran into a Soviet patrol. 'We had already torn off our rank badges,' said Axmann. 'The Russians challenged us and almost certainly took us for Volkssturm.' To his surprise, he added, 'They offered us cigarettes.'[29] Bormann, seizing the opportunity, ran off into the night and took his own life using cyanide. Fearing they were about to be taken prisoner, Axmann said, 'Slowly, we edged away from them.'[30] He later came across Bormann's corpse and recalled, 'I bent over him and found no evidence of breathing. There was no sign of wounds or blood … Suddenly we came under heavy rifle fire, and had to go on.'[31] Both Axmann and Kempka managed to escape the city but were later arrested by the Americans. Linge, who had become separated, was caught by the Soviets in the subway alongside Rochus Misch, who had set out on his own.[32] When they came to the surface, Misch threw away his pistol, but Linge was amazed that he was initially allowed to keep the two weapons he was carrying and offered cigarettes.

At midnight that day, as promised, the defenders of the main flak tower by the zoo surrendered. Artillery commander Colonel Wöhlermann had met with General Weidling and other officers beforehand, and it had been agreed that further fighting was useless. There were an estimated 29,000 civilians crammed in the zoo bunkers as well as 2,000 troops, including 350 men under Colonel Haller. Everyone was desperate to get out. Red Cross worker Ursula Stalla recalled the stench of 'perspiration, smelly clothes, babies' diapers, all mixed with the smell of disinfectants from the hospital.'[33] The general in command of the zoo garrison shot himself after drinking a glass of champagne. A number of others took their lives in the flak tower, including two elderly women who nobody noticed were dead.

At first light, Wöhlermann emerged at the head of those still in uniform. To his dismay, several of them were killed by machine-gun fire glancing off the concrete walls. This was not the work of the Red Army, but diehard SS. Luftwaffe Lieutenant Gerda Niedieck was grateful to escape the confines of the neighbouring communications tower. She had the heart-breaking task of relaying the last of Hitler's messages from the Führerbunker. Most of these had been desperate pleas for help to Generals Steiner and Wenck. They had reduced her to tears. Still in the Führerbunker, Generals Burgdorf and Krebs shot themselves. Krebs may have felt dishonoured by his failure to gain terms from the Soviets and dismayed by the realization that Germany had collapsed. Over in the New Chancellery bunker, true to his word, SS-Lieutenant Colonel Schädle placed a pistol in his mouth and pulled the trigger.

Weidling surrendered to Chuikov on the morning of 2 May, officially signalling the end of the battle for Berlin. He made a radio broadcast stating, 'I hereby order that all resistance be ceased immediately.'[34] Goebbels' deputy and well-known Nazi radio announcer, Hans Fritzsche, also made an appeal for the surviving defenders to lay down their weapons. 'The fighting in the area of the Reichstag and the Imperial Chancellery as well as along the entire Tiergarten had come to an end,' noted Chuikov with satisfaction. 'Everything was quiet in Berlin.'[35] However, Germany's war with the Soviet Union would not end until six days later when Field Marshal Keitel met with Zhukov, by which time the Germans had already surrendered to the Western Allies.

Officially, the first Soviet officer to enter the Führerbunker was Lieutenant Colonel Ivan Klimenko. However, a dozen female Red

German prisoners of war in Berlin marching past Soviet troops.

Army medics had gone in at 0900 hours looking to loot the wardrobe of 'Hitler's Frau'. They reportedly left with black bras and lace lingerie from Paris as well as other valuable souvenirs. The medics were followed by two Soviet officers, who were horrified when shown Goebbels' dead family by Johannes Hentschel, who had remained behind. The officers recoiled at the sight and slammed the door shut. 'To see the children was horrid. The only one who seemed disturbed was the eldest, Helga. She was bruised ... but the rest were lying there peacefully,'[36] recalled Major Boris Polevoi. 'I must admit,' said Zhukov, 'I had not the heart to go down and look at the children killed by their own mother and father.'[37]

Hentschel then found himself drinking champagne with about 20 young Red Army officers, believed to be from the 301st Rifle Division, after they had looted the wine cellar. The men were all boisterously singing a Soviet drinking song. 'They danced around me as if I were King of the May,'[38] said Hentschel. Following two mugs of champagne, he was grateful that he had eaten a hearty breakfast of black bread, marmalade and *Liverwurst* all washed down with coffee and bottled spring water. He had even diligently cleaned the dishes. After 15 minutes, having had a bottle of champagne poured over his head, the engineer slipped away and staggered up to the surface and out into the sunlight. There, he was arrested and carted off as a prisoner of war. He was the last German to leave the Führerbunker.

'On 2 May, when the Berlin garrison ceased resistance, a surrender of weapons took place in the streets,' wrote Yelena Rzhevskaya. 'German soldiers were formed into columns and marched off into captivity.'[39] Soviet cameramen were there to record the forlorn-looking prisoners dumping their firearms, most of whom very wisely retained their greatcoats and field caps. The men's expressions ranged from sullen indifference to one of pensive relief. Although they had been defeated, at least the carnage was at an end. German wounded, particularly the stretcher cases, were gathered in the centre of Unter den Linden ready for collection.

Most Nazi Party officials and members of the SS divested themselves of their insignia and any documentation that would identify them as such. Rochus Misch and Heinz Linge, although not influential members of the SS, both got rid of their expensive wristwatches. This was not only in order to deny them to looting Soviet soldiers, but also to prevent their immediate identification as members of Hitler's personal staff. In the case of Linge's watch, it had a personal inscription from Hitler.

In some places, a few fanatics fought on. 'In the Reich Chancellery, however,' adds Rzhevskaya, 'there was intermittent gunfire from SS soldiers who refused to surrender.'[40] Nonetheless, the Red Army occupied the Reich Chancellery at 1500 hours on 2 May with little resistance. 'As far as I can see are Russians … not a single shot,' said SS-Captain Fenet, 'the Reich Chancellery walls are dumb, there is no

Red Army tankers celebrate the surrender of Berlin.

one around, it is all over!'[41] Rzhevskaya was amazed when she arrived. 'The Reich Chancellery building,' she noted, 'dented by shells, pitted by shrapnel, its windows gaps with jagged glass, had nevertheless survived mainly intact.'[42] Everywhere she looked was debris, 'Mangled enemy vehicles had crashed into the wall of the Reich Chancellery or were scattered over the ravine of the street.'[43]

After the German surrender, Zhukov called Nikita Khrushchev. 'I won't be able to keep my promise after all,' Zhukov informed him. 'That snake Hitler is dead. He shot himself, and they burned his corpse. We found his charred carcass.'[44] Khrushchev was elated by the news and recalled the words of legendary Russian warrior Alexander Nevsky: 'He who comes to us with a sword shall perish by the sword.'[45] Berlin had fallen after 11 days of unrelenting fighting.

Chapter 18

The Butcher's Bill

'The fall of Berlin and the link-up between the Soviet Army and the troops of our allies,' wrote Zhukov, 'led to the final collapse of Nazi Germany and its armed forces.'[1] The butcher's bill for taking the city was appalling. The Red Army suffered at least 305,000 casualties, which included almost 80,000 dead. Some sources put the figure in excess of 350,000. Their commanders claimed rather disingenuously that they had willingly gone to their deaths. 'These men burnt with a passionate and impatient desire to end the war as soon as possible,' observed Konev. 'Those who want to judge how justified or unjustified the casualties were must remember this.'[2] Zhukov expressed similar sentiments: 'The Soviet soldier ... was consumed with hatred for the enemy and wanted only to finish him off as quickly as possible.'[3] Equipment losses were 2,156 tanks and self-propelled guns, 1,220 field guns and mortars and 527 aircraft. Some 1,082,000 Soviet troops were awarded the Berlin Medal for taking part. Not all Soviet soldiers agreed with Konev and Zhukov. Gregori Arbatov, who was a company commander during the battle, felt that Berlin should have been surrounded, then bombed and shelled into submission. 'But not that son of a bitch Stalin,' he said bitterly. 'He sent us into the city, with all those crazy Nazi kids, and we bled.'[4]

German losses amounted to half a million with a similar number captured. Among the German casualties were 125,000 civilians thanks to Hitler's refusal to evacuate. The dead included 4,000–6,000 who took their own lives.[5] An estimated 20,000 people died of heart attacks and

The symbol of the Red Army's victory, the hammer and sickle, hoisted over the Reichstag.

tens of thousands of women were raped by the rampaging Red Army. There were 40,000 wounded in the city's hospitals, though the number of hospital beds had fallen from 33,000 to 8,500. Around 3 million civilians were left without food or clean drinking water. Estimates for the number of rapes in Berlin range from 20,000 to 100,000. Some sources even put the figure as high as 500,000. This would have represented almost a third of the women in the city. In the final stages of the war, Soviet soldiers are estimated to have raped over 2 million German women.

On occasions, pleas for help had reached the Führerbunker switchboard. Rochus Misch received such a call from a distressed and barely coherent woman. 'Her neighbour was being raped, she sobbed. "Help, help! – come and help us!"' recalled a horrified Misch. 'In the background I could hear terrible screams.'[6] In a panic, he had handed the caller over to Joseph Goebbels. There was nothing they could do. One of the soldiers involved in Mohnke's breakout, who was an Eastern Front veteran and knew what to expect, recalled seeing 'a terrified, naked woman running along a roof top, pursued by half-a-dozen soldiers … then leaping five or six stories to certain death.'[7] SS-Grenadier Alfred Blombach recalled how after he had been captured at Halbe, Soviet troops singled out female signallers and Red Cross nurses. 'We lent them our coats, trying to make them unrecognisable as women,' said Blombach. 'Some, sadly, didn't escape and I'll never forget the screams of those unfortunate girls.'[8] Major Brand, who was also captured at Halbe, recalled, 'Women were being raped to death by Russians in the forests and on the roads.'[9]

When the bestial behaviour of Soviet forces was raised with Stalin, he responded dismissively, 'You have imagined the Red Army to be ideal. And it is not ideal, nor can it be.'[10] It is very important though to remember that Soviet soldiers were not the only perpetrators of such crimes. 'The behaviour of some troops was nothing to brag about,' recalled American officer Saul Padover, 'particularly after they came across cases of cognac and barrels of wine. I am mentioning it only because there is a tendency among the naive or malicious to think only Russians loot and rape.'[11] For example, during the occupation of Berchtesgaden there were allegations that US troops gang-raped a 16-year-old girl.

By 1500 hours on 2 May 1945, the Red Army claimed that the survivors of Berlin's garrison numbering over 134,000 men had surrendered. This figure presumably included troops caught around greater Berlin as the number rounded up in the city according to Zhukov amounted to 70,000. Prior to the surrender, the Red Army captured 8,000 prisoners in Spandau, 13,000 in Schöneberg, 10,000 in the Alexanderplatz area and 14,000 on the north bank of the Spree. It also captured a total of 1,500 tanks and assault guns, 8,600 field guns and mortars and 4,500 aircraft. During the battle, the Soviets claimed to have destroyed 1,232 enemy planes.

The tragedy of the ill-prepared Hitler Youth and Volkssturm was that they not only died at the hands of the Red Army. Some were the victims of the brutal flying court-martials operated by the vindictive SS in the dying days of the Third Reich. Their job was to punish deserters with the death penalty. When Johannes Hentschel was escorted from the Führerbunker by Soviet soldiers on 2 May, he saw on Vossstrasse half a dozen Germans dangling from the lampposts. Each had a placard accusing them of being cowards or traitors. 'They were all so young. The oldest may have been twenty, the others in their mid-teens,' recalled Hentschel. 'Half of them wore Volkssturm armbands or Hitler Youth uniforms.'[12] He realized they had been hung by the SS that very morning. Once on board a Soviet truck, he noted, 'I saw that I could almost reach out and touch one of those lifeless boys … I shuddered, looking away. I was ashamed…'[13]

The remains of General Busse and General Wenck's 9th and 12th Armies, numbering about 100,000, crossed the Elbe and surrendered to the Americans in the hope of a better future. Many years later, Konev visited the Halbe battlefield and wrote, 'Everything there was a reminder of the last days of the breakthrough by the remnants of the German 9th Army, in which the futility of the losses was combined with the courage of desperation and the grim resolve of those doomed to destruction.'[14] 'Even now no one knows how many 9th Army personnel and refugees in the Halbe pocket,' recalled a survivor, 'managed to breach the encirclement, and we will likely never find out.'[15]

'I would never have believed that a great city could be reduced to mere rubble,'[16] wrote Lieutenant Gennady Ivanov. 'The imperial palace, all the splendid castles, the prince's palace, the Royal Library, Tempelhof, the buildings along the Unter den Linden – hardly anything was left,'[17] recalled Swedish Red Cross official Sven Frykman. According to Zhukov, during the battle for Berlin, a fifth of the city's 250,000 buildings were either destroyed or severely damaged. Another 150,000 buildings were partially damaged.

However, the Royal Air Force had already destroyed up to 75 per cent of the city centre, having dropped 65,000 tons of bombs on Berlin. These killed thousands of people. Soviet artillery, rockets and bombers certainly added to the destruction. In the space of two weeks, the Red Army fired 40,000 tons of shells into the city. The Red Air Force flew 91,000 combat sorties during the Berlin offensive. On 25 April, over 2,000 Soviet aircraft had dropped hundreds of tons of bombs on the already ruined Reich Chancellery and the Reichstag to help blast a way for the ground troops. Zhukov also states that 225 bridges were blown up by the Germans, though Speer recorded a much lower figure of 84.[18] Over a third of Berlin's underground stations were flooded. The ruined city was left facing a major humanitarian crisis.

The Prussian State Library lost 700,000 books either stolen or destroyed. Berlin and many other German cities were systematically looted not only by Soviet soldiers, but also by the Soviet authorities. Evacuated secret caches were stolen, many of which had been looted by the Nazis. Some of these treasures were carted off by the Red Army to a top-secret museum known as the State Special Trophy Archive hidden in a Moscow suburb. Housed in large hangars, like at the end of the movie *Raiders of the Lost Ark*, most of the contents were left crated and uncatalogued until the end of the Cold War.

Despite his socialist principles, Zhukov was not above such activities. During his time in Germany, he claimed to have been gifted or purchased 3,700 m (2.3 miles) of silk, 740 pieces of silverware, 320 furs, 70 items of gold, 60 pictures and 50 rugs.[19] It is not clear why he needed or wanted such large quantities of these things. High-level hoarding by Zhukov and other senior Soviet commanders did little to encourage good discipline in the Red Army.

General Berzarin was appointed military commandant of Berlin with 22 district commanders under him. This effectively placed the city under martial law. One of his first tasks was to try to ward off the threat of famine. The Soviet response was to ship 50,000 cattle, 60,000 tons of potatoes and 96,000 tons of grain and other foodstuffs into the city. When the Red Army first arrived, it had not been quite so accommodating. 'Whatever food they found, they ruined deliberately,' recalled Waltraudt Williams. 'They filled bath tubs with edible food and defecated all over it. They didn't want us to have it because they didn't think we were entitled to it.'[20]

Red Army guards in the Chancellery garden where Mr and Mrs Hitler were cremated.

By the end of May 1945, the Soviets claimed to have restored gas and water supplies to Berlin's central districts. They worked to get some of the underground and surface railways as well as the trams running. At the end of the following month, they claimed 580 schools had been opened with 233,000 pupils. Over 120 cinemas were operating but these were showing Soviet propaganda films and documentaries as a prelude to the creation of communist East Germany.

Despite the international agreement to divide Berlin into four occupation zones, the Red Army was left in control for two whole months. American, British and French troops did not arrive until 4 July 1945. They were led by the 'Hell on Wheels' US 2nd Armored Division and the 'Desert Rats' of the British 7th Armoured Division. The arrival of the Division in Berlin was a great personal thrill,' recalled British Signaller Ronald Mallabar. 'The city was, of course, in ruins, thanks to the efforts of RAF Bomber Command and the Red Army.'[21]

The Western Allies were not impressed by ongoing Soviet attempts to get the city up and running. 'Berlin in July 1945 beggars description,' noted Captain Tom Ritson with 7th Armoured. 'No serious attempt had been made to clean it up ... There was no electricity, water or drainage'[22] Many of the streets remained strewn in hazardous debris. 'Of the buildings left standing, many were in a dangerous condition,' observed Signaller Mallabar, 'with adjacent footpaths fenced off with wire in case of falling masonry.'[23] Furthermore, the city and surrounding lakes were still full of rotting corpses, the stench from which fouled the air. 'We were continuously warned of the dangers of polluted water,' adds Captain Ritson, 'mosquitoes and rats.'[24] The men of 7th Armoured became aware of how their former allies had treated Berlin's women following the conquest of the city. 'Apart from wholesale looting and violence, "raped eight times" was a typical report,'[25] noted Signaller Mallabar.

When 7th Armoured took over the Olympic stadium, they were appalled by the state the Soviets had left it in. Private Verdon Besley recalled 'a lovely barracks but in a filthy condition with huge bugs going up the walls and human excrement on the floor.'[26] The men were ordered to live in their tents until the place could be fumigated. Likewise, when British troops occupied the German military barracks at Spandau, they discovered the Soviets had bequeathed them an equally disgusting mess. Soviet soldiers had been there for a month with no running water or latrines. The smell was so bad that it made some of the new inhabitants vomit. Anything not fixed down, the Soviets had carted off. Everything else, they had smashed. The division soon found it faced another menace and had to mount regular patrols to stop Soviet soldiers from looting in the British sector. Understandably, those out on patrol did not feel entirely safe. 'Amidst the ruins a feeling of isolation as being on an island surrounded by Russians,'[27] said Trooper Clifford Smith. In the meantime, Allied leaders gathered for the Potsdam Conference to agree the fate of post-war Germany and indeed the rest of Europe.

The old British warhorse Prime Minister Winston Churchill wanted to see where his Nazi enemy had been vanquished before meeting with US President Harry Truman and Stalin. He and his daughter Mary flew from Bordeaux on the afternoon of 15 July planning to tour the remains of the Reichstag, Reich Chancellery and the Führerbunker. The following day, to the alarm of his entourage and accompanying Soviet officers, Churchill posed for a photograph with his trademark cigar while perched precariously on a damaged chair outside the Führerbunker's emergency exit. Churchill made one of his characteristic quips and everyone laughed. However, one of the officers leant forwards and gently took his arm, fearful that the prime minister might take a tumble. Certainly, if he had leant back, the chair would have given way.

'I went down to the bottom and saw the room in which he and his mistress had committed suicide,' Churchill later recalled, 'and when we came up again they showed us the place where his body had been burned.'[28] However, Churchill, according to Lord Moran, his accompanying doctor, never made it all the way down. He descended one flight of stairs, but when he learnt there were more came back up. Once back on the surface he had turned to his entourage and said with some glee, 'Hitler must have come out here to get some air, and heard the guns getting nearer and nearer.'[29] Looking round at the devastation of Berlin, he knew that had Hitler got across the English Channel in 1940 this would have been the fate of London. Churchill was dismayed when he heard of the Soviets, having systematically looted their sector in Berlin, were now trying to do the same with the American and British sectors. 'They will grind their zone, there will be unimaginable cruelties,' he observed. Churchill knew that Berliners would be made to suffer. 'It is indefensible,' he added, 'except on one ground: that there is no alternative.'[30]

'A sordid and unromantic spot,' observed Field Marshal Alanbrooke, the British Chief of the Imperial General Staff, when he visited the Führerbunker three days later. 'Absolute chaos outside of concrete mixers, iron reinforcing bars, timber … Down below even worse chaos.'[31] Despite being shown where Hitler and Eva's bodies had been found, he noted that his Soviet host did not believe Hitler had died in the Führerbunker but had escaped to Argentina. Nor did his host believe the female body was Eva Hitler, but rather Goebbels' mistress.

The smartly turned-out US 2nd Armored was reviewed in Berlin by the American chief-of-staff, General George C. Marshall, on 18 July. Three days later, British troops paraded through the city past outgoing Prime Minister Churchill; Labour leader and Churchill's imminent successor, Clement Attlee; and Field Marshal Bernard Montgomery. Soviet troops in the city easily outnumbered them. 'They were quite smart in their loosely cut service dress, flat hats, gold or silver epaulettes, and polished jack-boots,' recorded Captain Bill Bellamy, 'and they all had so many medals!'[32] The Red Army conducted its own parade through Berlin on 7 September 1945.

There had been no right or wrong way to defend Berlin in 1945. Hitler's generals knew that everything rested on holding the Oder and the Seelow Heights. Their failure to prevent Zhukov creating the Küstrin bridgeheads or indeed to crush them clearly showed that all was lost. Only the ill-fated German Stargard operation slowed things down because it distracted Stalin into first clearing the Baltic balcony before assaulting Berlin. If Hitler had done everyone a favour and fled or taken his life sooner, that could have reduced the Berliners' suffering. Instead, his inertia in the final months of the war consigned the Nazi capital to prolonged agony and bloodletting. Part of that inertia and the rages was fuelled by the cocktail of toxic drugs pumped into him by the charlatan Dr Morell.

Ultimately, the German armies were exhausted by the spring of 1945 and only capable of defensive action. They simply did not have the strength to seal Soviet penetrations on the collapsed Eastern Front. If Hitler had withdrawn his forces from the Baltic ports and occupied territories, then the battle would have been even costlier for the Red Army. However, the outcome would have been the same. The bulk of the occupation units were second-rate infantry divisions that lacked mobility and armour, so would have not solved the German armed forces' fundamental inability to conduct large-scale manoeuvre warfare. Even the tough forces trapped in the Baltic balcony and Courland, which were worn down, could not have prevented defeat. If Hitler had agreed to the withdrawal of his forces from Courland and the Samland Peninsula, they might have been able to reach Berlin in time. Crucially, though they were short of ammunition and fuel and lacked air support.

Should Zhukov and Stalin have acted decisively in February 1945 as Chuikov contends? 'I happened to hear arguments that the fighting in Berlin could have been conducted with less fury, fierceness and haste, and therefore with fewer casualties,' recalled Konev. 'There is an outer logic in this reasoning but it ignores the main thing – the actual situation, the actual strain of the fighting and the actual state of the men's morale.'[33] Zhukov's armies had been weakened during the assault from the Vistula to the Oder and needed time to recoup. Konev's forces on reaching the Neisse were in a similar condition. They might have got into Berlin sooner and taken the city. However, there would have been considerable German forces still at large to the north and Stalin could have faced continued large-scale fighting after the surrender. This is exactly what happened in the Prague area where Army Group Centre remained intact and fought on for another week after the fall of Berlin. Hitler, thanks to his actions, had ensured the fall of Berlin was inevitable. It would rise from the ashes but as a divided city and the epicentre of the Cold War for the next 44 years.

Finally, could Hitler have escaped Berlin and made a last stand at Obersalzberg? The easy answer to this is no, as there never was an Alpine Redoubt. Furthermore, he could have been shot down on the way to Munich or caught on the open road. General von Hengl, in charge of all the troops in the region, reported at the end of the war that he had 38,000 uniformed personnel in his area of responsibility. However, 90 per cent of them were non-combatants and most were military refugees. Eisenhower could call on five entire armies plus the Red Army. None of Hitler's battered army groups ever managed to reach the Alps and even if they had, they were not in a condition to continue the fight.

If Hitler had somehow escaped Berlin it is hard to imagine resistance in Bavaria lasting very long in the face of the Allies' overwhelming firepower. 'From a purely military standpoint the Alpine Fortress would only have had value if it had been defended, not for its own sake,' wrote Field Marshal Kesselring, 'but as a means to an end.'[34] By April 1945, there really was no point in continuing the war, especially once Berlin had fallen. General von Hengl concluded: 'In modern warfare high mountains, deficient in roads and influenced by the seasons are utterly unsuited as bases for operations … The Alpine Redoubt existed merely on paper.'[35] Hitler deliberately avoided the hangman's noose at Nuremberg by taking his own life in the Führerbunker.

Bibliography

Allen, W.E.D & Muratoff, Paul. *The Russian Campaigns of 1944-45.* Harmondsworth: Penguin, 1946.

Ambrose, Stephen E. *Citizen Soldiers: The US Army from the Normandy Beaches to the Surrender of Germany.* London: Pocket Books, 2002.

Arthur, Max. *Churchill: The Life.* London: Cassell, 2017.

Arthur, Max. *Forgotten Voices of the Second World War.* London: Ebury Press, 2004.

Axell, Albert. *Russia's Heroes.* London: Constable, 2001.

Ballard-Whyte, Paul. *Lucky Hitler's Big Mistakes.* Barnsley: Pen & Sword, 2022.

Baumgart, Eberhard. *Halbe 1945: Eyewitness Accounts from Hell's Cauldron.* Barnsley: Greenhill, 2022.

Baxter, Ian. *The Fall of Berlin.* Barnsley: Pen & Sword, 2019.

Beevor, Antony & Vinogradova, Luba (ed & trans). *A Writer at War: Vasily Grossman with the Red Army 1941-1945.* London: Pimlico, 2006.

Beevor, Antony. *Berlin: The Downfall 1945.* London: Viking, 2002.

Beevor, Antony. *The Second World War.* London: Weidenfeld & Nicolson, 2012.

Bellamy, Chris. *Absolute War: Soviet Russia in the Second World War.* London: Pan, 2008.

Bessonov, Evgeni. *Tank Rider: Into the Reich with the Red Army.* London: Greenhill, 2003.

Bialer, Seweryn (ed). *Stalin and His Generals: Soviet Military Memoirs of World War II.* London: Souvenir Press, 1970.

Bormann, Martin. *Hitler's Table-Talk.* Oxford: Oxford University Press, 1988.

Butler, Rupert. *The Black Angels: The Story of the Waffen-SS.* Barnsley: Pen & Sword, 2005.

Caddick-Adams, Peter. *1945 Victory in the West.* London: Hutchinson Heinemann, 2022.

Carruthers, Bob (ed). *Ten Years at Hitler's Side: The Testimony of Wilhelm Keitel.* Barnsley: Pen & Sword, 2018.

Catherwood, Christopher. *Churchill and Tito.* Barnsley: Frontline, 2017.

Chaney, Otto Preston. *Zhukov.* Newton Abbot: David & Charles, 1972.

Chant, Christopher (ed). *Hitler's Generals and their Battles.* London: Salamander, 1976.

Clark, Alan. *Barbarossa: The Russian German Conflict 1941-45.* London: Cassell, 2001.

Cornish, Nik. *Berlin: Victory in Europe.* Barnsley: Pen & Sword, 2010.

Danchev, Alex & Todman, Daniel, (ed). *War Diaries 1939-1945: Field Marshal Lord Alanbrooke.* London: Phoenix Press, 2002.

Davies, Norman. *Europe at War 1939-1945: No Simple Victory.* London: Macmillan, 2006.

De Boer, Sjoerd J. *Escaping Hitler's Bunker: The Fate of the Third Reich's Leaders.* Barnsley: Frontline, 2021.

Delaforce, Patrick. *Churchill's Desert Rats: From Normandy to Berlin with the 7th Armoured Division.* London: Chancellor Press, 1999.

Delaforce, Patrick. *Monty's Iron Sides: From the Normandy Beaches to*

Bremen with the 3rd Division. London: Chancellor Press, 1999.

Delaforce, Patrick. *The Black Bull: From Normandy to the Baltic with the 11th Armoured Division.* Barnsley: Pen & Sword, 2010.

D'Este, Carlo. *Patton: A Genius for War.* New York: Harper Perennial, 1996.

Djilas, Milovan. *Wartime.* London: Martin Secker & Warburg, 1977.

Eberle, Henrik & Uhl, Matthias. *The Hitler Book.* London: John Murray, 2006.

Eisenhower, Dwight D. *Crusade in Europe.* London: William Heinemann, 1948.

Erickson, John. *The Road to Berlin: Stalin's War with Germany.* London: Weidenfeld and Nicolson, 1983.

Fest, Joachim. *Inside Hitler's Bunker: The Last Days of the Third Reich.* London: Pan, 2005.

Gehlen, Reinhard. *The Gehlen Memoirs.* London: Collins, 1972.

Gooderson, Ian. *A Hard Way to Make a War: The Italian Campaign in the Second World War.* London: Conway, 2008.

Grant, Roderick. *The 51st Highland Division at War.* Shepperton: Ian Allan, 1977.

Green, Michael. *Red Army Weapons of the Second World War.* Barnsley: Pen & Sword, 2022.

Hastings, Max. *All Hell Let Loose: The World at War 1939-45.* London: Harper Press, 2012.

Hastings, Max. *Armageddon: The Battle for Germany 1944-45.* London: Macmillan, 2004.

Holland, James. *Italy's Sorrow: A Year of War, 1944-1945.* London: Harper Press, 2008.

Horrocks, Lieutenant-General Sir Brian. *A Full Life.* London: Collins, 1960.

Horrocks, Lieutenant-General Sir Brian, Belfield, Eversley & Essame, Major-General H. *Corps Commander.* London: Magnum, 1979.

Irving, David. *The Rise and Fall of the Luftwaffe.* London: Weidenfeld and Nicolson, 1973.

Jackson, Robert. *Unexplained Mysteries of World War II.* Royston: Eagle Editions, 2000.

Jones, Michael. *After Hitler: The Last Days of the Second World War in Europe.* London: John Murray, 2015.

Kempka, Erich. *I Was Hitler's Chauffeur: The Memoirs of Erich Kempka.* Barnsley: Frontline, 2012.

Khrushchev, Nikita. *Khrushchev Remembers.* London: Andre Deutsch, 1971.

Klemperer, Victor. *To the Bitter End: The Diaries of Victor Klemperer 1942-1945.* London: Weidenfeld & Nicholson, 1999.

Le Tissier, Tony. *Race for the Reichstag: The 1945 Battle for Berlin.* Barnsley: Pen & Sword, 2021.

Le Tissier, Tony. *Soviet Conquest: Berlin 1945.* Barnsley: Pen & Sword, 2014.

Le Tissier, Tony. *SS-Charlemagne: The 33rd Waffen-Grenadier Division of the SS.* Barnsley: Pen & Sword, 2019.

Linge, Heinz. *With Hitler to the End: The Memoirs of Adolf Hitler's Valet.* Barnsley: Frontline, 2021.

Linklater, Eric. *The Campaign in Italy.* London: Her Majesty's Stationary Office, 1977.

Loringhoven, Bernd Freytag von. *In the Bunker with Hitler: 23 July 1944 – 29 April 1945*. London: Weidenfeld & Nicolson, 2006.

Lucas, James. *Kommando: German Special Forces of World War Two*. London: Cassell, 1998.

Lucas, James. *Last Days of the Third Reich: The Collapse of Nazi Germany, May 1945*. London: Cassell, 2000.

Lucas, James. *Storming Eagles*. London: Canelo, 2022.

Mayo, Jonathan & Craigie, Emma. *Hitler's Last Day: Minute by Minute*. London: Short Books, 2016.

McDonough, Frank. *The Hitler Years: Disaster 1940-1945*. London: Head of Zeus, 2020.

McKay, Sinclair. *Berlin: Life and Loss in the City that Shaped the Century*. London: Viking, 2022.

McKay, Sinclair. *The Lost World of Bletchley Park*. London: Aurum, 2013.

Merridale, Catherine. *Ivan's War: The Red Army 1939-1945*. London: Faber and Faber, 2005.

Misch, Rochus. *Hitler's Last Witness: The Memoirs of Hitler's Bodyguard*. Barnsley: Frontline, 2021.

Mitcham, Samuel W. *Hitler's Field Marshals and their Battles*. London: William Heinemann, 1988.

Moran, Lord. *Winston Churchill: The Struggle for Survival 1940-1965*. London: Constable, 1966.

Neillands, Robin. *The Desert Rats: 7th Armoured Division 1940-45*. London: Aurum, 2005.

O'Donnell, James. *The Berlin Bunker*. London: J.M. Dent, 1979.

Read, Anthony & Fisher, David. *The Fall of Berlin*. London: Pimlico, 1993.

Reitlinger, Gerald. *The SS: Alibi of a Nation 1922-1945*. London: Arms and Armour Press, 1981.

Roberts, Geoffrey. *Stalin's General: The Life of Georgy Zhukov*. London: Icon, 2013.

Roland, Paul. *The Secret of the Nazis: The Hidden History of the Third Reich*. London: Arcturus, 2017.

Ryan, Cornelius. *The Last Battle*. London: Collins, 1966.

Rzhevskaya, Yelena. *Memoirs of a Wartime Interpreter: From the Battle for Moscow to Hitler's Bunker*. Barnsley: Greenhill, 2018.

Schroeder, Christa. *He Was My Chief: The Memoirs of Adolf Hitler's Secretary*. Barnsley: Frontline, 2012.

Seaton, Albert. *Stalin as Warlord*. London: B.T. Batsford, 1976.

Seaton, Albert, *The Fall of Fortress Europe 1943-1945*. London: B.T. Batsford, 1981.

Sereny, Gitta. *Albert Speer: His Battle with Truth*. London: Macmillan, 1995.

Service, Robert. *Stalin: A Biography*. London: Pan, 2005.

Shirer, William L. *The Rise and Fall of the Third Reich: A History of Nazi Germany*. London: Secker & Warburg, 1960.

Shtemenko, S.M. *The Last Six Months: Russia's Final Battles with Hitler's Armies in World War II*. London: William Kimber, 1978.

Simms, Brendan. *Hitler: Only the World Was Enough*. London: Allen Lane, 2019.

Speer, Albert. *Inside the Third Reich.* London: Phoenix, 1995.

Subbotin, Vassili. *We Stormed the Reichstag: A War Correspondent Remembers.* Barnsley: Pen & Sword, 2017.

Terraine, John. *The Right of the Line: The Royal Air Force in the European War 1939-1945.* London: Hodder and Stoughton, 1985.

Toland, John. *Adolf Hitler.* Ware: Wordsworth, 1997.

Trevor-Roper, H.R. *Hitler's War Directives 1939-1945.* London: Pan, 1983.

Trevor-Roper, H.R. *The Last Days of Hitler.* London: Pan, 1965.

Tucker-Jones, Anthony. *Battle of the Cities: Urban Warfare on the Eastern Front.* Barnsley: Pen & Sword, 2023.

Tucker-Jones, Anthony. *Churchill Master and Commander: Winston Churchill at War 1895-1945.* Oxford: Osprey, 2021.

Tucker-Jones, Anthony. *Hitler's Armed SS: The Waffen-SS at War 1939-1945.* Barnsley: Pen & Sword, 2022.

Tucker-Jones, Anthony. *Slaughter on the Eastern Front: Hitler and Stalin's War 1941-1945.* Stroud: The History Press, 2017.

Turner, John Frayn & Jackson, Robert. *Destination Berchtesgaden.* Shepperton: Ian Allan, 1975.

Weigley, Russell F. *Eisenhower's Lieutenants: The Campaign of France and Germany 1944-1945.* London: Sidgwick & Jackson, 1981.

Whiting, Charles. *Warriors of Death.* London: Canelo, 2022.

Williams, Andrew. *D-Day to Berlin.* London: Hodder, 2004.

Winters, Major Dick. *Beyond Band of Brothers.* London: Ebury, 2011.

Zhukov, G. *Marshal Zhukov's Greatest Battles.* London: Macdonald, 1969.

References

Introduction: Capital of the World

1 Brendon, *The Dark Valley*, p.90.
2 Bormann, *Hitler's Table-Talk*, p.680.
3 Ibid.
4 Simms, *Hitler*, p.277.
5 Bormann, *Hitler's Table-Talk*, p.710.
6 Ibid.
7 Simms, *Hitler*, p.301.
8 Speer, *Inside the Third Reich*, p.203.
9 Ibid., p.122.
10 Ibid., p.230.
11 Ibid.
12 Bormann, *Hitler's Table-Talk*, p.523.
13 Ibid., p.83.
14 Ibid., p.361.
15 Ibid., p.668.
16 Speer, *Inside the Third Reich*, p.224.
17 Ibid., p.221.
18 Hitler responded by sending 300 bombers plus fighter cover to attack London on 7 September 1940.
19 Irving, *The Rise and Fall of the Luftwaffe*, p.102.
20 Sereny, *Albert Speer*, p.550.
21 Harris, *Bomber Offensive*, p.187.
22 See Tucker-Jones, *Stalin's Revenge*, for more on the scale of this massive and decisive victory.

Prologue: Last Flight from Berlin

1 O'Donnell, *The Berlin Bunker*, p.127.
2 Speer, *Inside the Third Reich*, p.637.
3 Kempka, *I was Hitler's Chauffeur*, p.132.
4 Ibid., p.135.
5 Ibid.
6 Trevor-Roper, *The Last Days of Hitler*, p.186.
7 Ibid., p.187.
8 Kempka, *I was Hitler's Chauffeur*, p.135.
9 Von Loringhoven, *In the Bunker with Hitler*, p.164.
10 Fest, *Inside Hitler's Bunker*, p.96.
11 Bullock, *Hitler A Study in Tyranny*, p.788.
12 Ibid., p.789.
13 Le Tissier, *Race for the Reichstag*, p.137.
14 Ibid.
15 Shirer, *The Rise and Fall of the Third Reich*, p.1122.
16 Ibid.
17 Bullock, *Hitler A Study in Tyranny*, p.790.
18 Shirer, *The Rise and Fall of the Third Reich*, p.1122.
19 Trevor-Roper, *The Last Days of Hitler*, p.205.
20 Toland, *Adolf Hitler*, p.882.
21 Misch, *Hitler's Last Witness*, p.164.
22 O'Donnell, *The Berlin Bunker*, p. 129.
23 Mitcham, *Hitler's Field Marshals and their Battles*, p.361.

Chapter 1: Delay at Küstrin

1 Werth, *Russia at War*, p.857.
2 Guderian, *Panzer Leader*, p.425.
3 Zhukov, *Reminiscences and Reflections*, Vol 2, p.322.
4 Bialer, *Stalin and his Generals*, p.502.
5 Zhukov, *Reminiscences and Reflections*, Vol 2, p.322.
6 Ibid., pp.333–4.
7 Ibid., p.334.

8   Merridale, *Ivan's War*, p.282.
9   Bialer, *Stalin and his Generals*, p.504.
10 Ibid., p.505.
11 Guderian, *Panzer Leader*, p.412.
12 Reitlinger, *The SS*, p.406.
13 Gehlen, *The Gehlen Memoirs*, p.120.
14 Speer, *Inside the Third Reich*, p.594.

Chapter 2: Busse is Not to Blame

1   Guderian, *Panzer Leader*, p.425.
2   Ryan, *The Last Battle*, p.80.
3   Ibid.
4   Ibid., p.171.
5   Ibid.
6   Guderian, *Panzer Leader*, p.427.
7   Ryan, *The Last Battle*, p.171.
8   Guderian, *Panzer Leader*, p.427.
9   Ryan, *The Last Battle*, p.173.
10 Guderian, *Panzer Leader*, p.428.
11 Loringhoven, *In the Bunker with Hitler*, p.141.
12 Ryan, *The Last Battle*, p.172.
13 Chant, *Hitler's Generals and their Battles*, p.214.
14 Seaton, *The Fall of Fortress Europe 1943-1945*, p.192.
15 Zhukov, *Reminiscences and Reflections*, Vol 2, p.346.
16 Ibid., p.349.
17 Ibid., p.353.
18 Bialer, *Stalin and his Generals*, p.516.
19 Zhukov, *Reminiscences and Reflections*, Vol 2, p.347.
20 Roberts, *Stalin's General*, p.223.
21 Bialer, *Stalin and his Generals*, p.500.
22 Ibid.
23 Speer, *Inside the Third Reich*, p.618.
24 Ibid., p.619.
25 Ibid.

Chapter 3: Firestorm on the Seelow

1   Weighley, *Eisenhower's Lieutenants*, p.699.
2   For a fuller account of the fall of Magdeburg, see Caddick-Adams, *1945 Victory in the West*, pp.362–5.
3   Wilmot, *The Struggle for Europe*, p.694.
4   Weigley, *Eisenhower's Lieutenants*, p.699.
5   Ibid.
6   Zhukov, *Reminiscences and Reflections*, Vol 2, pp.365–6.
7   Ibid., p.366.
8   Ibid.
9   Trevor-Roper, *Hitler's War Directives*, p.301.
10 Ryan, *The Last Battle*, p.269.
11 Merridale, *Ivan's War*, p.283.
12 Zhukov, *Reminiscences and Reflections*, Vol 2, p.364.
13 Ryan, *The Last Battle*, p.271.
14 Ibid.
15 Ibid., p.210.
16 Beevor, *Berlin The Downfall 1945*, p.218.
17 Merridale, *Ivan's War*, p.283.
18 Ryan, *The Last Battle*, p.273.
19 Hastings, *Armageddon*, p.535.
20 Subbotin, *We Stormed the Reichstag*, p.10.
21 Ibid., p.11.
22 Zhukov, *Reminiscences and Reflections*, Vol 2, p.364.
23 Hastings, *Armageddon*, p.537.
24 Ibid., p.535.
25 Speer, *Inside the Third Reich*, p.625.

Chapter 4: Get Moving

1 Zhukov, *Marshal Zhukov's Greatest Battles*, p.285.
2 Ryan, *The Last Battle*, p.283.
3 Le Tissier, *Soviet Conquest*, p.8.
4 Ibid.
5 Ibid., p.9.
6 Beevor, *The Second World War*, p.738.
7 Zhukov, *Reminiscences and Reflections*, Vol 2, p.366.
8 Ibid., p.367.
9 Ibid., p.365.
10 Bialer, *Stalin and his Generals*, p.514.
11 Le Tissier, *Soviet Conquest*, p.11.
12 Beevor, *Berlin The Downfall 1945*, p.237.
13 Ryan, *The Last Battle*, p.210.
14 Le Tissier, *Soviet Conquest*, p.12.
15 McDonough, *The Hitler Years*, p.555.
16 Zhukov, *Marshal Zhukov's Greatest Battles*, p.286.

Chapter 5: The Poison Chalice

1 Ryan, *The Last Battle*, p.176.
2 Ibid.
3 Ibid., p.337.
4 Ibid., p.168.
5 Ibid.
6 Shirer, *The Rise and Fall of the Third Reich*, p.1109.
7 Trevor-Roper, *The Last Days of Hitler*, p.143.
8 Ibid., p.142.
9 Ryan, *The Last Battle*, p.293.
10 Ibid., p.294.
11 Ibid.
12 Zhukov, *Reminiscences and Reflections*, Vol 2, p.357.
13 Ibid., p.375.
14 Speer, *Inside the Third Reich*, p.625.

15 Ryan, *The Last Battle*, p.314.
16 Ibid.
17 Zhukov, *Marshal Zhukov's Greatest Battles*, p.285.
18 Ryan, *The Last Battle*, p.325.
19 Ibid., p.337.
20 Von Loringhoven, *In the Bunker with Hitler*, p.156.
21 Fest, *Inside Hitler's Bunker*, p.60.
22 Jones, *After Hitler*, p.16.
23 Beevor, *Berlin The Downfall 1945*, p.287 & Hastings, *Armageddon*, p.543 record the garrison at this point numbering 45,000 soldiers, including the SS, 40,000 Volkssturm and 3,000 Hitler Youth.
24 Jones, *After Hitler*, p.17.

Chapter 6: Boys on a Bridge

1 Hastings, *Armageddon*, p.543.
2 Le Tissier, *Race for the Reichstag*, p.99 cites the higher figure.
3 Hastings, *All Hell Let Loose*, p.624.
4 Bullock, *Hitler a Study in Tyranny*, p.786, Ryan, *The Last Battle*, p.56 & Roper, *The Last Days of Hitler*, p.181.
5 Bialer, *Stalin and His Generals*, p.527.
6 Hastings, *All Hell Let Loose*, p.624.
7 Ibid.
8 Beevor, *Berlin The Downfall 1945*, p.181.
9 Bialer, *Stalin and His Generals*, p.531.
10 Ryan, *The Last Battle*, p.313.
11 Ibid.
12 Fest, *Inside Hitler's Bunker*, p.48.
13 Ryan, *The Last Battle*, p.317.
14 Fest, *Inside Hitler's Bunker*, p.48.
15 Le Tissier, *SS-Charlemagne*, p.95.
16 Bialer, *Stalin and His Generals*, p.531.
17 Shirer, *The Rise and Fall of the Third Reich*, p.1137.

18 Loringhoven, *In the Bunker with Hitler*, p.179.
19 Le Tissier, *Race for the Reichstag*, p.163.
20 Ibid., p.184.
21 Lucas, *Last Days of the Reich*, p.40.
22 Beevor, *Berlin The Downfall 1945*, p.374.
23 Ibid., p.376.

Chapter 7: This Attack is Murder

1 Butler, *The Black Angels*, p.260.
2 Ryan, *The Last Battle*, p.335.
3 Butler, *The Black Angels*, p.260.
4 Lucas, *Hitler's Commanders*, p.199.
5 Toland, *Adolf Hitler*, p.868.
6 Ryan, *The Last Battle*, p.336.
7 Bullock, *Hitler A Study in Tyranny*, p.783.
8 Ryan, *The Last Battle*, p.336.
9 Ibid., p.374.
10 Reitlinger, *The SS*, p.433.
11 Lucas, *Hitler's Commanders*, p.199.
12 Toland, *Adolf Hitler*, p.868.
13 Lucas, *Hitler's Commanders*, p.199.
14 McDonough, *The Hitler Years*, pp.557–8.
15 Shirer, *The Rise and Fall of the Third Reich*, p.1113.
16 Loringhoven, *In the Bunker with Hitler*, p.147.
17 Eberle & Uhl, *The Hitler Book*, p.240.
18 Whiting, *Warriors of Death*, p.235.
19 Ibid., p.236.
20 Ryan, *The Last Battle*, p.374.
21 Mitcham, *Hitler's Field Marshals and their Battles*, p.172.
22 Whiting, *Warriors of Death*, p.236.
23 Loringhoven, *In the Bunker with Hitler*, p.154.
24 Ibid., p.155.
25 Toland, *Adolf Hitler*, p.873.
26 Ibid.
27 Ibid.

Chapter 8: Where is Wenck?

1 Ryan, *The Last Battle*, p.350.
2 Bialer, *Stalin and His Generals*, p.529.
3 Ibid., p.529.
4 Zhukov, *Reminiscences and Reflections*, Vol 2, pp.376–7.
5 Ibid., p.377.
6 Ibid., p.373.
7 Bessonov, *Tank Rider*, p.222.
8 Ibid.
9 Ibid., p.223.
10 Baumgart, *Halbe 1945*, p.36.
11 Ibid., p.38.
12 Ibid., p.115.
13 Loringhoven, *In the Bunker with Hitler*, p.168.
14 Linge, *With Hitler to the End*, p.191.
15 Ibid.
16 Eberle & Uhl, *The Hitler Book*, p.254.
17 Toland, *Adolf Hitler*, p.876.
18 Loringhoven, *In the Bunker with Hitler*, p.168.
19 Toland, *Adolf Hitler*, p.876.
20 Ibid., p.879.
21 Fest, *Inside Hitler's Bunker*, p.92.
22 Bullock, *Hitler A Study in Tyranny*, p.790.
23 Rzhevskaya, *Memoirs of a Wartime Interpreter*, p.126.
24 Loringhoven, *In the Bunker with Hitler*, p.168 & p.170.
25 Shtemenko, *The Last Six Months*, p.391.

Chapter 9: Northwest Frontier

1 Trevor-Roper, *Hitler's War Directives*, p.292.
2 Montgomery, *The Memoirs*, p.332.
3 Ibid., p.278.
4 Eisenhower, *Crusade in Europe*, p.438.
5 Ibid.
6 Ryan, *The Last Battle*, p.212.
7 Horrocks, Belfield & Essame, *Corps Commander*, p.190.
8 Trevor-Roper, *Hitler's War Directives*, p.299.
9 Ryan, *The Last Battle*, p.335.
10 Loringhoven, *In the Bunker with Hitler*, p.153.
11 Grant, *The 51st Highland Division at War*, p.158.
12 Horrocks, Belfield & Essame, *Corps Commander*, p.178.
13 Horrocks, *A Full Life*, p.264.
14 Loringhoven, *In the Bunker with Hitler*, p.152.
15 Ibid.
16 Misch, *Hitler's Last Witness*, p.146.
17 Ibid., p.157.
18 Ryan, *The Last Battle*, p.212.

Chapter 10: Alpine Fortress

1 Eisenhower, *Crusade in Europe*, p.433.
2 Ibid., p.434.
3 Ibid.
4 Lucas, *Kommando*, p.204.
5 Ibid., p.213.
6 D'Este, *Patton*, pp.723–24.
7 Eisenhower, *Crusade in Europe*, p.434.
8 Ibid.
9 Ambrose, *Citizen Soldier*, p.454.
10 Speer, *Inside the Third Reich*, p.622.
11 Ibid., p.633.
12 Wilmot, *The Struggle for Europe*, p.700.
13 Speer, *Inside the Third Reich*, p.633.
14 Ibid.
15 Toland, *Adolf Hitler*, p.865.
16 Schroeder, *He was my Chief*, p.178.
17 Ibid., p.181.
18 Linge, *With Hitler to the End*, p.189.
19 Ibid., p.190.
20 Read & Fisher, *The Fall of Berlin*, p.361.
21 Ibid.
22 Ibid.
23 McDonough, *The Hitler Years*, p.557.
24 Ibid.
25 Toland, *Adolf Hitler*, p.865.
26 Schroeder, *He was my Chief*, p.181.
27 Ryan, *The Last Battle*, p.218.
28 Ibid., p.162.
29 Wilmot, *The Struggle for Europe*, p.690.
30 Shirer, *The Rise and Fall of the Third Reich*, p.1106.
31 Shtemenko, *The Last Six Months*, p.387.
32 Ibid.
33 Ibid.
34 Eisenhower, *Crusade in Europe*, p.434.
35 Ibid., p.453.
36 Winters, *Beyond Band of Brothers*, p.213.
37 Turner & Jackson, *Destination Berchtesgaden*, p.171.
38 Winters, *Beyond Band of Brothers*, p.215.
39 Ibid., p.216.
40 Klemperer, *To the Bitter End*, p.426.
41 Wilmot, *The Struggle for Europe*, p.698.
42 Kesselring, *The Memoirs of Field Marshal Kesselring*, p.276.
43 Loringhoven, *In the Bunker with Hitler*, p.188.

Chapter 11: Pinned Down

1   Misch, *Hitler's Last Witness*, p.105.
2   Kesselring, *The Memoirs of Field Marshal Kesselring*, p.277.
3   Ibid., p.283.
4   Djilas, *Wartime*, p.442.
5   Ibid., p.446.
6   Ibid., p.441.
7   Ibid., p.442.
8   Ibid., p.440.
9   Lucas, *Last Days of the Reich*, p.122.
10 Ibid.
11 Holland, *Italy's Sorrow*, p.517.
12 Ibid., p.516.
13 Lucas, *Storming Eagles*, p.268.
14 Lucas, *The Last Days of the Reich*, p.158.
15 Kesselring, *The Memoirs of Field Marshal Kesselring*, p. 288.
16 Ibid., p.289.

Chapter 12: Escape from Halbe

1   Bailer, *Stalin and his Generals*, p.531.
2   Ibid.
3   Ibid.
4   Beevor, *Berlin The Downfall 1945*, p.332.
5   Baumgart, *Halbe 1945*, p.133.
6   Ibid., p.63.
7   Ibid., p.150.
8   Ibid., p.153.
9   Ibid., p.75.
10 Ibid., p.133.
11 Ibid., p.141.
12 Ibid.
13 Le Tissier, *Race for the Reichstag*, p.155.
14 Ibid.
15 Beevor, *Berlin The Downfall 1945*, p.397.
16 Fest, *Inside Hitler's Bunker*, p.108.
17 Ibid.
18 Baumgart, *Halbe 1945*, p.118.
19 Ryan, *The Last Battle*, p.403.
20 Ibid., p.404.
21 Roger Moorhouse in his introduction to *Baumgart's Halbe 1945*, p.ix, says 20,000 escaped.
22 Beevor, *Berlin The Downfall 1945*, p.379.
23 Ibid.
24 Bellamy, *Absolute War*, p.658.
25 Misch, *Hitler's Last Witness*, p.178.
26 Beevor, *Berlin The Downfall 1945*, p.398.
27 Bialer, *Stalin and His Generals*, p.532.

Chapter 13: Death in the Tiergarten

1   Toland, *Adolf Hitler*, p.887.
2   Kempka, *I was Hitler's Chauffeur*, p.76.
3   Ryan, *The Last Battle*, p.382.
4   Beevor, *Berlin The Downfall 1945*, p.340.
5   Bialer, *Stalin and His Generals*, pp.527–8.
6   Ibid., p.528.
7   Ibid.
8   Merridale, *Ivan's War*, p.284.
9   Ryan, *The Last Battle*, p.381.
10 Beevor, *Berlin The Downfall 1945*, pp.372–3.

Chapter 14: Avalanche of Fire

1   McDonough, *The Hitler Years*, pp.547.
2   Read & Fisher, *The Fall of Berlin*, p.213.
3   Ibid.
4   Ibid.
5   Toland, *Adolf Hitler*, p.570.
6   Shtemenko, *The Last Six Months*, p.387.
7   Zhukov, *Reminiscences and Reflections*, Vol 2, p.381.

8   Ibid., p.382.
9   Subbotin, *We Stormed the Reichstag*, p.55.
10 Ibid.
11 Le Tissier, *SS-Charlemagne*, p.119.
12 Davies, *Europe at War*, p.343.
13 McDonough, *The Hitler Years*, p.73.
14 Beevor, *Berlin The Downfall 1945*, p.406.
15 Shirer, *The Rise and Fall of the Third Reich*, p.946.
16 Roland, *The Secret Lives of the Nazis*, pp.218–9.
17 Speer, *Inside the Third Reich*, p.438.
18 Eisenhower, *Crusade in Europe*, p.444.
19 Ibid.

Chapter 15: Storming the Reichstag

1   Le Tissier, *Soviet Conquest*, p.123.
2   Ibid.
3   Erickson, *The Road to Berlin*, p.601.
4   Ryan, *The Last Battle*, p.237.
5   Le Tissier, *SS-Charlemagne*, p.122.
6   Zhukov, *Reminiscences and Reflections*, Vol 2, p.385.
7   Beevor, *Berlin The Downfall 1945*, pp.349–50.
8   Shtemenko, *The Last Six Months*, p.391.
9   Beevor, *Berlin The Downfall 1945*, p.355.
10 Erickson, *The Road to Berlin*, p.605.
11 Subbotin, *We Stormed the Reichstag*, p.29.
12 Ibid., p.25.
13 Ibid.
14 Erickson, *The Road to Berlin*, p.605.
15 Zhukov, *Reminiscences and Reflections*, Vol 2, p.385.
16 Ibid.
17 Fest, *Inside Hitler's Bunker*, p.119.
18 Zhukov, *Reminiscences and Reflections*, Vol 2, p.385.
19 Zhukov, *Marshal Zhukov's Greatest Battles*, p.287.
20 Ibid.
21 Subbotin, *We Stormed the Reichstag*, p.37.
22 Zhukov, *Reminiscences and Reflections*, Vol 2, p.385.
23 Beevor & Vinogradova, *A Writer at War*, p.339.
24 Rzhevskaya, *Memoirs of a Wartime Interpreter*, p.172.
25 Hastings, *Armageddon*, p.548.
26 Subbotin, *We Stormed the Reichstag*, p.37.
27 Ibid., p.28.
28 Zhukov, *Reminiscences and Reflections*, Vol 2, pp.386–7.
29 Subbotin, *We Stormed the Reichstag*, p.47.

Chapter 16: Beneath the Reich Chancellery

1   Speer, *Inside the Third Reich*, p.638.
2   Misch, *Hitler's Last Witness*, p.160.
3   Ibid.
4   Loringhoven, *In the Bunker with Hitler*, p.169.
5   Ibid.
6   Shirer, *The Rise and Fall of the Third Reich*, p.1123.
7   Kempka, *I Was Hitler's Chauffeur*, p.71.
8   Loringhoven, *In the Bunker with Hitler*, p.171.
9   Linge, *With Hitler to the End*, p.194.
10 Fest, *Inside Hitler's Bunker*, p.97.
11 Ryan, *The Last Battle*, p.392.
12 Loringhoven, *In the Bunker with Hitler*, p.173.

13 O'Donnell, *The Berlin Bunker*, p.171.

14 Loringhoven, *In the Bunker with Hitler*, p.173.

15 Fest, *Inside Hitler's Bunker*, p.100.

16 O'Donnell, *The Berlin Bunker*, p.172.

17 Trevor-Roper, *The Last Days of Hitler*, p.217.

18 Mitcham, *Hitler's Field Marshals and their Battles*, p.352.

19 Trevor-Roper, *The Last Days of Hitler*, p.226.

20 Ibid.

21 Le Tissier, *Soviet Conquest*, p.127.

22 Zhukov, *Reminiscences and Reflections*, Vol 2, p.388.

23 Ibid., p.383.

24 Ibid.

25 Bialer, *Stalin and his Generals*, p.515.

26 Speer, *Inside the Third Reich*, p.196.

27 Ibid., p.197–8.

28 Ibid., p.204.

29 O'Donnell, *The Berlin Bunker*, p.148.

30 Ibid.

31 Ibid.

32 Linge, *With Hitler to the End*, p.197.

33 Fest, *Inside Hitler's Bunker*, p.111.

34 Misch, *Hitler's Last Witness*, p.170.

35 Speer, *Inside the Third Reich*, p.640.

Chapter 17: Time to Surrender

1 Ryan, *The Last Battle*, p.394.

2 Bialer, *Stalin and his Generals*, p.535.

3 Ibid., p.536.

4 Zhukov, *Reminiscences and Reflections*, Vol 2, p.390.

5 Khrushchev, *Khrushchev Remembers*, p.218.

6 Bialer, *Stalin and his Generals*, p.539.

7 Read & Fisher, *The Fall of Berlin*, p.459.

8 Ibid.

9 Ibid., p.461.

10 Ryan, *The Last Battle*, p.396.

11 Read & Fisher, *The Fall of Berlin*, p.461.

12 Bialer, *Stalin and his Generals*, p.540.

13 Read & Fisher, *The Fall of Berlin*, p.463.

14 Ibid.

15 Le Tissier, *SS-Charlemagne*, p.146.

16 Ibid., p.151.

17 Zhukov, *Reminiscences and Reflections*, Vol 2, p.393.

18 O'Donnell, *The Berlin Bunker*, p.216.

19 Rzhevskaya, *Memoirs of a Wartime Interpreter*, p.137.

20 McKay, *The Lost World of Bletchley Park*, p.145.

21 Trevor-Roper, *The Last Days of Hitler*, p.240.

22 Le Tissier, *SS-Charlemagne*, p.149.

23 Ibid.

24 O'Donnell, *The Berlin Bunker*, p.283.

25 Ibid., p.218.

26 Kempka, *I was Hitler's Chauffeur*, p.90.

27 O'Donnell, *The Berlin Bunker*, p.218.

28 Kempka, *I was Hitler's Chauffeur*, p.95.

29 Jackson, *Unexplained Mysteries of World War II*, p.60.

30 Ibid.

31 Ibid.

32 For a fuller account of the breakout by senior Nazis, see De Boer, *Escaping Hitler's Bunker: The Fate of the Third Reich's Leaders*.

33 Ryan, *The Last Battle*, p.381.

34 Zhukov, *Reminiscences and Reflections*, Vol 2, p.392.

35 Bialer, *Stalin and his Generals*, p.549.

36 Ryan, *The Last Battle*, p.398.

37 Zhukov, *Reminiscences and Reflections*, Vol 2, p.395.

38 O'Donnell, *The Berlin Bunker*, p.288.

39 Rzhevskaya, *Memoirs of a Wartime Interpreter*, p.155.

40 Ibid.

41 Le Tissier, *SS-Charlemagne*, p.154.

42 Rzhevskaya, *Memoirs of a Wartime Interpreter*, p.155.

43 Ibid.

44 Khrushchev, *Khrushchev Remembers*, p.219.

45 Ibid.

Chapter 18: The Butcher's Bill

1 Zhukov, *Marshal Zhukov's Greatest Battles*, p.290.

2 Axell, *Russia's Heroes*, p.249.

3 Zhukov, *Marshal Zhukov's Greatest Battles*, p.289.

4 Ambrose, *Citizen Soldiers*, p.457.

5 McKay, *Berlin*, p.239 quotes 3,996 female and 3,091 male suicides citing Christian Goeschel, 'Suicide at the End of the Third Reich,' *Journal of Contemporary History*, Vol 41, No.1, January 2006.

6 Misch, *Hitler's Last Witness*, p.159.

7 O'Donnell, *The Berlin Bunker*, p.228.

8 Baumgart, *Halbe 1945*, p.125.

9 Ibid., p.118.

10 Service, *Stalin*, p.473.

11 Mayo & Craigie, *Hitler's Last Day*, p.269.

12 O'Donnell, *The Berlin Bunker*, p.291.

13 Ibid.

14 Bialer, *Stalin and His Generals*, p.532.

15 Baumgart, *Halbe 1945*, p.185.

16 Hastings, *Armageddon*, p.550.

17 Hastings, *All Hell Let Loose*, p.625.

18 Ryan, *The Last Battle*, records 120 bridges being blown, p.379.

19 Roberts, *Stalin's General*, p.242.

20 Arthur, *Forgotten Voices of the Second World War*, p.425.

21 Neillands, *The Desert Rats*, p.275.

22 Delaforce, *Churchill's Desert Rats*, p.190.

23 Neillands, *The Desert Rats*, p.275.

24 Delaforce, *Churchill's Desert Rats*, p.190. When Konev visited Berlin in 1962, he noted 'it was still impossible to use the water from one of the lakes that had been packed with corpses.' Bialer, *Stalin and His Generals*, p.532.

25 Neillands, *The Desert Rats*, p.275.

26 Delaforce, *Churchill's Desert Rats*, p.190.

27 Ibid.

28 Arthur, *Churchill: The Life*, p.216.

29 Moran, *Winston Churchill*, p.270.

30 Ibid., p.278.

31 Danchev & Todman, *War Diaries 1939-1945*, p.707.

32 Delaforce, *Churchill's Desert Rats*, p.193.

33 Axell, *Russia's Heroes*, p.249.

34 Kesselring, *The Memoirs of Field Marshal Kesselring*, p.277.

35 Lucas, *The Last Days of the Reich*, p.147.

Index

Index

Index

Index

Index

329